KU-266-245

THE IMAGE OF AFRICA

VOLUME TWO

LEEDS BE

Leeds Metropolitan University

17 0574327 5

LEEDS BE

THE
IMAGE OF AFRICA

British Ideas and Action, 1780–1850

VOLUME TWO

PHILIP D. CURTIN

The University of Wisconsin Press

LEEDS METROPOLITAN
UNIVERSITY
LIBRARY

1705743275
GC-B
CC-130412
15. 10. 12
966.22 CUR

Published 1964
The University of Wisconsin Press
Box 1379, Madison, Wisconsin 53701
The University of Wisconsin Press, Ltd.
70 Great Russell Street, London

Copyright © 1964
The Regents of the University of Wisconsin
All rights reserved

Printings 1964, 1973

Printed in the United States of America
ISBN 0-299-03020-2 cloth (2 vols. in one)
Vol. 1, 0-299-83025-x paper; Vol. 2, 0-299-83026-8 paper
LC 64-10922

CONTENTS · VOLUME 2

PART III

The Age of Humanitarianism, 1830–1852

FIGURES · VOLUME 2

MAPS · VOLUME 2

*Maps by the University of Wisconsin
Cartographic Laboratory*

PART III

The Age of Humanitarianism

1830–1852

KEY TO ABBREVIATIONS

IN THE NOTES

Ad. Mss.   Additional Manuscripts, British Museum

AG   National Archives of Ghana, Accra

ASP   Papers of the Anti-Slavery Society and the Aborigines Protection Society, Rhodes House, Oxford

BT   Board of Trade series, Public Record Office

CMSA   Archives of the Church Missionary Society, Salisbury Square, London. (Microfilm series also available at Memorial Library, University of Wisconsin.)

CO   Colonial Office series, Public Record Office

DNB   Dictionary of National Biography

HO   Home Office series, Public Record Office

H   Hansard

IA   Nigerian National Archives, Western Regional Repository, Ibadan

PP   Parliamentary Papers

PRO   Public Record Office, London

SLA   National Archives of Sierra Leone, Freetown

T   Treasury series, Public Record Office

THE ERA

OF

THE NIGER EXPEDITION

LEEDS METROPOLITAN UNIVERSITY LIBRARY

Eighteen hundred and thirty seems to mark the end of an era in Anglo-West African relations. To the well-informed contemporary observer, it must have appeared that even the unsubstantial British effort of past decades was to be written off. From the side of government, the 1830 Parliamentary Committee and the decision to reduce commitments seemed final. In exploration, the Landers had settled the Niger problem, but the route from Tripoli was now closed. Private missionary efforts went on, but only on a very small scale, and the well-publicized mortality figures were a strengthened deterrent to any kind of activity. Yet other events of 1830 were to lead, indirectly and only after a decade of gestation, to a reversal of the apparent trend.

These events took place in Europe, not Africa. The July Revolution in France, the death of George IV, the election of a new Parliament, and the growing threat of revolution in England itself all conspired to bring about the Reform Act of 1832—though the importance of Parliamentary reform can easily be exaggerated. The act of 1832 was no revolution, but it brought a shift in the balance, and in the method and spirit, of English political life. The Whigs and their allies who came into office in the 1830's were mainly old-line politicians operating in old-line ways, but they could sometimes be made to respond to the opinions of the new electorate. The effective voice of Evangelicals, Non-Conformists, and Radicals was stronger than it had been.

This new balance of Parliamentary opinion first made itself felt on colonial issues with the act of 1833, emancipating the slaves in the British colonies. Even if the anti-slavery movement had gone no further, emancipation in itself changed the basic alignment of British interests on either side of the South Atlantic. Some of the consequences were not apparent for a decade or more, but some were immediate. The victory over colonial slavery proved that a well-organized political agitation could influence national policy. The impetus of the victory carried the humanitarians further into colonial affairs. Their parliamentary leaders kept a watching brief over the transition from slavery to freedom in tropical America, and they looked with renewed concern to the continuing slave trade from tropical Africa.

During most of the 1830's and 1840's, humanitarian opinion had more effective access to the Colonial Office than ever before, or ever again. In part, this was mere chance—the fact that James Stephen became Assistant Under-Secretary for Colonies in 1834 and Permanent Under-Secretary in 1836. As the son of an anti-slavery leader, he had been active in the anti-slavery cause. He had left his private law practice in 1825 to become Permanent Counsel of the Colonial Office, partly in order to work against slavery from within the administration. Once in the higher posts of the permanent staff, he was able to dominate many routine decisions of the Office. Parliamentary Secretaries of State came and went, but Stephen stayed on; and his influence on colonial affairs remained important even after he was succeeded in office by Herman Merivale in 1847.

Humanitarian influence reached the Colonial Office in other ways as well. Stephen served under a succession of Secretaries of State who were responsive to humanitarian suggestion. Lord Glenelg in 1835–39 was a convinced humanitarian, as zealous as Stephen himself. The succession of Lord Normanby in 1839 and Lord John Russell in 1839–41 was also favorable, and the six years 1835 to 1841 can be taken as the high-water mark of humanitarian dominance in British colonial affairs. The wave receded in the administrations of Lord Stanley and William Gladstone under the Tory Government of

1841–46, but it rose again when the Government of Lord John Russell in 1846–52 put the third Earl Grey into the Colonial Office. Grey was far too much the aristocrat to be dominated by "Exeter Hall," (the collective name for the missionary and philanthropic societies, many of which held their annual meetings at Exeter Hall in the Strand). The third Earl, however, was a son of the second Earl Grey, whose Government had passed the Reform Bill. As Lord Howick, he had served in the Colonial Office during the 1830's. When he returned as head of the Office in 1846, his administration continued in the spirit of the humanitarian era. When he left it in 1852, that era came to an end.

If the winds from Exeter Hall blew strongly through the Colonial Office in the years between 1833 and 1852, they were also in competition with new breezes from other directions. Two distinct, and sometimes contradictory, tendencies became stronger after 1830. One of these was the vaguely Benthamite belief that legislation could correct some of the evils of society. It was not a belief in "planning" in a modern sense—not intervention in economic and social processes by regular and continuous administration. It called, rather, for the creation of legislative guide lines, setting limits, so that self-interested individuals would act in socially desirable ways. Most of the Benthamite Radicals had little interest in the colonies, but an off-shoot group, commonly called the "Colonial Reformers," wished to apply the same principles overseas. The best known publicist of this group was E. Gibbon Wakefield. Their principal interest was the land policies of Australasia and Canada. Their efforts to manipulate land policies in order to create a "good society" in the settlement colonies could, however, be extended to other matters. In time, some of their suggestions for colonial reform were applied in the tropical dependencies as well. Both the spirit of their suggestions and the means they proposed could be used in West Africa, though rarely by the Colonial Reformers themselves.

The second tendency was the economic doctrine of laissez faire, the belief that maximum economic productivity and social benefit will be achieved through the least possible government interference in the economic process. By any rigorous use of logic, laissez faire was incompatible with Benthamite tinkering with society, but individual politicians and publicists could create their own mixture of Ricardian and Benthamite doctrine. In the political debate of the 1830's and

1840's, the issue was not laissez faire as a general policy, but free trade—more specifically the abolition of the Corn Laws. The demand for cheap food was perfectly compatible with any degree of Benthamite Radicalism. Free trade could even become a moral issue, and the Anti-Corn-Law League brought to bear the same moral fervor shown by the anti-slavery agitation. It was not initially a colonial issue, much less an African issue, but the abolition of the Corn Laws in 1846 was immediately followed by the Sugar Act; and the Sugar Act did affect West Africa. By providing for the gradual removal of the duties which had formerly protected British West Indian sugar in the British domestic market, it destroyed the traditional British economic policy toward the tropical Atlantic. The economic relations of tropical America with tropical Africa, and of both with Britain, had to be reconsidered from the roots upward.

None of these major tendencies of British thought—none of the major issues of colonial policy—were concerned principally with Africa. Humanitarians took some interest in Africa, but this interest was secondary to their broader, world-wide missionary effort, or to their special concern with West Indian slavery. Colonial Reformers and the Anti-Corn-Law League hardly thought about West Africa at all. Thought and writing about West Africa remained what it had been—a field of great interest for a small group of enthusiasts, supported by the occasional excursions of major theorists or major statesmen.

There was reason enough for this relative neglect. British North America, Australia, and New Zealand after 1840 were much more promising centers for overseas Britons. India was by now a great empire, under British control, and a much more promising scene for missionary activity, or the investment of British capital. On the African continent itself, Britain had acquired new interests and responsibilities. The Cape had been in British hands since 1806, though its importance was merely strategic until the 1820's, when frontier wars pointed to the fact that South Africa also had a hinterland. Missionary work and missionary publicity in Britain, the attempt to reform Boer society, and finally the Great Trek carried British interests further and further north during the 1830's and 1840's. By 1850 the Boers had spread far into the interior, and the missionaries even further. Livingstone had set out on his greatest missionary journey, and West Africa had to share the limelight with the rest of the continent.

In this respect a dividing line occurs in the mid-forties: before that time, West Africa dominated British thought about Africa; it never did so again, except in moments of particular crisis.

Because of West Africa's continued position in the shadow of greater issues, the greater issues set the physical and intellectual environment in which West African policy was formed. This was the "Age of Reform," the "Age of Improvement," and also the age of the greatest relative economic success for the British Isles. During the two decades from 1830 to 1850, Great Britain became the first nation to build a general railway network. Industrial production was still increasing at the annual rate established during economic "take-off" at the end of the eighteenth century. Other countries were now industrializing; but they were only entering take-off, and they were not to catch up for some decades to come.

One of the concomitants of British industrial power and security in that power, was a free hand in international affairs. With no major war between 1815 and the Crimean War, the 1830's and '40's were the apogee of *pax britannica*. They were also a period of relatively slack tensions within the European state system. Though there might be alarms in the eastern Mediterranean, neither France nor Russia was a serious threat to British security. The unifications of Italy and Germany had not yet raised the need for delicate adjustment to change. The absence of serious diplomatic concerns freed the Foreign Office for its endless negotiations to end the Atlantic slave trade—and freed the Navy for blockade duty off the African coast. These activities, both naval and diplomatic, were, indeed, the only source of sustained interest keeping West Africa before the British public and Parliament.

Still another result of economic development was a continuous increase in national self-confidence, beginning shortly after the victory of 1815 and continuing to a peak of self-satisfaction in the 1850's. Doubts and difficulties were, of course, present even in the first half of the nineteenth century. The working classes complained. The Irish complained. But the Chartist agitation passed without breaking the accustomed order of society. Eighteen-forty-eight was hardly more than a ripple, at least compared with the Continent. No wonder, then, that the Great Exhibition of 1851 marked such a pinnacle of pride. No wonder, also, that the pride of achievement should carry with it pride of race, pride in British religion and British culture and British morality, and, in the face of African "barbarism," a rise in arrogance and cultural chauvinism even surpassing the clear beginnings already visible during the first three decades of the century.

In West Africa itself, the scale of British activity was indeed small in the 1830's. Fewer British subjects of European extraction were resident on shore than in any recent decade—and fewer than would ever be there again. In the early decades of the century, a military force of one to three hundred soldiers had been the usual thing. After 1830 it was reduced to a few officers, usually less than ten, in command of African troops. In Sierra Leone there were about eighty to a hundred white merchants and officials, about two dozen in the Gambia, and the same on the Gold Coast. Making allowance for those beyond the sphere of direct British control, the total number of British Europeans on the Coast could seldom have exceeded two hundred.[1] By contrast, the mean annual strength of the anti-slavery squadron off West Africa was at least five hundred and sometimes as high as a thousand men, but the squadron stayed at sea as much as possible to escape the "climate" on shore.

British trade was another matter—though not one for precise discussion. There were too few customs houses and too many creeks and inlets where unofficial trade could go on. Masters of ships clearing from Britain were not always accurate in stating their destinations, and they sometimes gave intentionally misleading information. To all appearance, however, the 1830's and 1840's were a period of increasing British trade. The annual average declared value of British exports to the Western Coast of Africa rose from £270,000 in 1829–33 to £591,000 in 1847–52. Some of the optimistic sheen is taken off these figures, however, if they are compared with British exports as a whole. West Africa took only .72 per cent of British exports in 1829–33 and only .89 per cent in 1847–52. West Africa, in short, kept its place in the pattern of British trade, but that place was small indeed compared with 1783–87, when the equivalent figure had been 4.4 per cent of the whole. In the eighteen century, furthermore, West Africa had been the most important region for British trade on the African continent. By 1847–52, West Africa took only about a quarter of British exports to Africa. A trans-Atlantic comparison is also indicative: in these same years, Brazil took more British exports than

1. R. R. Kuczynski, *Demographic Survey of the British Colonial Empire, Volume I: West Africa* (London, 1948), pp. 187 and 318.

all of Africa. Brazil, the British West Indies, and the Foreign West
Indies together took ten times as much as West Africa—and this at
a period when the British West Indies were in the depths of a prolonged depression. In 1829–33, at the height of the pre-emancipation
prosperity, the British West Indies had imported from Britain 100
times more than West Africa.[2]

But the economic importance of West Africa was increasing
sharply in certain commodities, principally palm oil from the tropical
forest belt. Demand in Britain, both for lubricating oil and for soap,
had risen sharply with the rise of British industry. British imports of
palm oil doubled between 1827 and 1830, then trebled again during
the course of the 1830's. Almost the whole of this supply came from
West Africa, and mainly from the Niger Delta. By the mid-thirties,
half the value of West African exports to Britain was in this single
commodity.[3]

The rise of the palm oil trade shifted the economic center of grav-
ity in West Africa markedly to the east—away from the Windward
Coast and the Gold Coast and toward the Bights. But this shift implied no absolute decline in the far west. The Gambia found its own
staple of legitimate trade, and the first groundnuts were shipped in
1835. Gambian groundnuts, however, went mainly to France, and the
trade was dominated by French merchants. The region was therefore
not recognized in London as one of increasing British economic activity. In Sierra Leone, the recaptives were moving out into the
coastal trade and into the interior, but the total trade of the colony
was relatively stable. It hardly increased during the 1830's, and by
1850 the level of combined imports and exports was barely 25 per
cent higher than it had been in 1830.[4]

While the trends of West African trade were mildly encouraging,
they were not encouraging enough to prompt the government to further action. During the 1830's indeed, the discouragement of the
1820's lived on, and the series of government exploring expeditions
came to an end. The Admiralty limited itself to coastal surveys,

2. J. R. McCulloch, *A Descriptive and Statistical Account of the British Empire*,
2 vols. (London, 1837 and subsequent editions), edition of 1839, II, 19; edition of
1854, II, 20.
3. K. O. Dike, *Trade and Politics in the Niger Delta, 1830–1885* (London, 1956),
pp. 50, 57, and 63; M. Laird and R. A. K. Oldfield, *Narrative of an Expedition into
the Interior of Africa by the River Niger in 1832–4*, 2 vols. (London, 1837), II, 356.
4. N. A. Cox-George, *Finance and Development in West Africa. The Sierra Leone
Experience* (London, 1961), p. 142.

linked to the needs of the anti-slavery squadron. Only minor private expeditions tried to reach the far interior—such as the Davidson expedition, which set out from southern Morocco for Timbuctu and disappeared in the desert in 1836.

In the Niger valley, the only substantial new explorations of the 1830's were those sponsored by merchants. Of these, the most important was an expedition mounted by the African Inland Commercial Company in 1832–33, with the leadership and principal financial support of Macgregor Laird. Up to 1832, Laird had been connected with his family's firm of shipbuilders in Birkenhead. He now shifted his interest to African trade, and especially to river navigation on the Niger. For the next thirty years, he was the prime mover in a whole series of efforts to develop the Niger route to the interior, and he became one of the principal publicists for the cause of African commerce.

Two iron steamers were especially designed and built for the expedition of 1832–33. Richard Lander was hired as a guide to the river, and Lt. William Allen, R.N., went along as a representative of the Admiralty. The principal aim was to establish a trading post at the confluence of the Niger and Benue, where a supercargo would remain on shore to collect produce between the projected regular visits of the steamers. Laird's steamers sailed up the Niger in two successive seasons of high water, proving that the river was open to steam navigation. The expedition also brought back the first detailed European knowledge of African trade on the Niger, but it was not a commercial success. Forty of the forty-nine Europeans who took part died, including Richard Lander, and Laird himself returned to England after the first season.[5]

Laird was ruined financially by this first attempt, but the Niger effort was continued by other merchants. When the African Inland Commercial Company dissolved in 1834, it sold one of the ships, the *Quorra*, to Robert Jamieson of Glasgow. The *Quorra* had been left in Fernando Po, where the British had established a small post in the expectation of being able to buy the island from Spain. One of the commercial agents attracted to the island during the brief British

5. Laird and Oldfield, *Narrative of an Expedition.* The most authoritative recent account of this and the subsequent Niger expeditions is C. C. Ifemesia, "British Enterprise on the Niger, 1830–1869 " (Unpublished Ph.D. thesis, London, 1959). Lt. (later Rear-Admiral) William Allen (1793–1864) should not be confused with William Allen, the Quaker philanthropist (1770–1843).

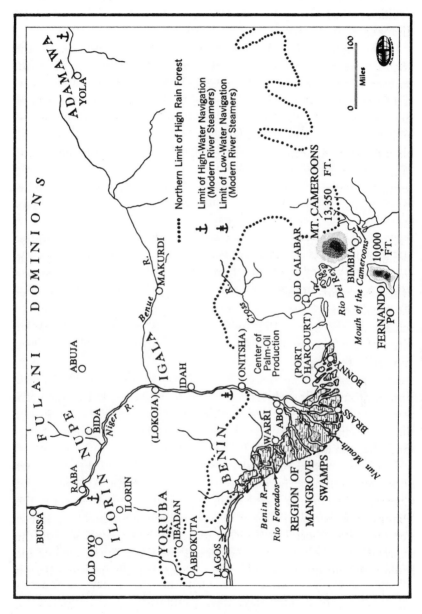

Map 17. The Lower Niger, c. 1840

occupation was Captain John Beecroft. When the government post was evacuated in 1834, Beecroft stayed on as a merchant with a small trading post on the island and another at Bimbia in the Cameroons. Jamieson now secured Beecroft's services as Captain of the *Quorra*. With a crew of six Europeans, including two survivors of Laird's expedition, and some thirty Africans, Beecroft took her up the Niger again in 1835. In 1836 he moved east to the Cross River, hoping (incorrectly, as it turned out) that the Cross might prove a more useful entrance into the Niger than the Nun mouth, which steamers had been using up to this time.[6] *Quorra* was subsequently wrecked, but Jamieson sent out another small steamer, *Ethiope,* which first began operating on the Niger in 1840.

These smaller Niger expeditions of the 1830's showed what might be done with steam navigation, but they were only indirectly a precedent for the great government-sponsored Niger Expedition of 1841–42. That effort was no mere exploring expedition. It was the first step toward a general "forward policy" in West Africa, reversing the established doctrine of minimum commitments. Its origins went back to the stream of projects put forward during the first three decades of the century; and it was carried out in the face of Jamieson's violent and vocal opposition, since Jamieson believed it would ruin the commercial opening he had developed at so much trouble and expense.

Although the plan for a forward policy was drawn from African enthusiasts of many shades of political opinion, the impetus for the Niger Expedition came from Exeter Hall, and specifically from the leadership of T. Fowell Buxton. The victory over colonial slavery had been only one part of a much broader humanitarian program: at its most radical and far-reaching it was nothing less than the intention to use British national power in the cause of world-wide Christian morality—the same kind of Christian morality which had moved the Clapham Sect a half century earlier. The humanitarians of the 1780's may not have seen the road ahead as a Fabian campaign against one evil at a time, but each achievement opened new worlds to be conquered, first the British slave trade, then the foreign slave trade, then colonial slavery. Even after the Emancipation Act of 1833 the job was not finished. The foreign slave trade continued; so did slavery in the United States and much of tropical America. There was also a new

6. Ifemesia, "British Enterprise," pp. 56–67.

concern with the plight of the aborigines in British settlements, and finally the broadest missionary objective of carrying Christianity and civilization to the whole world.[7]

Buxton, as Parliamentary leader of the humanitarian faction moved on to the aborigines question in 1835–37, when he became chairman of a Select Committee of the House of Commons during successive sessions. The Committee's responsibility was to investigate government policy in regard to "Native Inhabitants of Countries where British Settlements are made, and to the neighbouring Tribes, in order to secure to them the due observation of Justice, and the protection of Rights; to promote the spread of Civilization among them; and to lead them to the peaceful and voluntary reception of the Christian religion."[8] West Africa was not directly concerned in these terms of reference; but the Committee's investigation led to a general discussion of the moral position of non-Western peoples in the face of expanding Europe.

After the end of 1837, Buxton was again free to move on to other topics, and he turned his attention to the foreign slave trade. Inevitably, this led him to a further concern with West Africa. By August, 1838, he had completed a detailed plan, which was submitted to the government. After further elaboration it was published in two fat volumes.[9] The point of departure was clear enough. In spite of thirty years of British effort, the African slave trade had not ended. Instead, it appeared to be increasing. According to Buxton's estimate, it was then running at about 150,000 slaves exported by Europeans each year. The figure may have been slightly exaggerated, but in certain years the trade certainly came close to this order of magnitude.

Buxton's crucial point, however, was not the number of slaves exported. It was the failure of the Navy to render the trade unprofitable. In its best year, 1837, the Navy had been able to capture and liberate only 8,652 slaves in transit—surely no more than 10 per cent of those shipped, and probably a good deal less.[10] The Navy's problem was formidable. The commanders of the squadron had to work with reference to an intricate set of regulations, based on treaties the

7. For the political background of the Niger expedition see J. Gallagher, "Fowell Buxton and the New African Policy," *Cambridge Historical Journal*, X, 36–58 (1950).
8. PP, 1837, vii (425), p. 3.
9. T. Fowell Buxton, *The African Slave Trade* (London, 1839) and *The Remedy: Being a Sequel to the African Slave Trade* (London, 1840).
10. Christopher Lloyd, *The Navy and the Slave Trade* (London, 1949). pp. 275–77.

Foreign Office had been able to sign with individual foreign powers. These treaties gave varying rights of search, capture, and condemnation, and the slavers could switch from one flag to another according to the diplomatic situation of the moment. Up to 1835, when the so-called equipment clause was inserted into the treaty with Spain, slave ships could be condemned only when found with slaves actually on board. Furthermore, Brazil and the Spanish government of Cuba were unwilling at most times to enforce their own anti-slave-trade legislation. Naval forces at sea could impede the slave trade, but Buxton was correct in believing that naval force alone could not stop it, at least without a radical change in the size of the force or its mode of operation. Others agreed that some change to policy was called for—either to make the blockade effective, to give it up altogether, or to supplement it with other kinds of action—but there was far less agreement about which course to follow.

Buxton said his own proposed solution came to him suddenly in the summer of 1837. Perhaps so, but it was modified so much during the next two years that no part of the final published version was really new. All the elements were present in the West African literature of the earlier nineteenth century, and Buxton enlisted the help of James MacQueen, whose knowledge of that literature was second to none. Buxton's real contribution was to draw up a coherent plan, based on many sources in fact and theory, and to present it to the public with the organized weight of Exeter Hall behind it.[11]

The substance of Buxton's plan was a four-point program. Its first item was an intensified campaign against the slave trade at sea and along the coasts, based on a strengthened naval blockade and the co-operation of the African authorities, to be obtained through a series of anti-slave-trade treaties. The treaties were to bind African states to help put down the slave trade, to open their frontiers to European commerce, and to permit agricultural settlement. The net of treaties was to stretch into the interior, until it had created a "confederacy with the chiefs from the Gambia in the West to Begharmi [Bagirmi, now in the Chad Republic] in the East; and from the Desert on the North to the Gulf of Guinea on the South."[12]

This first point had diverse origins. The blockading squadron was

---

11. Charles Buxton (Ed.), *Memoirs of Sir Thomas Fowell Buxton, Baronet* (London, 1848), pp. 429–34; T. F. Buxton, *The Remedy*, pp. 236–37.
12. Buxton, *The Remedy*, p. 17.

now an old policy, pursued in practice since 1808, and even older in Wadström's suggestion. The treaty policy was also old. Treaties had been signed in the past, if less systematically. T. Perronet Thompson, Sir Charles MacCarthy, and Charles Turner, among the Governors of Sierra Leone, had all wanted to create a more systematic network of treaties. Both the practice of granting subsidies in return for favors, and the assumption that Africans would willingly sign such treaties were an ancient aspect of European action and thought in West Africa. The Buxtonian strategy for penetration inland was equally old. It was his suggestion to establish a series of posts in the interior, which would serve as centers of trade and influence. The British would not directly administer the territory around the posts. Instead, they would sign a series of treaties binding African authorities to each other and to the British government. In essence it was precisely the kind of overland trading-post establishment used by the Hudson's Bay Company or by the Russian fur traders in seventeenth-century Siberia. With variations, it had already been suggested for West Africa by Banks, Golbéry, Corry, MacQueen, and the anonymous project presented by the African Institution—among others.

Buxton's second point was even more familiar. It was to use the power of the government to encourage legitimate commerce as a key to the "civilization" of Africa, and it incorporated the assumption of the early nineteenth century, that legitimate commerce could not thrive without some form of intervention to hold the ring free of slavers.

The third point called for the development of African agriculture. By this, Buxton meant agricultural production managed by Africans, but modeled on European plantations to be established as an example. He thus took the side of agriculture in the old controversy of trade vs. agriculture. He argued that commerce alone could not "civilize" Africa, since commerce could only call forth the "spontaneous productions of nature." Real civilization demanded "habits of settled industry," which could only be formed by regular agricultural labor.[13] Buxton's thought on this point closely followed the project put forward by the African Institution in 1808, and repeated with variations by MacQueen, but the base lay even further back in the ideas of Wadström, Beaver, or, less precisely, in the hopes of Malachy Postlethwayt.

13. Buxton, *The Slave Trade*, pp. 55–56.

Finally, and primarily, Buxton counted on direct exhortation through moral and religious instruction. The primacy he gave to this factor may have been a bow to the missionary movement, since Buxton's principal discussion focused on the other three points. In any event, the missionary movement was too strong to be set aside, even if Buxton himself had not been closely associated with Christian humanitarianism.

In short, Buxton's plan was little more than a pulling together of certain strands, and often the dominant strands, from the mass of older suggestion. It could hardly have struck the permanent officials at the Colonial Office as a revelation of new insights. James Stephen, in spite of his humanitarian connections, was opposed to it, as he was opposed to all increased British intervention in West Africa. Lord Melbourne, the Prime Minister, was not favourably impressed. Nor was Palmerston, who believed in diplomatic negotiation with the European slaving powers as the best weapon against the slave trade. The Parliamentary position of the Government, however, was very weak in 1838 and continued so until it finally fell in 1841. It was so weak that Melbourne had been forced to resign briefly in May, 1839, when a block of Radicals deserted. A similar revolt of the humanitarians would have brought down the Government.

Buxton's plan was therefore accepted in principle in the autumn of 1838, but not without elaborate modification. James MacQueen gave further advice directly to the government. Several other authorities were consulted, among them Governor Rendall of the Gambia. James Bandinel, the Foreign Office specialist on anti-slave-trade treaties, prepared a new draft plan, and the higher officials of the Colonial Office, both permanent and Parliamentary, took a hand in whittling down the grandiose all-West-Africa concept until it became a modest trial expedition bound for the Niger. Finally, with more pressure from Buxton, the project grew again—but not to its original size, even though it gained the crucial support of Lord John Russell, who had meanwhile become Secretary of State for Colonies.[14]

While the Government was investigating, Buxton organized a major public agitation to mobilize opinion in support of the project. For the future British image of Africa, this publicity was almost as important as the expedition itself. West African affairs were more

14. Gallagher, "Fowell Buxton," pp. 44–45.

widely discussed between 1839 and 1842 than at any previous time—and not entirely in a pro-Buxton vein. The original suggestion led to many differing projects, objections, and counter-proposals, though these were drowned in the first instance by the voice of the humanitarians. The Buxton supporters organized a series of mass meetings, one of them with the Prince Consort himself in the chair. They formed the African Civilization Society, under Buxton's chairmanship, to carry out certain parts of the plan. The missionary societies joined in with their own projects for West Africa. Even when they were not directed to the Niger, they were able to ride the crest of enthusiasm and raise funds where no funds had been available.

The government expedition sailed in April 1841 in a mood of high hope. Every care was taken. The steamers were especially constructed and placed under the command of experienced naval officers. They were ordered to explore the Niger, making the fullest possible report of political and commercial conditions. They were also to sign anti-slave-trade treaties with the African authorities and establish one or more trading posts, plus a "model farm" on land purchased from the Africans at the juncture of the Niger and Benue. The government supplied the ships. The African Civilization Society supplied the scientific staff. The Church Missionary Society sent representatives to make a missionary reconnaissance. A separate Agricultural Association, organized as a private firm, took responsibility for the model farm.[15]

To a point, it all worked according to plan. The ships sailed up the river. The Commissioners signed treaties in the recommended form. The scientists and observers gathered a great deal of new information. Everything else failed in the face of high mortality. Forty-eight of the Europeans died during the first two months in the river, and 55 of the 159 who went along died before the expedition returned to England in 1842.[16] In fact, this mortality was no higher than should have been expected; but it was higher than the planners had anticipated, and the disaster was magnified in the public mind by the false hopes of the enthusiasts.

The initial withdrawal from the Niger to Fernando Po in 1841 was ordered by the commanders of the expedition, but the final decision not to repeat the effort came from England. Melbourne had

15. Buxton, *Memoirs,* pp. 514–16.
16. PP, 1843, xxxi (83), p. 1.

resigned while the expedition was still in Africa, and in 1841 the Peel Government brought Lord Stanley to the Colonial Office. The new Government was less responsive to humanitarian pressure than its predecessor had been. During the dry season of 1841–42, while the ships and survivors waited at Fernando Po for the next season of high water, they were ordered to evacuate the inland post and abandon the effort.[17] One ship re-entered the river in 1842, but that was the end. The normal Colonial Office disenchantment with West Africa returned, and the upsurge of public zeal ebbed away during the course of 1842, exposing the mud flats of apathy and disappointment.

But it would be a mistake to write off the expedition as just another failure of the Europeans to survive in Africa. The government and the broader public were disillusioned, but apathy about West Africa was their usual state of mind. However temporary, the unusual enthusiasm of 1840 and 1841 provided the impetus for a new round of African activity, and the activity remained even after the general enthusiasm died away. In time, it was to alter the whole of British relations with West Africa.

Even from the side of the government, there were by-products that could not be wiped out. Further exploration on the Niger was out of the question, but the Niger expedition in a narrow sense had been only one part of a broader policy. In response to the Niger agitation, Parliament passed the "Equipment Act" in 1839, legalizing the capture (without Portuguese consent) of Portuguese vessels equipped for the slave trade, even when there were no slaves on board. Expenditure for the blockading squadron rose by 50 per cent between 1829 and 1841, and the tactics were changed. Ships now began to cruise close inshore. In 1840 they began raiding barracoons where slaves were kept waiting shipment. Anti-slave-trade treaties with African states, legalizing such raids, were signed as part of the Niger effort, and they remained in force. As a result, the annual average numbers of slavers captured rose from thirty-one in the quinquennium 1834–38 to sixty-five in 1839–43,[18] and still higher in the later 1840's. Even though the right of search and seizure was never legally perfect, and though the policy of raiding barracoons was abandoned between

---

17. Ifemesia, "British Enterprise," pp. 326–27.
18. Gallagher, "Fowell Buxton," pp. 54–55; Lloyd, *Navy and the Slave Trade,* p. 275.

1842 and 1848 on account of legal qualms, the commitment of the Navy remained at its new, post-Niger level.

As another facet of the new policy, the Government began to reconsider the status of the older posts and settlements. Dr. R. R. Madden was sent out as a commissioner to visit the Gambia, Sierra Leone, and the Gold Coast—with orders drafted in November 1839, one month before those of the Niger Expedition. Madden was a medical man who had served in post-emancipation Jamaica as a Special Magistrate, had written on slavery in Cuba, and had the confidence of the humanitarians. It was a natural choice. His orders called for special attention to rumors that British merchants on the Coast were selling supplies to foreign slavers, to the operations of the merchants' government on the Gold Coast, to European mortality, and to the possibilities either of expanding the existing settlements or of creating a system of organized labor emigration to the West Indies.[19]

His report, when presented toward the end of 1841, was full of humanitarian zeal and harsh strictures. It was unfavorable to the merchants' government on the Gold Coast and to the administration of the Gambia, though Madden was rather better pleased than most with the recent progress of Sierra Leone. Like the Niger Expedition itself, the report fell in badly with the timing of English political change. It was well received by Lord John Russell, but Russell immediately left the Colonial Office, to be replaced by Lord Stanley. Stanley disliked humanitarian meddling; he was also deluged with the angered protests of the merchants and others who had borne the brunt of the Commissioner's zeal. In spite of James Stephen's efforts on his behalf, Madden was quietly dropped from the public service, and in 1842 a Parliamentary Select Committee reconsidered his report.[20]

The Committee's recommendations were framed to suit the new, and less humanitarian, political climate—if not the post-Niger apathy of the public. The Committee's attitude, however, was far different than that of its predecessor in 1830. It played down the pessimism of the recent Niger failure and the pseudo-scandals that Madden had unearthed. Instead, it called for a more active British role in West

19. Lord John Russell to R. R. Madden, 26 November 1840, PP, 1842, xii (551), p. 1.
20. See Russell's minute of 26 August 1841, Stanley's minute of 25 September 1841, and James Stephen's minute of 5 October 1841 in CO 267/170.

Africa to exploit existing commercial openings. Without explicit
credit to Buxton, it intended to keep some aspects of his plan, shifting
the focus away from the Niger and back to the Windward Coast. The
new strategy called for new coastal strongpoints. Among others, the
Committee recommended the reoccupation of Bulama, the erection of
small blockhouses along the Gambia and the coasts near Sierra Leone,
and the reoccupation of several Gold Coast forts abandoned in 1828,
including Ouidah in Dahomey. British interest in the Bights was to
be protected by buying one of the Portuguese islands, either Principe
or São Thomé.[21]

The administration of the Gold Coast was a matter of special concern. Under the merchants' government from 1828 onward, Gold
Coast affairs had largely dropped from public sight in Britain, except
for extraneous matters like the romantic and mysterious death of
Letitia Landon ("L.E.L."), the popular poetess and wife of George
Maclean, President of the Council at Cape Coast. Serious interest had
revived with the case of Dos Amigos, a slaver whose capture and condemnation at Freetown in 1839 revealed that she had bought supplies
from British merchants on the Gold Coast. The scandal was one of
the special subjects for Madden's investigation and it was soon apparent that British merchants on the Gold Coast made a regular practice of outfitting foreign slavers who called there. It was equally
apparent that, in their anomalous legal position, the merchants' government had no clear power to prevent this.[22] Partly because James
Stephen was suspicious of merchants, partly because of Madden's
damning report, and largely in order to clear the legal ground for
stronger measures against the slave trade, the government accepted the
Committee's recommendation. The Gold Coast forts were returned to
the direct control of the Crown, but as a separate colony and no
longer as a mere dependency of Sierra Leone.

The investigations of Madden and the 1842 Committee also publicized other, and positive, achievements on the Gold Coast. Because
of its peculiar legal position, the merchants' government under
George Maclean had been able to carry out practical innovations in

21. PP, 1842, xi (551), pp. iv–x.
22. Gold Coast Council Minutes, 12 November 1839, AG, Acc. 68/1954. The
authoritative study of the Gold Coast under the merchants' government is G. E. Metcalfe, Maclean of the Gold Coast (London, 1962). For Gold Coast administration after
the return of royal government, see Freda Wolfson, "British Relations with the Gold
Coast, 1843–1880" (Unpublished Ph.D. thesis, London, 1952).

the process of "civilizing" Africa. Maclean, as effective ruler for the merchants between 1830 and 1844, had used his personal prestige to create an *ad hoc* judicial protectorate extending well beyond the forts themselves. With the informal consent of the African authorities, he began by arbitrating disputes, especially those between the tiny Fante states. After this initial opening, he began to sit on certain African courts administering African law, while at the same time urging the Africans to modify their law. By 1840, he had gone far toward illegalizing human sacrifice, and he had secured a wide, if informal, sphere of British judicial influence.

When the forts were taken over in 1843 by the royal government, the judicial protectorate was preserved. The new office of Judicial Assessor was created to continue Maclean's informal jurisdiction, with Maclean himself holding the post until his death in 1847. The informal jurisdiction was formalized by treaty. In 1844 the first of the series of "Bonds" was signed by the Gold Coast government and the African authorities. The Bonds empowered the Gold Coast government to put down human sacrifice and the practice of "panyarring" (kidnapping an individual in order to force his family to pay a debt or redress a grievance), and to try certain other cases. These treaties were the first extension of British legal authority beyond the walls of the forts, the first significant move forward in two hundred years, and they established the Gold Coast "protectorate"—though it was a protectorate for judicial purposes only in the first instance. Dutch and Danish forts were still interspersed with the British, but the new quality of the British presence after 1844 fostered a new habit of thought: the Gold Coast began to be talked of as British "territory," and not simply a series of British posts. In 1850, the British purchased the Danish forts, thus extending their influence eastward from Accra to the Volta. On the Gold Coast at least, the Niger failure and the 1842 Committee marked the beginning of a new British advance, however slow.

South Atlantic migration was another interest of Madden's mission, and of the 1842 Committee. Here again the impetus for change came from events in Europe and America. The legal emancipation of the West Indian slaves in 1834 was followed by a period of "apprenticeship," ending with complete freedom in 1838. After that date, the ex-slaves in many colonies were unwilling to work the sugar and coffee estates—not, at least, on terms the planters offered.

One obvious and early suggestion was to establish a paid-labor equivalent of the slave trade and bring contract workers from the African coast. The 1842 Committee accepted the idea in principle, and justified its morality as a benefit to Africa. Emigrants would return to Africa with some of the "civilization" they had acquired working in the cane fields of the Caribbean.[23] In this sense too, the Committee paid lip service to the goal of Buxton's plan, while radically altering the method.

Meanwhile, the impetus of the Niger Expedition was felt in other ways as well. One was the increased pace of African exploration—not, of course, in government hands, since the Government had sworn off any such effort, but with the support of private commercial, scientific, or humanitarian interests. On the Niger itself, the commercial explorers, who had been there before the government, were still exploring after the government ships left. Jamieson's *Ethiope* under Beecroft's command explored three new mouths of the Niger in the season of 1840 and ascended the main river as far as Raba, which turned out to be the practical limit of navigation. During part of the next season, *Ethiope* helped the government steamers. Later in the year Beecroft moved east again to the Cross River where he had earlier explored with *Quorra*. Again in 1842, he took *Ethiope* to the limit of navigation on the Cross, and in 1845 he was back on the Niger. *Ethiope* later met with an accident, and Niger exploration was given up for almost a decade; but the hiatus had little connection with the spectacular government failure of 1841.[24]

Other new exploration was more closely associated with the Buxton plan. William Cooper Thomson, a CMS missionary, was sent by the government of Sierra Leone in 1841 to try again along the old route to Timbo, first used by Watt and Winterbottom a half century earlier. The object was to keep Sierra Leone in the Niger game by opening a land route from Freetown to the headwaters of the river. An uncertain royal succession in Timbo delayed the party, and finally Thomson died there after a residence of almost two years. His twelve-year-old son brought his journal back to the coast.[25]

The same strategy of reaching toward the upper Niger had its repercussions in the Senegambia. A French expedition under Huard-

---

23. PP, 1842, xi (551), pp. x–xv.

24. *Journal of the Royal Geographical Society*, XI, 184–92 (April, 1841) and XIV, 260–63 (1844).

25. *Journal of the Royal Geographical Society*, XVII, 106–138 (1846).

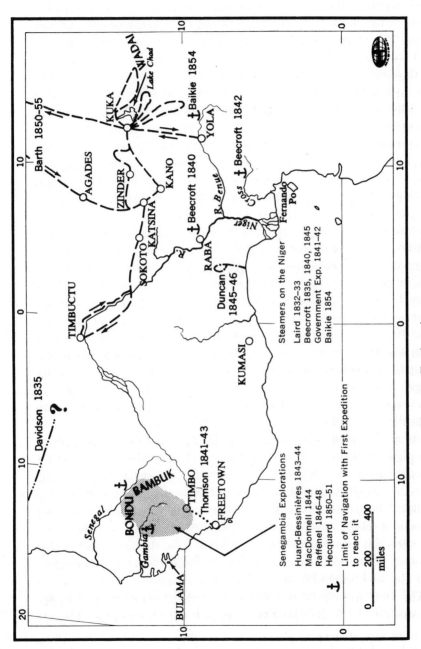

Map 18. Explorations, 1830–1855

Bessinières moved inland to the Falémé River in 1843–44, principally to investigate the prospect of gold trade from the mines of Bambuk, but also (in the aspiration of its members) to prepare for further French expansion eastward from the Senegal. A simultaneous British expedition under the Governor of Gambia, Richard Graves MacDonnell, travelled overland from the Gambia to the Falémé to sign a commercial treaty with Bondu. This time the object was not British expansion, but the security of the caravan routes from the Niger to the Gambia. Between 1846 and 1851, two French expeditions under A. Raffenel and L. H. Hecquard explored the regions inland from Futa Jallon, the upper Gambia, and the upper Senegal as far as Kaarta.[26] The western approaches to the Niger were certainly not neglected.

More consequential new explorations started at the Mediterranean coast. Even here, the impulse of the Niger agitation had an influence. Buxton had emphasized the slave trade from coastal Guinea, but he had also attacked the Muslim-dominated trans-Sahara slave trade. The British government responded by sending Vice-Consuls to a number of posts in the Sahara, and the Anti-Slavery Society sent James Richardson to the Maghrib as an observer, where he occasionally functioned as a government representative as well. He was in Morocco in 1843–44, then in Tunis, and finally in Tripoli in 1845. There he met Warrington and was appointed Vice-Consul for Ghadames. The Turkish conquest of Libya was now secure enough to allow travel to the south, and Richardson visited Ghat, Ghadames, and Murzuk in 1845–46. His journal, published in 1848, in turn pro-

Another short-range exploration of the mid-1840's was based on Dahomey. The traveller was John Duncan, who had served in the Life Guards and resigned in 1839 to become master-at-arms of the Niger Expedition. He now returned to Africa with the support of the Royal Geographical Society to try an overland route from Ouidah north to the "Kong Mountains." His travels in 1845–46 took him into the central part of the modern Republic of Dahomey, but no further. Like the journeys of Thomson and MacDonnell, Duncan's expedition added something to geographical knowledge, but provided small encouragement for further efforts in these particular regions.[27]

---

26. A Raffenel, *Voyage dans l'Afrique occidentale exécuté en 1843 et 1844* (Paris, 1846) and *Nouveau voyage dans le pays des nègres*, 2 vols. (Paris, 1856) ; MacDonnell to Grey, 16 June 1849, PP, 1849, xxxvi [C. 1126], pp. 325–27; L. H. Hecquard, *Voyage sur la côte et dans l'intérieur de l'Afrique occidentale* (Paris, 1853).

27. J. Duncan, *Travels in Western Africa*, 2 vols. (London, 1847).

voked a further British interest in the suppression of the trans-Sahara slave trade.[28]

The Government accepted Richardson's proposal for a major expedition to the Western Sudan. Richardson was put in command, accompanied by two German scholars, Heinrich Barth and Adolf Overweg. The three set out from Tripoli early in 1850, but disease followed its usual course: Richardson died in Bornu in 1851; Overweg died in 1852, and Barth was left to continue alone. Richardson's journal was recovered and published, and Barth was joined from 1853 to 1856 by Edouard Vogel; but the real accomplishment of the expedition was Barth's. His investigations were those of an experienced scholar, based on five years of travel from Wadai on the east to Timbuctu on the west. His five published volumes still remain the greatest single contribution to European knowledge of West Africa.[29]

It was the Richardson-Barth-Overweg expedition that reawakened the Government's interest in the Niger. Barth reached the upper course of the Benue in 1851 and reported that it was navigable for steamers as far as Adamawa. His message reached London early in 1853, where it coincided with the renewed interest of Macgregor Laird. Partly in the hope of finding Barth, Laird was able to persuade the Admiralty to furnish a subsidy for a private venture up the Niger and Benue. He had the *Pleiad* especially designed and built in his brother's yard at Birkenhead. John Beecroft was selected for command, and the Admiralty sent along three naval officers as observers. Beecroft died before the expedition could actually sail, but Dr. W. B. Baikie of the Navy took his place and the expedition steamed up the Niger and Benue in the summer of 1854. It was not a commercial success, but for the first time in Niger exploration no lives were lost. This achievement was possible for a variety of reasons, among others the use of prophylactic quinine, but its crucial importance was to demonstrate, on the very scene of widely publicized death from the "climate," that the Niger was now open.[30] The success of the *Pleiad*

28. J. Richardson, *Travels in the Great Desert of Sahara*, 2 vols. (London, 1848). See A. A. Boahen, "British Penetration of North-West Africa and the Western Sudan, 1788–1861" (Unpublished Ph.D. thesis, London, 1959), pp. 506–8.

29. J. Richardson, *Narrative of a Mission to Central Africa*, 2 vols. (London, 1853); H. Barth, *Travels and Discoveries in North and Central Africa*, 5 vols. (London, 1857–1858).

30. For accounts of the expedition see W. B. Baikie, *Narrative of an Exploring Voyage up the Rivers Kwora and Binue (Commonly Known as the Niger and Tsadda) in 1854* (London, 1856); T. J. Hutchinson, *Narrative of the Niger, Tshadda, &*

marked the end of the experimental era for steam navigation on the Niger, just as Barth's work opened the Western Sudan to a new depth of scientific investigation.

Missionary activity during the 1830's and 1840's followed much the same pattern as exploration. The missionary awakening was now moving at full speed in Europe, though work in West Africa was halting and uncertain during the 1830's. Missionaries died at the usual rate, and the effort suffered from the past reputation of the Coast. Some projects, however, foreshadowed the kind of broad effort the Niger Expedition was to represent. An "Institution for Benefitting the Foulah Tribe" worked in the Gambia from 1831 onward, in close cooperation with the Wesleyan mission. The object was to settle pastoral Fulbe on MacCarthy's Island (the same island which had seemed attractive for the convict project of the 1780's). The missionaries were to teach both agriculture and Christianity in a way suggestive of Buxton's plan for a "model farm." The project failed. Missionaries and agents died, and the Fulbe showed little interest in the sedentary life.

Once the Niger agitation began in Britain, however, the missionary societies used the glare of publicity to highlight missionary opportunities throughout West Africa. Since only the CMS was allowed to send its agents up the river with the government steamers, the other societies chose other regions. The Wesleyans picked Ashanti, and the Rev. T. B. Freeman from their Gold Coast mission made a tour of reconnaissance to Kumasi in 1839, returning again in 1842 to establish the first Christian mission. The Basel Mission, which had been working in the hinterland of Accra since 1828, had only one missionary still alive in 1840; but they launched a new effort in 1843, built around a nucleus of Christian West Indian settlers. This time the foundation was permanent. The Baptist Missionary Society of England followed a similar policy of staffing their missions from the West Indies. The first, established on Fernando Po in 1841, was based on a small group of Jamaican Baptists. In 1846 they moved to the Cameroons mainland. In the same year the Scottish Missionary Society began work in Calabar, again with a missionary transferred

---

Binuë Exploration (London, 1855); S. Crowther, *Journal of an Expedition up the Niger and Tshada in 1854* (London, 1855). See also Ifemesia, "British Enterprise," esp. pp. 342–47 and 402–3.

from Jamaica. The Catholic missions were also re-established in 1842, leading to the creation of a lasting Vicarate-Apostolic in 1847, with initial efforts directed toward Liberia and the French posts.[31]

In point of future British involvement, however, the most important missionary departure of the 1840's was in Yoruba. As early as the 1830's, some degree of order began to return out of the anarchy which followed the collapse of Oyo and the Fulani incursions from the north. The cities of southern Yoruba, some of them newly founded, began to function as nuclei of a returning stability. A new Egba state centered on Abeokuta and the new city of Ibadan began to attract and assimilate refugees from the north. The return of moderate stability presented an unusual opportunity for missionary work. During the period of anarchy the Yoruba had been the largest single group sold into slavery, hence the largest single group to be captured from the slave ships and landed in Sierra Leone. By 1838, a few of them had made their way back to Badagri as coastal traders. In 1839, with an impetus quite separate from that of the Niger Expedition, three liberated Africans in Sierra Leone bought a ship and sailed with trade goods and sixty-seven passengers for Badagri. By 1844, several hundred returnees from Sierra Leone had moved inland and settled in Abeokuta. Since they were already Christian and partly Western in culture, they found ready-made congregations and centers for further proselytizing; and those in Badagri appealed on their own initiative for British protection and missionary assistance. The Methodists answered with a mission station at Badagri in 1842. The CMS established one at Abeokuta in 1846, hoping to extend this mission field overland to the Niger in the vicinity of Raba. The Southern Baptist Convention in the United States followed in 1851 with their own Yoruba Mission.[32]

31. Ifemesia, "British Enterprise," p. 357; T. B. Freeman, *Journal of Various Visits to the Kingdoms of Ashanti, Aku, and Dahomi*, 2nd ed. (London, 1844); J. Beecham, *Ashantee and the Gold Coast* (London, 1841); Basler Evangelische Missions Gesellshaft, *The Basel Mission on the Gold Coast, Western Africa* (Basel, 1879); R. M. Wiltgen, *Gold Coast Missionary History* (Techny, Illinois, 1956), pp. 109–26. The most authoritative recent study of the missionary follow-up of the Niger expedition is J. F. Ade Ajayi, "Christian Missions and the Making of Nigeria, 1841–1891" (Unpublished Ph.D. thesis, London, 1958).

32. This account of missions and British intervention in Yoruba is based on Ajayi, "Christian Missions"; S. O. Biobaku, *The Egba and their Neighbours 1842–1872* (Oxford, 1957); Dike, *Trade and Politics*; A. N. Cook, *British Enterprise in Nigeria* (Philadelphia, 1943); C. W. Newbury, *The Western Slave Coast and its Rulers* (London, 1961); and C. Fyfe, *A History of Sierra Leone* (London, 1962), esp. pp. 212–13.

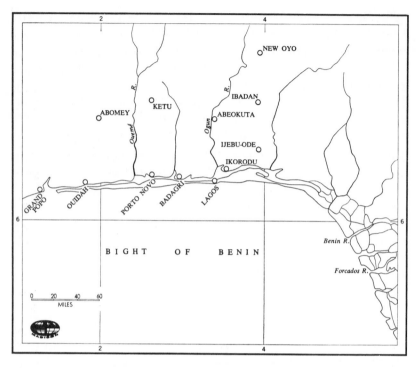

Map 19. The Slave Coast

The spread of British mission stations inevitably involved the British government. The Navy was always present off shore, and officers of the squadron were accustomed to political dealings with African authorities in connection with the anti-slave-trade treaties. By 1849 John Beecroft was appointed Consul for the Bights, with his residence on the still-Spanish island of Fernando Po. In spite of the official policy of no further commitments, the presence of British interests on shore, British power at sea, and the continued intention to suppress the slave trade easily led to more forceful intervention. The decisive action occurred in 1851, and it grew out of the missionary interest in the Yoruba hinterland of Lagos and Badagri. The principal rivals in this region were the new Abeokuta, with its contingent of British missionaries, and the older power of Dahomey. Dahomey controlled its own exit to the sea through Ouidah, while Abeokuta had to deal through one of the independent city-states, either Lagos, Porto Novo, or Badagri. When Dahomey invaded Abeokuta, the policy of no commitment broke down. How could the British government withstand the appeal made (for public consumption) by the Reverend Henry Townsend to the Church Missionary Society? "Can England stand by, and look on and see Christians who have become so through England's love of the Gospel, filling the barracoons of the slave merchant first, and then suffering and dying under the cruel usage of the taskmaster?"[33]

Consul Beecroft decided for action, first by sending military supplies inland to Abeokuta, then by ordering a blockade of all ports except Badagri (at that time Abeokuta's principal avenue to the sea), finally by landing a naval force to reduce Lagos. It was believed at the time that a single intervention could install a more cooperative ruler in Lagos. "Legitimate trade" could then flow freely to Abeokuta, and British power would no longer be needed. In fact, this belief was mistaken. A fresh landing at Lagos was necessary in 1853, and, in 1861, intervention was followed by outright British annexation of the port; but the annexation merely confirmed the *de facto* relations established in 1851. Once the British had thrown their weight on the balance of African rivalries, they could not withdraw without accepting the defeat of their allies, and the defeat of their allies would have meant victory for those who were now the enemies of Britain as well. However firmly the Government may have decided in 1842 to withdraw from the Niger, within a decade they were firmly established on the Bight of Benin. Only a decision to abandon the effort to suppress the slave trade by naval force could have loosened that commitment.

A final ripple from the foundering of the Niger Expedition almost brought about such a change. The necessity of maintaining the blockade had hardly been questioned before 1840. More than once the needs of the squadron had saved the West African posts from evacuation. Buxton, however, exposed the fact that blockading the African coast had not, in fact, stopped or even seriously discouraged the foreign slave trade. His own recommendation to reinforce the squadron was not the only possibility. A movement to remove it altogether grew in strength during the 1840's.

One source of opposition was humanitarian. It was alleged that the blockade increased the suffering of the slaves in transit, by forcing

33. Townsend to Secretary of the Church Missionary Society, 17 October 1849, PP, 1852, liv [C. 1455], p. 33.

the shippers to pack them even more tightly and treat them less humanely than they had done in the days of the legal slave trade. Many Quakers also objected to the use of force by the Navy, even in a good cause. A pacifist wing led by Joseph Sturge broke more or less openly with the Buxton group in 1839 and formed the British and Foreign Anti-Slavery Society to work for emancipation everywhere—but only by peaceful means.

Another and stronger objection came from those who disliked the cost in money and lives of a naval operation that seemed to accomplish nothing. In 1848, William Hutt, a free-trader formerly associated with the Colonial Reformers in the settlement of New Zealand, mustered a Parliamentary following and moved for a Select Committee of the House of Commons to investigate the foreign slave trade and its prevention. The Hutt Committee took evidence during two sessions and recommended in 1849 that the squadron should be withdrawn. Supporters of the squadron in turn organized their own following and moved for a similar Committee of the House of Lords. The Lord's Committee heard evidence under the chairmanship of Samuel Wilberforce, Bishop of Oxford and son of the great anti-slavery leader. It recommended that the squadron should be maintained and strengthened.

The issue drawn between the two Committees had broader implications than appear on the surface. The evidence they took represented a broad spectrum of British attitudes. In matters far beyond the issue at stake, it revealed a fundamental revision since 1830 of British thought about African problems. Some of the old fire was gone from the supporters of humanitarian action. A new faith in the efficacy of the "unseen hand" of economic interest was replacing the earlier faith in British morality and British gunboats as twin arbiters of the South Atlantic. But the humanitarians were not yet defeated. They rallied their friends, and conducted a new political agitation in Parliament and in the country. In March 1850 they once more won a decisive victory in the House of Commons—and in the face of the adverse report of the Hutt Committee.[34]

It was not, perhaps, their last victory, but it was the last victory they needed on this particular issue. Not quite by coincidence, the

---

34. The evidence and reports of the two Committees are found in PP, 1847–1848, xxii (272) (336) (536) (623); PP, 1849, xix (308) (410); PP (Lords), 1849, xviii (32); PP (Lords), 1850, xxiv (35).

Brazilian government accepted the inevitable later in 1850. Under anti-slavery pressure from the British and the Brazilians alike, Brazil began enforcing her own anti-slave-trade legislation. The estimated numbers of slaves imported into the country dropped from 54,000 in 1849, to just over 3,000 in 1851, to a mere trickle of smuggled slaves after 1852.[35] This change broke the back of the Atlantic slave trade. It continued for another fifteen years, but in vastly diminished quantity, and with cargoes drawn mainly from Lower Guinea.

For most of West Africa the era of the slave trade had come to an end. The era of the Niger expedition was thus the last era of humanitarian dominance in British policy, the last era of important slave trade, and the last era in which British investigators stood off from West Africa as a continent they hardly dared to enter.

35. Lloyd, *Navy and the Slave Trade*, pp. 139–48, 176.

13

REPORTING WEST AFRICA:

SOURCES

AND USES OF INFORMATION

Even during the disinterested decade of the 1830's, some new data continued to flow from West Africa to Britain, but the quality and quantity were both altered. Exploration no longer had its old appeal. With the Niger problem solved and "Timbuctu the mysterious" visited by two expeditions, the quarterlies turned to other matters. Travellers' accounts were limited to the now-familiar regions of the Guinea coast.

Buxton's *Slave Trade,* however, awakened a new kind of interest, beginning in 1839. A new stream of literature began to appear, growing into a small flood during the course of the 1840's, but publishers of that decade had nothing equivalent to the earlier classics of Mungo Park or Clapperton. Instead, they seemed to make up the deficiency in sheer quantity, turning out books, pamphlets, and secondary surveys designed to summarize what was known or to plead the case for a specific policy.

The boom in West Africana lasted through the 1840's, declining slowly as the decade progressed. After a short revival timed with the meeting of the Hutt Committee, it died away in the course of the

1850's to the level of popular disinterest shown in the 1820's or early 1830's. The decline was apparent as early as 1851.[1] The reviews carried less and less African material. *Blackwood's,* which had published so many of MacQueen's essays in the great era of exploration, published nothing at all about West Africa in the whole decade of the 1850's.

Richard Burton himself wrote in 1858 that readers were becoming bored with "the montonous recital of rapine, treachery, and murder; of ugly savages . . . of bleared misery by day, and animated filth by night, of hunting adventures and hairbreadth escapes, lacking the interest of catastrophe."[2] He was, perhaps, a little pessimistic, since he was to have a large audience for his accounts of East Africa and the Arab lands. Still, he was correct, contrasting this period with the 1820's.

David Livingstone's report of 1857 on his first great missionary journey, however, struck the right mixture of "hunting adventures and hairbreadth escapes" combined with moral purpose, and Livingstone himself helped to draw public attention from the Niger to the Zambezi. By contrast, Barth's masterpiece of West African scholarship and exploration, published in the same year as Livingstone's, was a commercial failure. The first three volumes sold so poorly that the modest print order of 2,250 copies was reduced to 1,000 for the later volumes.[3]

In part, Barth's lesser popularity was to be expected. He was a scholar writing for a scholarly as well as a popular audience, and his work was translated from German in a way that made it stylistically unattractive. In addition, Livingstone visited totally new country. He could report its marvels and horrors to an astonished public, even as Park or Bowdich had once done in West Africa. By contrast, Barth was going over old ground, although he went over it far more thoroughly than any of his predecessors had done. Park, Clapperton, and Denham had, nevertheless, set the initial image of the Western Sudan —and at a time when such reports were widely read and commented on. Barth's work might alter the knowledge of the specialists, but it could not change the superficial image of the broader public.

1. *Westminster Review,* XLV, 1 (1851).
2. R. Burton, "Zanzibar; and Two Months in East Africa," *Blackwood's Magazine,* LXXXIII, 282 (1858).
3. A. H. M. Kirk-Greene, "Barth: A Centenary Memoir," *West Africa,* XLII, 1231 (27 December 1958).

The new generation of explorers also began to write to a new pattern. They were, in part, reduced to retelling an old story. Buxton's agitation, for example, created a public demand for books about the Niger, and publishers appeared willing to meet this demand over and over again. Twelve of the seventeen book-length accounts by British explorers in West Africa in this period were concerned with the lower course of the Niger.[4] With so many narratives in the field, the most apparent excuse for still another was a new story of adventure. The Niger travellers of the 1840's were thus more personal and less inclined than their predecessors to describe people and places.

Exploration on the Niger posed still another problem. Travel by steamer necessarily followed a pattern of rapid penetration and withdrawal, before the river could fall at the onset of the dry season. Only Laird and Oldfield in the early 1830's enjoyed a relatively leisurely trip followed by detailed publication. Beecroft saw more of the river than anyone else, but very little of his information was published. Many of the scientists of the government expedition of 1841–

4. William Allen and T. R. H. Thomson, *A Narrative of the Expedition to the River Niger in 1841*, 2 vols. (London, 1848); W. Allen, *Picturesque Views on the River Niger* (London, 1840); W. B. Baikie, *Narrative of an Exploring Voyage up the Rivers Kwora and Binue (Commonly Known as the Niger and Tsadda) in 1854* (London, 1856); H. Barth, *Travels and Discoveries in North and Central Africa*, 5 vols. (London, 1857–1858); Samuel Crowther, *Journal of an Expedition up the Niger and Tshada in 1854* (London, 1855); John Duncan, *Travels in Western Africa*, 2 vols. (London, 1847); F. E. Forbes, *Dahomey and the Dahomans*, 2 vols. (London, 1851); T. B. Freeman, *Journal of Various Visits to the Kingdoms of Ashanti, Aku, and Dahomi*, 2nd ed. (London, 1844); T. J. Hutchinson, *Narrative of the Niger, Tshadda & Binuë Exploration* (London, 1855); S. W. Koelle, *Narrative of an Expedition into the Vy Country of West Africa* (London, 1849); R. and J. Lander, *Journal of an Expedition to Explore the Course and Termination of the Niger . . .*, 3 vols. (London, 1832); M. Laird and R. A. K. Oldfield, *Narrative of an Expedition into the Interior of Africa by the River Niger in 1832–4*, 2 vols. (London, 1837); J. O. M'William, *Medical History of the Expedition to the Niger during the years 1841–42 . . .* (London, 1843); James Richardson, *Narrative of a Mission to Central Africa*, 2 vols. (London, 1853); J. F. Schön and S. Crowther, *Journals of the Rev. James Frederick Schön and Mr. Samuel Crowther, who with the Sanction of Her Majesty's Government Accompanied the Expedition up the Niger in 1841* (London, 1842); William Simpson, *Private Journal Kept During the Niger Expedition* (London, 1843). The Niger coverage represented here includes one report from Lander's successful descent of the river in 1830, two from the 1832–1834 expedition, five from the government Niger Expedition of 1841–1842, and three from the *Pleiad* expedition of 1854. In addition to the final reports of Barth and Richardson, the Richardson-Barth-Overweg-Vogel expedition was covered in an interim report by A. Peterman, *An Account of the Progress of the Expedition to Central Africa . . .* (London, 1854), and Dr. Vogel's journals were edited in Germany by Hermann Wagner as *Schilderung der Reisen und Entdeckungen des Dr. Eduard Vogel in Central-Afrika* (Leipzig, 1860).

42 died before they could finish their work. Although Allen and Thomson tried to pull together the threads in a brief report on botany, zoology, and ethnography for their semi-official account, they too were hampered by the shortness of their visit. Thus the Niger narratives bulked large, but they fell far below the intentions of the promoters—or the hopes of the scholars.

The professional background of the explorers continued to be non-scholarly and non-scientific. Only the three Germans, Schön, Koelle, and Barth, had scholarly training, all three in linguistics or philology. Of these, both Schön and Koelle were professional linguists employed by the Church Missionary Society, and their reports were often narrowly confined to their professional specialties. Two other inland explorers of the period were missionaries, Samuel Crowther of CMS and T. B. Freeman of the Wesleyan-Methodist Missionary Society. Both were Western in culture but African in descent. Freeman was born in Britain of a British mother and an African father. Crowther was born in Yoruba, emancipated from a slave ship, and educated in Sierra Leone. Perhaps because of their race, both Freeman and Crowther were less culture-bound than most Western explorers. They depicted real people with a comprehensible way of life, in place of the cardboard savages in the accounts of most of their colleagues; but they too measured Africa by Western standards and found it wanting. They were less successful than Barth in really penetrating the culture barrier.

Most of the explorers were either military or medical men. Duncan, Forbes, and Allen were officers in the forces. Baikie, M'William, Oldfield, Hutchinson, and Thomson were doctors, often with a military background as well. Both the medical and military travellers had a professional tradition of accurate reporting, but neither were well equipped to understand an alien society. The value of their data was therefore highly variable. The best of them, such as Allen, Baikie, and Forbes, simply reported what they saw, from a slightly ethnocentric point of view, but avoiding both theory and value judgements. Thomson and M'William tended to confine their reports to medical matters in which they specialized. At the other end of the scale, Hutchinson and Duncan were culture bound in the extreme and followed Lander's device of poking fun at African culture.

This particular technique for keeping the readers' interest was increasingly characteristic of travel writing as the government exploring missions gave way to a less official kind of visit. The naval blockade came, by the 1830's, to provide a special reservoir of leisured would-be literary talent, and military or naval reminiscences began to appear with greater frequency.[5] The authors rarely had any real interest in Africa as such. They wrote to give their fellow countrymen a vicarious enjoyment of their adventures—laced with occasional political recommendations about the blockade or other timely topics. Vignettes of life on shore were introduced for light amusement or sensationalism. Human sacrifice in Ashanti, the female army in Dahomey, the "humorous" attempts of the emancipated Africans in Sierra Leone to re-educate themselves in the ways of the Western world—all this was standard fare.

The memoirs of civilian visitors or residents formed another and allied class of literature,[6] but it was more diverse than the military memoirs. The worst were very bad indeed, and the worst of all was J. Smith's *Trade and Travel in the Gulph of Guinea,* where sensationalism reached a peak. The sub-heads under the chapter on Human Sacrifice give the flavor: "Nailing prisoners—Jack Ketch—Decapitation—Cooking and eating human flesh—Priests—King Pepple eats

5. The following are a representative selection of this class of literature: J. E. Alexander, *Narrative of a Voyage of Observation among the Colonies of Western Africa,* 2 vols. (London, 1837); [Horatio Bridge], Nathaniel Hawthorne (Ed.), *Journal of an African Cruiser by an Officer of the U.S. Navy* (London, 1845); F. E. Forbes, *Six Months' Service in the African Blockade* (London, 1849); Pascoe G. Hill, *A Voyage to the Slave Coasts of West and East Africa* (London, 1849); H. V. Huntley, *Seven Years' Service on the Slave Coast of Western Africa,* 2 vols. (London, 1850); Peter Leonard, *Records of a Voyage to the Western Coast of Africa . . . in the Years 1830, 1831, and 1832* (Edinburgh, 1833); T. E. Poole, *Life, Scenery, and Customs in Sierra Leone and the Gambia,* 2 vols. (London, 1850); "Reminiscences of the Gold Coast, Being Extracts from Notes taken during a Tour of Service in 1847-8," *Colburn's United Service Magazine,* 1850 (III), 67–68, 573–88, and 1851 (I), 93–103; H. I. Ricketts, *Narrative of the Ashantee War with a View of the Present State of Sierra Leone* (London, 1831).

6. See, for example, Robert Clarke, *Sierra Leone: Description of the Manners and Customs of the Liberated Africans . . .* (London, 1843); Hugh Crow, *Memoirs* (London, 1830); Brodie Cruickshank, *Eighteen Years on the Gold Coast of Africa, Including an Account of the Native Tribes, and Their Intercourse with Europeans,* 2 vols. (London, 1853); J. Fawckner, *Narrative of Captain James Fawckner's Travels on the Coast of Benin, West Africa* (London, 1837); James Holman, *A Voyage Round the World . . . ,* 4 vols. (London, 1834–1835); [Elizabeth Melville], *A Residence in Sierra Leone* (London, 1849); "Private Journal of a Voyage to the Western Coast of Africa," *Edinburgh New Philosophical Journal* (October, 1830); F. Harrison Rankin, *The White Man's Grave: A Visit to Sierra Leona in 1834,* 2 vols. (London, 1836); A. R. Ridgeway, "Journal of a Visit to Dahomey; or the Snake Country," *New Monthly Magazine,* LXXXI, 187–98, 299–309, 406–14 (1847); W. W. Shreeve, *Sierra Leone: The Principal British Colony on the Western Coast of Africa* (London, 1847); J. Smith, *Trade and Travel in the Gulph of Guinea* (London, 1851).

King Amacree's heart—Sacrifice human beings to the god of the Bar
—Shipwrecks." In other respects as well, Smith's attitude toward
Africans was uncordial. According to his recommendation, "the best
way to treat a black man, is to hold out one hand to shake hands
with him, while the other is doubled ready to knock him down."[7] Yet
the work seems to carry no overt propaganda message: it was simply
written to amuse.

A few of the civilian accounts, however, were minor classics of
nineteenth-century travel literature. Brodie Cruickshank's *Eighteen
Years on the Gold Coast* was one of these. Unlike most visitors,
Cruickshank stayed long enough to gain real understanding and at-
tachment for one part of Africa. The common attitude of the time,
for example, was to interpret the tropical environment as both alien
and forbidding. A romantic antithesis was often drawn between the
beauty of nature and the sinister shadow of tropical death: "But with
all that it is pleasing to the eye, it is but a painted sepulchre. It is
painful to the imagination to conceive that this very exuberance of
vegetation is the remote cause of that great destruction of European
life, for which the place [Sierra Leone] is so distinguished—contami-
nating the surrounding atmosphere with mephitic exalations by its
annual death and putrefaction."[8]

For Cruickshank, by contrast, the spell of the tropics was what it
had been for Smeathman, attractive in its exoticism, yet friendly:

> The Gold Coast of Africa, extending from Asinee to the River Volta, pre-
> sents a wide field for curious and varied speculation. Its sunny skies, but
> seldom disfigured by gloom or tempest; its modulating sweep of hill and dale;
> its deep impenetrable thickets; its magnificent forest trees, the ever-verdant
> freshness of its luxurious vegetation; the richness of its mineral wealth, still
> shrouded in the mysterious recesses of its mountains, or in the depths of its
> dark and muddy streams; its luscious fruits; the gorgeous plumage of its birds;
> and the endless variety of animal and insect life, which inhabit its wild jungle
> tracts; invest it with an indescribable charm of vague and wandering curiosity.[9]

Cruickshank was also able to discuss African culture from a base
of extensive experience. Though he was no scholar, his treatment of
Fante customs and religion was one of the best of the nineteenth
century. His judgments were often as unfavorable as those of his
contemporaries, but real understanding came first, and the judgment

7. Smith, *Trade and Travel*, p. 197.
8. Leonard, *Voyage to the Western Coast of Africa*, pp. 38–39.
9. Cruickshank, *Eighteen Years*, I, 1–2.

followed. Cruickshank also paid a price for staying in one place: he had few "adventures"—and few readers—and the image dominant in Britain came from other sources.

Rankin's *White Man's Grave* was of great importance as an unusually full account of Sierra Leone, widely read in the 1830's. The title became a famous catch phrase, though Rankin himself meant it ironically. He was, in fact, one of the very few advocates of European colonization. In other respects, his work was very nearly typical of the reports that well intentioned travellers produced over and over again. He defended the Sierra Leone experiment and opposed the slave trade and slavery. His attitude toward the Africans was kindly, without trace of racial fear or real dislike, but the two volumes are full of sly digs and small jokes at the Africans' expense. The total impression he gave was that of an amusing, pleasant, and childlike people, but a people whose ultimate capacity was very much in doubt.

The missionary image of Africa was again different from that of secular humanitarians like Rankin—and far more important in the sheer quantity of print that began to deluge the English public. Publication was essential to the missions. Unlike the government or the traders, they lived on voluntary contributions. If the missions in the field were to continue their day-to-day operations, the missionary societies at home had to maintain a regular flow of contributions: sole dependence on spectacular events, like the Niger Expedition, was not enough. The link between publicity and fund raising was established early in the century. Article VIII of the Wesleyan-Methodist "Instructions to Missionaries" read: "It is *preemptorily required* of every Missionary in our Connexion to keep a Journal, and to send home frequently such copious extracts of it as may give full and particular account of his labours, success, and prospects. He is also required to give such details of a religious kind, as may be generally interesting to the friends of the Missions at home; particularly accounts of conversions. . . ."[10] The Church Missionary Society had a similar requirement, and these two were the most important British societies on the West Coast.

By the 1830's, both had developed a systematic range of publications designed to carry their message to all groups and classes of their supporters. For the leaders of the movement there were annual reports, outlining administrative dispositions, the state of missionary affairs in all parts of the world, and the financial condition of the

---

10. Wesleyan-Methodist Missionary Society, *Annual Report*, 1827, pp. xiii–xiv.

organization.[11] Educated laymen and the clergy were given further information in religious journals like the *Methodist Magazine,* or, after 1849, the *Church Missionary Intelligencer.* The *Intelligencer* published reviews, articles on missionary work and methods, and the scholarly contributions of field missionaries. It was, in short, a medium of inter-communication among the elite of the movement.

A second type of publication was designed for the general public. Here the journals and letters from field missionaries came into their own, printed either as verbatim extracts or rewritten in a more popular style. In this way, each contributor could have a sense of vicarious participation in the righting of wrongs and the eradication of paganism. These periodicals were scaled to reach as many different levels of British society as possible. The monthlies, such as the *Church Missionary Record* or the *Wesleyan Missionary Notices,* were designed for the educated middle class. In the CMS series, the *Juvenile Instructor* carried the message to young people, while the CMS *Quarterly Paper* was designed for circulation "amongst our friends in the humbler ranks of life."[12]

The same range and type of material also appeared in the missionary book trade. One common form of publication was an edition of the letters and journals of a single missionary, either worked up by the missionary himself,[13] put together by a pious relative, or compiled by the missionary society as part of its public relations work.[14] These accounts were sometimes rewritten with embellishments for the more popular audience. Miss Tucker's *Abbeokuta: or Sunrise within the Tropics* was so successful as a secondary account of the CMS Yoruba mission, it was immediately copied by a similar popularization of W. A. B. Johnson's memoir of his work in Sierra Leone.[15] With a broader sweep, popular ethnography could be combined with exhorta-

11. Wesleyan-Methodist Missionary Society, *Annual Reports; Proceedings of the Church Missionary Society* (annual).

12. *Church Missionary Intelligencer,* I, 2 (1849). See J. F. Ade Ajayi, "Christian Missions and the Making of Nigeria 1841–1891" (Unpublished Ph.D. thesis, London, 1958), pp. 649ff. for a discussion of the missionary literature of the period.

13. See, for example, R. M. Macbrair, *Sketches of a Missionary's Travels in Egypt, Syria, Western Africa, &c., &c.* (London, 1839); J. L. Wilson, *Western Africa: its History, Condition, and Prospects* (New York, 1856); William Fox, *A Brief History of the Wesleyan Missions on the Western Coast of Africa* (London, 1851).

14. See Sarah Biller (Ed.), *Memoir of the Late Hannah Kilham* . . . (London, 1837); *A Memoir of the Rev. W. A. B. Johnson* (London, 1852); George Townsend (Ed.), *Memoir of the Rev. Henry Townsend* (London, 1887).

15. Sarah Tucker, *Abbeokuta, or Sunrise within the Tropics* . . . (London, 1853); [Maria Louisa Charlesworth], *Africa's Mountain Valley; or, the Church in Regent's Town, West Africa* (London, 1856).

tion to support missions;[16] or a narrower focus, appropriate to the children's trade, could be given through the life of a single convert. Samuel Crowther, the former Yoruba slave boy who became a CMS missionary, and later a bishop, was most useful for this purpose.[17] The message of racial equality was combined with moral exhortation and a brief sermon on "self help," exemplified by Crowther's rise from lowly origins. The sins of Portuguese slave traders were even associated with the fact that many were Catholic, thus teaching the superiority of Protestant Christianity.

The burden of the argument in all the popular missionary publications, however, was to demonstrate the overwhelming need for missionary work. They insisted on the ultimate racial equality of all men, but they also embodied the worst aspects of cultural chauvinism. It was not enough to show that the unconverted Africans were doomed hereafter as worshippers of idols and followers of false gods. They were doomed on this earth as well to a nasty and barbarous way of life from which only Christianity could save them. The darker the picture of African barbarism, the more necessary the work of the missionaries. While the cultural chauvinism of private missionary letters or the more scholarly missionary journals was no greater than that of other Western writers on African affairs, the popular missionary publications were selective. They consciously chose to report on those aspects of African culture most likely to be shocking to their readers, and they often omitted sections of journals and letters that stressed elements common to all human cultures.

The force of the argument was heightened by setting present misery against possible achievement. The contrast commonly drawn between West Africa as a land of beauty and a land of death became, in missionary hands, a contrast between natural beauty and the evil of man. In the version of the Reverend D. J. East it was given a further twist to set material riches against moral poverty: "Africa itself is one of the finest and most beautiful as well as the most fruitful portions of the globe. No other country surpasses it in native riches. Its fertile plains will raise almost every production peculiar to a tropical climate. . . . Its mineral wealth is immense. Some dis-

16. As in D. J. East, *Western Africa; Its Condition, and Christianity the Means of Its Recovery* (London, 1844).

17. See *The African Slave Boy, A Memoir of the Rev. Samuel Crowther, Church Missionary, at Abbeokuta, Western Africa* (London, [1852?]).

tricts are literally impregnated with precious metals, and their stores of gold, in particular are inexhaustible."

But he held that man had failed to develop what God gave him, because: "Africa is a moral wilderness, and her inhabitants, as they have been too correctly described, are wolves to each other."[18]

An even more common theme showed the Africans before and after their conversion, often in a way that drew on the older balance of virtue and vice in the "African character." The "before" image featured slave raiding, human sacrifice, lascivious dances, highly sexual religious ceremonies, and the wicked excesses of polygyny—incidentally providing a mild titilation to keep up the readers' interest. By contrast, the "after" image showed the mild and gentle disposition of the converted Africans, their respect for the white missionaries, their childlike innocence.[19]

The combined impression was ideal for missionary purposes and it repeated familiar elements. It recalled the old legend of Negro sexuality. It supported the possibility of rapid conversion by reference to the Christianized version of the noble savage—the belief that Africans were, in some sense, natural Christians. Fowell Buxton accepted this view, saying: "I have no hesitation in stating my belief that there is in the negro race a capacity for receiving the truths of the Gospel beyond most other heathen nations; . . . ."[20]

W. R. Greg explained it in greater detail: "The European is vehement, energetic, proud, tenacious, and revengeful: the African is docile, gentle, humble, grateful, and commonly forgiving. The one is ambitious, and easily aroused; the other meek, easily contented, and easily subdued. The one is to the other as the willow to the oak. The European character appears to be the soil best fitted for the growth of the hardy and active virtues hallowed by Pagan morality; the African character to be more especially adapted for developing the mild and passive excellencies which the gentle spirit of Christianity delights to honour."[21] Greg's statement was so apposite for missionary purposes, it was quoted in full (without credit to Greg) in the Reverend D. J. East's general work on missionary theory.

The greatest diffusion of the idea, however, came only with the

18. East, *Western Africa*, pp. 5–6.
19. See Ajayi, "Christian Missions," pp. 598–99.
20. T. Fowell Buxton, *The African Slave Trade* (London, 1839), p. xi.
21. *Westminster Review*, XXXIX, 5 (January 1843).

1850's, when Harriet Beecher Stowe gave it dramatic form in *Uncle Tom's Cabin*. *Uncle Tom* became the most widely read book ever produced on the subject of race relations, and many more copies were sold in England than in America.[22]

While the missionary literature preserved and extended the Christianized image of the noble savage, missionary ethnography killed once and for all the secular, eighteenth-century literary motif—so much so that a missionary commentator could even boast of the deed: "The universal degredation and misery of unreclaimed man, even of that boast of a false philosophy, the North American Indian—has chiefly, by the circulation of Missionary information, become a fact as fully accredited as that of his existence. In vain would it be for a certain class of Europeans to paint in glowing colours as they once did, the virtue of Asiatic pagans. . . ."[23]

The missionaries were not alone to blame for the increasing cultural arrogance of the British public, but they bear a special responsibility. The views presented in their popular press were unequivocal, and they were very widely circulated. By contrast, their more sophisticated reports and works of scholarship were circulated to a narrower public in journals like the *Church Missionary Intelligencer*—or else remained in the files. The broader public, furthermore, could easily miss the point that the sins of African culture were not caused by the race of those who practiced them. It is hard to escape the conclusion that the systematic misrepresentation of African culture in the missionary press contributed unintentionally to the rise of racial as well as cultural arrogance.

The missionary image was all the more important, because it reached its real flowering in the 1830's and '40's when the possible antidote of critical scholarly investigation based on first-hand information was lacking. From the death of Bowdich to the expedition which took Barth to Africa in 1849, the ethnography of Africa depended almost entirely on data supplied by men who happened to be in Africa for some other purpose. Dr. W. F. Daniell gave a report

---

22. East, *Western Africa*, pp. 102–4; J. C. Furnas, *Goodbye to Uncle Tom* (New York, 1956).

23. John Harris, *The Great Commission* (London, 1842), p. 233. See also *Eclectic Review*, XII (n.s.), 79–80 (1847). The missionary movement had even earlier opposed the image of the noble savage outside of Africa. (See Bernard Smith, *European Vision and the South Pacific 1768–1850. A Study in the History of Art and Ideas* [London, 1960], pp. 107–9 and 243–47.)

on the ethnography of Old Calabar to the British Association in
1845, and another scholarly paper on the Ga-Adangme peoples in
1842, which was followed by still another on Ga ethnography in
1849.[24] Otherwise, ethnographers were armchair scholars. Modern
field research was still many decades away, and the kind of work
done by a generation of enlightened travellers had died out. The
single exception was the research of linguists who came to West
Africa in the service of the missionary societies. Perhaps Guinea's
growing reputation as a land of death was enough to discourage
scholars who lacked the special drive of missionary zeal. In any event,
general ethnographers stayed at home.

Meanwhile, the social sciences in Europe were passing through a
period of development and reorganization. New lines of investigation
gradually became formalized into separate disciplines. One of the
first steps was the formation of a scholarly society, such as the Royal
Geographical Society, founded in 1831. The Society with its journal
set out to improve the quantity and quality of reporting from all
parts of the world, prepared special instructions for travellers, and
acted as a clearing house for the new data.

Other disciplines were less fortunate, lacking the traditional recognition geography already enjoyed. Scholars came to an interest in
African culture and history from many and diverse backgrounds—
from medicine, from moral philosophy, from botany, from linguistics,
or from a Christian humanitarian concern about government policy.
As these interests coalesced into a new and separate discipline, the
strongest pull came from the biological sciences. J. C. Prichard had
already established a precedent by annexing ethnography to his study
of man's physical nature. The first anthropological societies came from
a further merger of Prichard's biological orientation with the political concerns of the humanitarians.

The occasion arose in 1837, at the time of Buxton's Parliamentary
Committee on the Aborigines. Dr. Thomas Hodgkin, a Quaker
humanitarian, a friend of Prichard, and Professor of Anatomy at
Guy's Hospital, began to work informally, supplying the Committee

24. *Reports of the British Association for the Advancement of Science*, XV, 79–80
(1845); W. F. Daniell, "On the Natives of Old Callebar, West Coast of Africa,"
Journal of the Ethnological Society, I, 210–27 (1848), W. F. Daniell, "On the Ethnography of Akkrah and Adampe, Gold Coast, Western Africa," *Journal of the Ethnological Society*, IV, 1–32 (1856); *Reports of the British Association*, 1849 (II), 85.

with ethnological data. He then formed a permanent organization with a dual purpose: one objective was to save the aborigines in the British settlement colonies from possible extinction as a result of European immigration; the other was to study those peoples who seemed to be on the point of disappearance. The new society, called the Aborigines Protection Society (APS), was thus partly a political pressure group and partly an ethnological society. Buxton himself became the first chairman, though Thomas Hodgkin dominated its affairs until 1847.[25]

The first purely scientific ethnological society was founded in France rather than England, but it too was a direct outgrowth of Hodgkin's efforts. In 1838, Hodgkin wrote to W. F. Edwards in Paris, suggesting that he organize a French companion society to the APS. Edwards agreed, but the French scholars were more interested in scientific than humanitarian objectives. They therefore reversed the order of priority and formed the Société Ethnologique, with the preservation of the aborigines as a secondary objective.

Being first in the field, the French ethnologists set the earliest definition of its subject matter. Ethnology on either side of the Channel was already the study of human races. The crucial point was the precise definition of race. On the basis of Edwards' assumption that culture and history were largely determined by physical race, the Société Ethnologique held that races were to be distinguished by "physical organisation, intellectual and moral character, and historical traditions." Only the first of these items would be recognized today as a racial characteristic: the rest are cultural or historical. The mistaken identity of race and culture was thus incorporated in the very beginnings of the science, and physical and cultural anthropology were brought together in the unhappy marriage that has not yet dissolved.

British ethnologists would have agreed in linking race and culture, without assuming that one or the other was the dominant factor. They therefore accepted the essence of the French definition, but they added some assumptions of their own. The founders of the APS were convinced monogenists, and the motto of the Society was "Ab Uno Sanguine."[26]

25. Aborigines Protection Society, *Extracts from the Papers and Proceedings* . . . , I, 99–100 (August–September, 1839); *The Aborigines Protection Society, Chapters in its History* (London, 1899), pp. 3–14.

26. *Mémoires de la Société Ethnologique*, I (1), i–v (1841). The definition of

The English Society's curious double function as political pressure group combined with a scientific body was not to last. In its early years, the humanitarian side was dominant, so much so that the scientific members began to meet separately. In 1843 they formed a separate Ethnological Society—apparently in order to have a more efficient organization, not because of disagreement within the group. Early meetings of the Ethnological Society were held at Thomas Hodgkin's house, and Prichard still lent his scientific prestige to the humanitarian cause.[27]

Even the formation of a separate society could not rescue British ethnology from a special kind of limbo in the shadow of traditional humanities and the natural sciences. The Ethnological Society claimed an interest in linguistic studies, but so did the Philological Society of London, founded in 1842 and principally concerned with the languages of the Mediterranean basin. Until 1847, ethnological papers were presented to the British Association for the Advancement of Science under the heading of Physiology. Even after 1847, when an Ethnological sub-section was created, it fell under the general heading of Zoology and Botany. Ethnology was recognized, but not yet as an entity separate from its biological origins.

Ethnologists also had a problem of data. Few were able to make a full-time professional commitment to the new science. They began, therefore, by expanding and refining the technique of the questionnaire, following the practice of the Geographers. In 1834, Colonel John R. Jackson, a correspondent of the Royal Geographical Society living in St. Petersburg, had prepared a mammoth 500-page questionnaire for geography.[28] The ubiquitous Thomas Hodgkin presented a plan to the Philological Society for a similar language questionnaire as part of a large effort to record dying and out of the way languages.[29] In ethnology itself, Prichard presented a similar project to

ethnology and of culture developed in the same decade by Gustav Klemm in *Allegemeine Cultur-Geschicte der Menschheit*, 10 parts (Leipzig, 1843–1852) was considerably closer to modern anthropological usage, but it was not influential in England.

27. Richard King, "Anniversary Address, May 1844," *Journal of the Ethnological Society*, II, 14–16 (1854).

28. [J. R. Jackson], *Aide-mémoire du voyageur, ou questions relatives à la géographie physique et politique* . . . (Paris, 1834). See *Journal of the Royal Geographical Society*, IV, 229–339 (1834).

29. Thomas Hodgkin, "On the Importance of Studying and Preserving the Languages Spoken by Uncivilized Nations, with the View of Elucidating the Physical History of Man," *London and Edinburgh Philosophical Magazine and Journal of Science*, VII, 27–36, 94–106 (July–August, 1835).

the British Association in 1839, pleading the evidence of Buxton's Aborigines Committee that many peoples were moving rapidly toward extinction.

The result was a new ethnological questionnaire, published in 1841 by a committee of the Association working under the chairmanship of Thomas Hodgkin. It drew heavily on a similar questionnaire published in the same year by Edwards and the Société Ethnologique in Paris. Both questionnaires assumed a close connection between race and language. Both asked especially for descriptions and measurements of the head—following Edwards' predilection and the tenets of phrenology. Both requested detailed descriptions of individual and family life, including the life-cycle, which was to become standard fare in later ethnographic reports. On other points, they diverged in emphasis. Hodgkin was more interested in political institutions, while Edwards had a special concern about material culture, a greater variety of physical measurements, and his favorite hypothesis that most nations would be found to contain several different races whose identity might not be immediately obvious. Neither made a special point of kinship structure, but otherwise the future course of ethnographic investigation was laid out.[30]

It was also laid out in a way that suggested answers. The emphasis on physical measurement suggested racial interpretations—which were, indeed, explicit in Edwards' own work. His questions on language suggested that language was related to physical type and urged investigators to look for these connections. In Hodgkin's version, the policy concerns of the APS were also apparent. His question of "psychological character" asked not merely for information, but for suggestions which might "contribute to an estimation of the probable result of an effort to develop and improve the character."[31]

In later years British ethnology moved still more in the direction of Edward's interest in physical man. The Hodgkin questionnaire was revised and reprinted in 1852, with considerably enlarged sections on physical measurements, particularly of the shape of the skull. The language sections also grew, and both changes reflected the most recent tendencies of ethnological research: physical anthro-

30. *Mémoires de la Société Ethnologique*, I (1), vi–xv (1841); [Thomas Hodgkin and others], "Queries Respecting the Human Race, to be addressed to Travellers and others," *Reports of the British Association*, XI, 332–39 (1841).

31. Hodgkin and others, "Queries Respecting the Human Race," p. 339.

pology and linguistics shot ahead, while general ethnography lan-
guished.[32]

Questionnaires were more widely used for governmental than for
scientific purposes. Preparations for the Niger Expedition included
the circulation of a questionnaire to officials and travellers, but its
main concern was the physical problem of travel in Africa—naviga-
bility of rivers, availability of fuel for steamers, climatic dangers, and
the military capabilities of the African states. Cultural questions were
limited to language, belief in a supreme being, and the probable
reception of European missionaries. Even these were naive, for example: "Do they ever attempt to poison strangers? What species of
poison do they use?"[33]

The Expedition itself was designed to produce practical knowledge,
not to conduct basic research. In spite of James MacQueen's warning
that planned culture change required a careful study of the existing
way of life, the choice of scientific personnel sent by the African
Civilization Society clearly implied its intention to investigate the
country and not the people of Africa. The complement included a
botanist, mineralogist, geologist, gardener, zoologist, and drafts-
man—but no ethnographer. The Government's orders to the Niger
Commissioners were in the same vein. Commercial and political
matters were given highest priority. The Commissioners were asked
to report on the "state of civilization," but the emphasis was still on
useful knowledge—the habits and customs of the people and "any
striking virtues, vices, talents, or capabilities of which they are
possessed."[34]

By comparison, the fact-finding aspect of R. R. Madden's simultaneous Commission to the Windward Coast was much more elabo-
rately organized. In addition to his own enquiries, Madden circulated
five printed questionnaires to officials and to some private citizens.
One dealt with the state of the forts and settlements, a second with
commerce, a third with the slave trade, and a fourth with climate,
soil, and health conditions. Only the fifth and final questionnaire on

32. Thomas Hodgkin and Richard Cull, "A Manual of Ethnological Inquiry; being
a Series of Questions Concerning the Human Race," *Reports of the British Association*, XXII, 243–52 (1852).

33. *Queries Relating to the Coast of Africa*, 2 parts (London, 1840).

34. James MacQueen, Memorandum of 12 January 1839, CO 2/22; Lord John
Russell to Commissioners of the Niger Expedition, 30 January 1841, PP, 1843 xlviii
[C. 472], pp. 11–12.

schools and missions asked about African culture.[35] Madden's effort nevertheless reflects an understanding that both theory and policy required data not then available. His aim was more practical than scholarly, and the answers left much to be desired, but it was a comprehensive plan of investigation.

The systematic attempt to gather information from overseas was more common in the 1840's. The Admiralty followed up the earlier private questionnaires with its own guide to scientific enquiry, published in 1849. Individual chapters on the different branches of science were prepared by outstanding specialists—Geology by Charles Darwin, Ethnology by James Cowles Prichard, Medicine by Alexander Bryson.[36]

Thus, when the *Pleiad* expedition entered the Niger in 1854, it did so with much more exact preparation than was possible in 1841. A full set of particular instructions was prepared for each of the fields of geology, geography and meteorology, terrestrial magnetism, zoology and botany, and (for the first time) ethnography and philology. The ethnographic requests were now specific—not a general outline of useful subjects of enquiry, but a list of desiderata to fill in the existing knowledge.[37] Given the speed with which the expedition ascended the rivers and returned before the end of the high water, however, the results could hardly have been anything but disappointing.

Still another substitute for field investigation was to interrogate Africans who happened to be in Europe. The most thoroughgoing effort in this direction was that of d'Avezac-Macaya, who worked through Edwards' ethnological questionnaire with a Yoruba informant from Ijebu, then in Paris after a period of slavery in Brazil. The result was the most comprehensive account we now have of Yoruba culture in the early nineteenth century.[38] Other African accounts also found their way into print, either as narrated to a Western amanuensis or written by the African author himself.[39] The quality varied

35. The questionnaires and original answers are found in CO 267/171 and 173. They were printed for Parliament in PP, 1842, xii (551).

36. Sir John F. W. Herschel, (Ed.), *A Manual of Scientific Enquiry Prepared for the Use of Her Majesty's Navy and Adapted for Travellers in General* (London, 1849).

37. IA, Calprof 1/10.

38. M. A. d'Avezac-Macaya, "Notice sur le pays et le peuple des Yébous en Afrique," *Mémoires de la Société Ethnologique*, II (2) 1–196 (1845).

39. See, for example; "Narrative of Joseph Wright," in J. Beecham, *Ashantee and the Gold Coast* (London, 1841), pp. 349–58; "Narrative of Lamen Kebe," in T. Dwight, "On the Sereculeh Nation, in Nigritia," *American Annals of Education and*

considerably, since many of these narratives were the work of ex-
slaves who wrote down their experiences after many years of absence
from their homeland.

John Beecham of the Wesleyan-Methodist Missionary Society,
however, used the information of more recent arrivals from Africa.
His study of *Ashantee and the Gold Coast* sought to draw together
all that was known about Ashanti culture and history—from printed
accounts, from the missionary reports of T. B. Freeman—but corrected and supplemented with the aid of Joseph Smith and William
de Graft, African Methodist leaders who happened to be in London.
The result was not completely satisfactory by standards of modern
ethnography, and it was rarely pro-Akan in its judgment of African
culture, but it did portray one African society as a working whole.[40]

European penetration in North Africa also added to British knowledge about the Western Sudan. With the French occupation of
Algiers in 1830 and the conquest of Algeria in the following decades, French Islamic scholarship extended from its earlier interest
in Egypt to take in the Maghrib as well.

In the process, the three great medieval Arabic authorities, whose
works had been only partly known, came to light and were given
Western translations. The first short section of al-Bakri's geography
appeared in French in 1825 and another in 1831; but the most complete Arabic text was not known in Europe until 1851, when it was
found among other manuscripts captured by the French in Constantine.[41] In much the same way, ibn-Khaldūn's *History of the
Berbers and the Muslim Dynasties of North Africa* came to the attention of European scholars only in 1825; and even then it was
not available in full until after 1851, when Baron MacGurckin de

---

Instruction, V, 451–56 (1835); "Narrative of Sali-bul-Ali," in W. B. Hodgson, *Notes
on Northern Africa, the Sahara, and the Soudan* (New York, 1844), pp. 68–76;
"Narrative of Ali Eisami Gazir," in S. W. Koelle, *African Native Literature* (London,
1854), pp. 248–56; G. C. Renouard, "Routes in North Africa, by Abu Bekr es siddik,"
Journal of the Royal Geographical Society, VI, 100–113 (1836); "Narrative of Samuel
Crowther's Capture," in Schön and Crowther, *Journals*, pp. 371–85; Captain Wash-
ington, "Some Account of Mohammedu Seisei," A Mandingo of Nyani-Maru on the
Gambia," *Journal of the Royal Geographical Society*, VIII, 448–54 (1838).

40. J. Beecham, *Ashantee and the Gold Coast* (London, 1841).

41. The first fragment of al-Bakri's work appeared in Société de Géographie, Paris,
Receuil des voyages et mémoires, 8 vols. (1825–1866), II, issued in 1825. Another
appeared in M. Quatremère, "Notice d'un manuscrit arabe contennant la description de
l'Afrique," *Notices et extraits des mss. de la bibliotheque du roi*, XII, 437–664 (Paris,
1831). Baron de Slane's translation based in part on the Constantine text appeared as
Description de l'Afrique septentrionale par Abou-Obeid-el-Bekri (Algiers, 1857). See
Revue Africaine, II, 73 (1857).

Slane's translation began to appear.[42] Ibn-Battūta emerged in similar sequence—first a brief English translation in 1829, followed by the discovery of the full text in the Maghrib, and complete translation into French in 1858.[43] Arabic sources were also discovered south of the Sahara. Barth was shown a copy of Ahmad Baba's history of Songhai and had it in his possession long enough to copy extensive passages. These too were ultimately translated and published in Europe.[44]

Even before all these sources were fully translated, some of them were used by William Desborough Cooley for a new synthesis outlining the state of knowledge about the Western Sudan. Cooley was an Arabist with geographical interests. He worked with the known texts of al-Bakri, ibn-Khaldūn, and ibn-Battūta to produce *The Negroland of the Arabs* in 1841. This work both corrected and amplified the earlier geographical reconstructions of Rennell and MacQueen and presented a concise history of the Western Sudan. The vaguely rumored empires of Ghana, Mali, and Songhai were now seen to have a consecutive history; and those who read Cooley's work might have had cause to doubt the prevalent belief that African society was a changeless barbarism.[45]

British ethnology produced nothing to match the work of either Beecham or Cooley. Prichard still dominated the field. His *Researches into the Physical History of Man* reached five volumes in its third edition of 1836–47. His newer *Natural History of Man* passed through four editions between 1843 and 1852; but Prichard followed the fashion and concentrated on race and language, rather than giving a broader view of human culture. R. G. Latham, who came out with his own major ethnological survey in 1850, was even more narrowly concerned with the classification of human varieties,

42. Attention was first called to the work of ibn-Khaldūn by a note published in the *Journal Asiatique* in 1825. The French Ministry of War commissioned a translation by Baron de Slane in 1840, which began to appear in Paris in 1851. MacGurckin de Slane, "Introduction," ibn-Khaldūn, *Histoire des berbères et des dynasties musulmanes de l'Afrique septentrionelle*, 2nd ed., 4 vols. [Paris, 1925–1934], I, lxiv.

43. Sir Hamilton Gibb, "Forward," in Gibb (Ed.), *The Travels of Ibn Battuta*, 4 vols. (Cambridge, 1958), I, xiii–xiv.

44. Ahmad Baba, "Beiträge zur Geschiche und Geographie des Sudan. Nach dem Arabischen bearbeitet von C. Ralfs," *Zeitschrift der Deutschen Morgenländischen Gesellschaft*, IX, 518–94 (Leipzig, 1855).

45. W. D. Cooley, *The Negroland of the Arabs Examined and Explained* (London, 1841).

and the standard of his scholarship in discussing West African culture was a step downward from Prichard's work of more than twenty years earlier.[46]

Latham was nevertheless a respected scholar in his own time, and the deterioration of cultural anthropology is illustrated by his attempt to popularize the subject. In a series of six lectures on the "Ethnology of the British Colonies and Dependencies," delivered in Manchester in 1851, he devoted one to West Africa. In fact, his material was taken almost entirely from the Gold Coast, and it was anything but scholarly. Most of it was lifted bodily from the memoirs of a military officer, published the previous year in one of the service journals, and the borrowing was selective. Where the original had dealt generally with Akan culture, and even had an occasional word of praise, Latham picked out and quoted from those sections dealing with ordeals, human sacrifices, and "obscene" dances. He also forgot to say, as his source had done, that the human sacrifice he described had long since been abolished within the judicial protectorate on the Gold Coast.[47]

The lack of protest against distortion of this kind is a striking feature of the period. Only a very few commentators complained that the image they received at home was seriously wrong in the light of their experience in Africa itself.[48] Some Africans, however, tried to protest: Joseph Smith, an African merchant from Cape Coast and one of Beecham's informants, found his opportunity in giving evidence before the Hutt Committee.[49] Another protest was made, unexpectedly, in Africa itself. In 1848, when Governor Winniett went up to Kumasi as the first European of his rank to pay a formal visit, he found the Asantehene incensed at the false reports about Ashanti recently published in Britain. The Governor was reminded that good relations between his country and Ashanti could only be built on truthful information, and the Asantehene further pointed out that Africans had once thought Europeans were cannibals. Now

46. R. G. Latham, *Natural History of the Varieties of Man* (London, 1850).

47. Compare R. G. Latham, *The Ethnology of the British Colonies and Dependencies* (London, 1851), pp. 34–68 with "Reminiscences of the Gold Coast," *Colburn's United Service Magazine* (1850–51).

48. Curiously enough, Latham's source for his popular ethnology was one of these. See "Reminiscences of the Gold Coast," p. 410.

49. Evidence of 4 April 1848, PP, 1847–1848, xii (272), p. 150.

they had learned better, while Africans were still maligned in Europe.[50]

The lack of protest against error was merely one symptom of a deeper misunderstanding, and one associated with the general self-confidence of the age. Neither the scholars nor the publicists understood the limitations of their data. Only scholarly field work or careful observation by long-term residence could have given the kind of understanding needed to replace the false confidence that Europe had really come to understand something about Africa. The telling criticism was made by J. Leighton Wilson, an American missionary with almost twenty years' experience on the Coast: "little is known, even at the present day, of the actual state of the country. The interior life of the people, their moral, social, civil, and religious condition, as well as their peculiar notions and customs, have always been a sealed book to the rest of the world. There have been no lack of books on Africa, but most of them have been confined, in the information they give, to single and isolated districts, or been written by transient visitors, who could see nothing but the surface of things."[51]

The self-confidence of the observers, however, was passed on to the general public—and with lowered standards of care and accuracy, as the reading habits of the British public changed. More people were educated, and more people could afford to buy books. The book trade responded to the needs of middle-class readers with books consciously aimed at the lowest common denominator of the largest possible audience. The immense spread and diversity in the missionary publications was one symptom of the change.

Another was the decline of the great collections of travel literature which had appeared with such regularity in the past and had made available the first-hand accounts. Shorter collections and anthologies were now more popular, and specialized West African works were less common. With more of Africa to know about, the old area of contact was necessarily treated more briefly. Hugh Murray's editions had long since ceased to deal with West Africa alone. When James MacQueen revised his *Northern Central Africa*

50. W. Winniett, "Journal of a Visit to Kumasi," entry for 26 October 1848, PP, 1849, xviii (32), p. 179.
51. J. L. Wilson, *Western Africa*, p. iii.

in 1840 to catch the Niger enthusiasm, he also shifted ground to take in all of Africa, reducing the West African sections by half.

A similar change of emphasis came with the newer French editions of travel literature. *L'Univers,* published in 70 volumes between 1835 and 1863 claimed to be the history and description of the whole world, but it was a world seen in the eyes of mid-nineteenth-century France. Africa as a whole received only seven volumes, and West Africa only one.[52]

At the same time, West Africa began to find a small but significant place in a whole range of new British periodicals, designed mainly for middle-class readers, and often to promote a special cause or policy. On the side of the humanitarians, the *Anti-Slavery Reporter* had been published since 1823 as the organ of the Anti-Slavery Society, but the victory over West Indian slavery ended the real unity of the anti-slavery movement. With the split between Sturge and Buxton in 1839, Sturge led the pacifists into a new British and Foreign Anti-Slavery Society, which kept the *Reporter.* Buxton's Society for the Suppression of the Slave Trade and the Civilization of Africa (more commonly called the African Civilization Society) launched its own journal, *The Friend of Africa,* with the special purpose of supporting the Niger Expedition.

Buxton was also concerned with the Aborigines Protection Society, which had similar humanitarian interests, but the APS at first left West African affairs to the African Civilization Society, just as it left Indian affairs to the specialized British India Association. As long as the other societies flourished, APS could devote its principal attention to the Australian aborigines and the American Indians of Upper Canada. As the African Civilization Society weakened and died in the mid-forties, APS took over its concerns. Especially after 1847, when it began publishing its own journal, *The Aborigines Friend,* it took an increasing interest in West Africa.

Enthusiasm for converting the barbarians to Western civilization spread from the Niger effort and led to the formation of still another society. The Society for the Advancement of Civilization was, like the APS, world-wide in scope, but it was less concerned with specific

---

52. Hugh Murray, *The African Continent* (Edinburgh, 1853); James MacQueen, *A Geographical Survey of Africa* (London, 1840); *L'Univers. Histoire et description de tous les peuples,* 70 vols. (Paris, 1835–1863).

policies and projects and more concerned with broader problems of culture change. *The Journal of Civilization,* which it published during 1841, was more elaborate than the usual run of humanitarian journals. It offered a series of articles on popular ethnography, building on the fascination with the exotic and ostensibly designed to acquaint the British public with the barbarism still flourishing overseas.

Another group of periodicals served the interests of colonial enthusiasts. They were not specifically humanitarian, but they might express humanitarian attitudes along with their special interests in Colonial Reform, free trade, or some particular region of the world. The principal organ of the Colonial Reformers was the *Colonial Gazette,* the weekly publication of the Colonial Society from 1838 onward. Its first object was to promote overseas settlement, but it took at least a negative interest in West Africa, opposing the whole Sierra Leone experiment and favoring government-sponsored emigration of Africans to the West Indies. For the African continent, the semi-weekly *African Colonizer,* modeled on the *Gazette,* was published briefly in 1840–41. Its main concern was European settlement in South Africa, and editorial policy followed the Colonial Reformers' opposition to the Colonial Office in general and to James Stephen in particular. But the editors also believed in the protection of the aborigines, the equality of all races of men, and the future of a multi-racial Empire. To this end, they supported the Niger Expedition.

Still other colonial journals were mainly commercial in emphasis. *The Colonial Magazine and Commercial Maritime Journal* was founded by R. M. Martin, who was also one of the founders of the British India Association. Under his editorship between 1840 and 1843, it followed a line that was generally humanitarian and mildly favorable to further government activity in West Africa. The competing *Colonial Magazine,* edited by P. L. Simmonds between 1844 and 1848, was less humanitarian and less interested in West Africa, though it too provided a forum for the discussion of West African affairs.

In addition to the specialized periodical press, political pamphlets and books followed in the wake of each important debate on public policy. The appearance of these pamphlets was almost continuous during the 1840's; since the Niger Expedition was followed in 1842 by the West Africa Committee and the debate on emigration to the West Indies, and this by a prolific literature for and against the anti-slavery blockade.[53]

These periodicals and pamphlets were not published to convey information, but to argue questions of policy. They had little influence on the British image of Africa. The image was already formed by the travellers and the missionary press, which did convey information. But the secular press was important. It summarized and popularized and transmitted a stereotype to a wider public. In the process, the detail available from the new flow of data was lost. The understanding available in the best of the new scholarship was also lost, and the image became more uniform. The range of journalistic opinion had been narrowing gradually since the eigtheenth century, when only a few people knew much or cared to know much about Africa. By the middle of the nineteenth, few cared, but almost everyone knew a little. The little they knew was epitomized by a reviewer in *Blackwood's*, describing Negro Africa in general.

Thus is Central Africa; distinguished from all the earth by the unspeakable mixture of squalidness and magnificence, simplicity of life yet fury of passion, the savage ignorance of its religious notions yet fearful worship of evil powers, its homage to magic, and desperate beliefs in spells, incantations, and the *fetish*. The configuration of the country, so far as it can be conjectured, assists this primeval barbarism. . . . The very fertility of the soil, at once rendering

53. The controversy over the anti-slavery blockade was an especially rich source of pamphlets and books. See William Allen, *A Plan for the Immediate Extinction of the Slave Trade, for the Relief of the West India Colonies, and for the Diffusion of Civilization and Christianity in Africa, by the co-operation of Mammon with Philanthropy* (London, 1849); J. Bandinel, *Some Account of the Trade in Slaves from Africa* (London, 1842); Buxton, *The African Slave Trade;* Thomas, Lord Denman, *A Letter from Lord Denman to Lord Brougham, on the Final Extinction of the Slave Trade,* 2nd ed. (London, 1848), *A Second Letter . . . to Lord Brougham . . .* (London, 1849), and *Uncle Tom's Cabin, Bleak House, Slavery and the Slave Trade* (London, 1853); W. R. Greg, *Past and Present Efforts for the Extinction of the African Slave Trade* (London, 1840); Robert Jamieson, *Commerce with Africa: the Inefficiency of Treaties,* 2nd ed. (London, 1859); T. Kehoe, *Some Considerations in Favour of Forming a Settlement at the Confluence of the Niger and Tchadda* (Waterford, 1847); Macgregor Laird, *Remedies for the Slave Trade* (London, 1844); J. S. Mansfield, *Remarks on the African Squadron* (London, 1851); H. Matson, *Remarks on the Slave Trade and the African Squadron,* 2nd ed. (London, 1848); P. Read, *Lord John Russell, Sir Thomas Fowell Buxton, and the Niger Expedition* (London, 1840); J. Richardson, *The Cruisers* (London, 1849); Sir George Stephen, *The Niger Trade Considered in Connexion with the African Blockade* (London, 1849); Robert Stokes, *Regulated Slave Trade* (London, 1851); H. Townsend, *Letter to Capt. Trotter, R. N. on the African Coast Blockade* (London, 1849); J. L. Wilson, *The British Squadron on the Coast of Africa* (London, 1851); Sir Henry Yule, *The African Squadron Vindicated* (London, 1850).

them indolent and luxurious, excites their passions, and the land is a scene alike of profligacy and profusion.[54]

In this popular form, the image of Africa was less favorable and no more accurate than that of the later eighteenth century. A half century of exploration and investigation—and simply of British presence on the West African coast—had greatly increased British knowledge of Africa, but the best of the new knowledge was locked in the low-circulation works of Barth, Cruickshank, Beecham, and Cooley. The rarity of these work was, of course, no evidence of their lack of influence among men who specialized in West African affairs. To a degree, these men were better informed than other people, even among the educated classes. On the other hand, the well informed had also picked up some beliefs of the popular image, which they cherished in spite of their later and more specialized knowledge. Among the most important of these was undoubtedly the general attitude of cultural chauvinism, and it was fortified by new tendencies in British thought about the meaning of race. In general, the political classes in Britain were no better informed than ever, but they were more confident of their information. The errors once confined to a few specialized works had now become "common knowledge."

54. *Blackwood's Magazine*, LV, 291 (1844).

14

TROPICAL MEDICINE

AND

THE VICTORY OF EMPIRICISM

> I hinted that the climate—
> "The finest climate in the world!" said Mrs.
> Jellyby.
> "Indeed, ma'am?"
> "Certainly. With precaution," said Mrs. Jellyby.
> "You may go into Holborn, without precaution,
> and be run over. You may go into Holborn, with
> precaution, and never be run over. Just so with
> Africa."
> I said, "No Doubt."—I meant as to Holborn.
> Charles Dickens—*Bleak House*

When *Bleak House* was published, ten years after the sailing of the Niger Expedition, the memory of the famous failure was still fresh enough to serve Dickens' purpose. He chose it as the favorite philanthropy of Mrs. Jellyby, his parody of all that was narrow, impractical, and unhumane in the humanitarianism of Exeter Hall. It was a useful target. First of all, it was philanthropy at a distance, a convenient point for his attack on the "telescopic philanthropists," who righted wrongs only in the far corners of the world and ignored the evils on their own doorstep. Furthermore, it proved how impractical Exeter Hall could be, and in this case the impracticality was demonstrated by their apparent unconcern for the known facts of the African "climate." The high mortality, which had served as the excuse for recall, raised still higher West Africa's reputation as the most dangerous climate in the world. In 1848, *The Times* merely echoed the popular impression when it called the Bights, "the most deadly sea," and Fernando Po, "the most pestiferous land which the universe is known to contain."[1] When Dickens, the most popular writer of his day, chose the African climate for a further round of abuse, he helped to keep alive for later generations the image of the white man's grave.

The emphasis on high mortality was unfair to the Niger Expedition, which suffered no worse than the usual European experience in West Africa. Dickens' attack was also badly timed for another reason. During the decade between the Niger Expedition and the publication of *Bleak House,* tropical medicine passed through the most important series of practical reforms of the entire nineteenth century. Europeans would still die on the Guinea Coast at a higher rate than in England, but the death rate for newcomers was cut in half.

The Niger Expedition itself contributed greatly to these reforms, but the concentrated effort to solve the problem of survival went back to the earlier impact of European mortality in the 1820's. Before that time, medical practice in West Africa took its lead from other parts of the tropical world. From then on, empirical data was gathered in West Africa itself, and gathered far more systematically than ever before. The new trend appeared as early as 1826, when Commissioners Wellington and Rowan brought a new emphasis on health and survival to their investigation. The Navy also played a crucial role. Naval surgeons were ordered to report on the "medical topography" of foreign stations, the prevalent diseases, the mode of treatment, medicinal plants, and other information that might be of value to science.[2] As these reports accumulated they formed a mass of data about disease off the West African coast. They were further supplemented by Major Alexander Tulloch's detailed statistical surveys of military mortality in the Atlantic tropics, published in 1838 and 1840. Individual medical men with experience on the Coast also published more often than before. In 1831, James Boyle, a naval surgeon acting as Colonial Surgeon of Sierra Leone, brought out the *Practical Medico-Historical Account of the Western Coast of Africa,* the first full-length study actually based on African conditions since Winterbottom's work in the 1790's.[3]

1. *The Times,* 13 September 1848, p. 4.

2. *Regulations and Instructions for the Medical Officers of His Majesty's Fleet* (London, 1835), p. 40.

3. James Boyle, *A Practical Medico-Historical Account of the Western Coast of Africa* (London, 1831); A. Tulloch, "Statistical Reports on the Sickness, Mortality, and Invaliding among Troops," PP, 1837–1838, xl (138) and PP, 1840, xxx [C. 228].

With the preparations for the Niger Expedition, the effort was intensified. The government circulated questionnaires to recent African travellers, consulted medical authorities in England, and sent out Dr. R. R. Madden to the western portion of the Guinea coast with a commission that was both medical and political. The Niger Expedition itself spent more of its scientific effort on medical problems than on any other type of investigation. When the expedition was proclaimed a failure, and on medical grounds, the ships themselves were withdrawn, but the effort to solve the problem of survival in West Africa went on. The Navy in particular still had to protect the health of the anti-slavery squadron. Following a similar report already published by the French Navy, Dr. Alexander Bryson studied all of the data available on the health of the squadron and published a far-reaching series of recommendations in 1847.[4]

Meanwhile, in the later 1840's the half-century-old yellow fever controversy broke out again among British medical men. A special committee of the staff of the Army Medical Department held an inquiry on the disease in 1849–50. The Royal College of Physicians followed with its own investigation, and a third report was published by the General Board of Health in 1852. These discussions were especially marked by personal bitterness and factional rivalries. In the end, they may have done more to raise the temperatures of the British medical profession than to lower those of yellow fever victims in Africa, but they kept alive a general concern about tropical medicine. By the early 1850's, a very large body of empirical data, of a kind and quantity previously unknown, was available on disease in West Africa.

But the analytical tools for dealing with these data had not changed very greatly in fifty years. The principal cause of death was still "fevers," and the effort to classify fevers led relentlessly back to the yellow fever problem—in much the same form that Chisholm had raised it in 1795. The main questions were two: first, is yellow fever a disease *sui generis,* or is it a special form of the disease now called malaria? Second, is it contagious? The reason these questions touched off so much controversy was not simply the problem of survival in the tropics. These relatively simple problems in a single

4. J. P. F. Thévenot, *Traité des maladies des européens dans les pays chauds, et spécialement au Sénégal* (Paris, 1840); A. Bryson, *Report on the Climate and Principal Diseases of the African Station* (London, 1847).

disease led to other, more important questions about infection, contagion, and the nature of disease itself—as, indeed, they had done since the 1790's.

Two facts were universally recognized as empirically true. Some diseases seemed to have the power to spread from one person to another, as in the case of smallpox. Other diseases, such as tropical fevers, were confined to particular areas of the world, where they seemed to be endemic, affecting large numbers but without clearly established transmission from one individual to the next. From these observations, a distinction could be made between contagion and infection. Contagion was sometimes defined as the power of communicating a disease from one individual to another. Infection, on the other hand, was defined as the "principle which produces the disease, depending altogether upon *local* causes, and having no relation to emanations from persons labouring under the disease, or from bodies of those who have died of it."[5] Thus an epidemic outbreak might be started by the appearance of a diseased person, or it might be started by some subtle change in the state of the atmosphere.

To draw further conclusions from the empirical evidence, it was necessary to identify individual diseases. If a doctor distinguished between yellow fever and other tropical fevers, he produced one kind of data. Those who lumped all fevers together produced another kind that was in fact a description of at least two separate diseases—yellow fever and malaria—with dengue fever, typhus, and typhoid often thrown in for good measure. The case for a separate yellow fever was still unproved; and it remained so until after 1866–67, when J. J. L. Donnet in Jamaica developed the diagnoses based on quantitative albumin records.[6] Meanwhile, it was forcefully sustained by William Pym, already a thirty-year veteran of the controversy and now Inspector General of Naval Hospitals. He was supported by the Army Medical Service and contradicted by both the Royal Society of Physicians and the General Board of Health. After some initial uncertainties, however, Alexander Bryson established the distinction in the practice of the Navy off the African

<hr/>

5. Dr. Gilkrest, in Board of Health Report, PP, 1852, xx [C. 1473], p. 157.
6. S. F. Dudley, "Yellow Fever as seen by the Medical Officers of the Royal Navy in the Nineteenth Century," *Proceedings of the Royal Society of Medicine*, XXVI, 443–56 (1932), p. 447.

coast, and yellow fever entered the official naval terminology along-side remittent and intermittent fevers.[7]

Even the common distinction between remittent and intermittent fevers beclouded the issue in its own way. The fever which doctors saw most often in West Africa was *Plasmodium falciparum,* a form of malaria which produces apparently different symptoms at different phases of infestation. Remittent fever, as the name suggests, was a very high fever marked by regular intervals of remission, and it was descriptive of the symptoms of an initial attack of *P. falciparum.* Intermittent fever, on the other hand, was the term used to describe the later appearance of clinical symptoms, in a milder form among those who had already survived the "seasoning sickness." Thus most medical men failed to distinguish yellow fever from malaria, but made a false distinction between different phases of malaria.[8]

Some, however, were trying to break out of the old framework of fever classifications. One escape was to argue that fever was not a disease at all, but a symptom of some more specific pathological condition. Perhaps it was caused by inflammation of the brain, or, according to Broussais and his followers, by infection of the mucous membrane and the alimentary canal. Bascombe took the position that fever was even more generally a symptom of some "condition inimical to vitality" and "nothing more than Nature's effort to attempt the curative process."[9] Even though these views led to no immediate changes in medical practice, they marked the path that modern medicine was to follow.

On the West African coast, James Boyle initiated a new classification of fevers, which did nothing to improve clinical description or understanding of disease but did lead to changes in medical practice. Boyle was influenced by the earlier habit of classifying tropical fevers

7. W. Pym, *Observations upon Bulam, Vomito Negro or Yellow Fever* (London, 1848); PP, 1852, xx [C. 1473]; Bryson, *Principal Diseases,* p. 250; A. Bryson, *Account of the Origin, Spread, and Decline of the Epidemic Fevers of Sierra Leone* (London, 1849), pp. 173–74.

8. Report of Commissioner R. R. Madden, PP, 1842, xii (551), p. 423; E. J. Burton, "Observations on the Climate, Topography, and Diseases of the British Colonies in Africa," *Provincial Medical and Surgical Journal,* 1841-1842 (I), pp. 219 ff., 265 ff., 287 ff., 306 ff., 323 ff., 346 ff., 365 ff., 392 ff. (25 December 1841 to 12 February 1842), p. 309; Bryson, *Principal Diseases,* p. 250.

9. Burton, "Observations," pp. 323–24; E. Bascombe, *On the Nature and Causes of Fever, Especially that Termed Yellow Fever* (London, 1852), pp. 8–9.

according to their geographical homes. He held, therefore, that two different fevers occurred near Sierra Leone, though the symptoms were identical. One of these, the "climatorial bilious remittent fever," occurred only at sea. The other, the "African local bilious remittent" occurred only on land and only in Africa. Subsequent attacks, again with identical symptoms, were called "irregular bilious fever" on the first return of symptoms, and "intermittent fever" on still later occurrences. By giving African fevers new names, Boyle was able to break with the authority of British medicine and its recommended treatment with large doses of calomel and copious bloodletting. This reaction against dangerous treatments and the return to those which seemed empirically more sound was the beginning of a major medical reform.[10]

In spite of the bitter quarrels at home, new evidence about yellow fever emerged from West Africa. Doctors in Sierra Leone were especially well placed to study the epidemiology of the disease. Serious epidemics broke out in Freetown in 1823, 1829, in 1836 to 1839, and again in 1847. There were others on the Gambia and the Gold Coast and aboard the ships of the anti-slavery squadron. In spite of the uncertainty about diagnoses, careful study established a new base of empirical knowledge. It was recognized that epidemics tended to come in the dry season, rather than during the rains when malaria was most prevalent. It was established that the disease spread rapidly among Europeans, but in a way that was difficult to explain. Its course could be traced through a town, with relatively short jumps from one victim to the next. Yet it might skip several houses, and those in daily contact with a victim might escape altogether. When, in 1829, Lt. MacKinnial of H.M.S. *Sybille* drank a glass of black vomit from a yellow fever victim, it was proven that, at the very least, the disease was not contagious in the same way smallpox was. At the same time, it was known that whole ships' companies could come down with it at once. It was therefore clearly epidemic, if not contagious.[11]

This description of a yellow fever epidemic was empirically accurate, and it can be explained in the light of modern knowledge. *Aedes aegypti,* the carrier of yellow fever, breeds in small containers

10. Boyle, *Medico-Historical Account,* pp. 84–137 and 188.
11. R. R. Madden, Commissioner's Report, PP, 1842, xii (551), pp. 427–30; Bryson, *Epidemic Fevers,* pp. 173–74; Boyle, *Medico-Historical Account,* pp. 201–7; PP, 1842, xx [C. 1473]; Dudley, "Yellow Fever," p. 444.

and is found in large numbers around human habitation. Unlike *Anopheles gambiae* and *A. funestus*, the principal West African carriers of malaria, *A. aegypti*, could breed aboard ship. Epidemics in the dry season are possible because this mosquito does not depend on rain water alone. The pattern of transmission through a town came about because *Aedes aegypti* has both a short life and a short range. A single infected mosquito might not carry the disease more than a few yards, but the parasite is then left to develop in the human host, only to be picked up again by another mosquito of a later generation.

When these facts were fully understood, yellow fever turned out to be one of the easiest to control of all mosquito-borne diseases, but the bitterness of the yellow fever controversy limited the use that could be made of the knowledge already available. The Army Board of Inquiry, for example, recognized that all yellow fever victims were immune to further attack, but the information was obscured by many incorrect opinions to the contrary. More important, the isolation of yellow fever victims might well have saved a number of lives and stopped the spread of the disease, but the violently anti-quarantine report of the General Board of Health in 1852 tended to cut off action in this direction. One important reform was made in naval practice. On Bryson's recommendation, orders were issued that any ship in the tropics with a case of fever marked by early yellowness of the skin and black vomit was to proceed immediately to a cold climate. In some instances, this measure was enough to stop the epidemic which might otherwise have carried off most of the crew.[12]

The search for the causes of fevers followed the pattern set earlier in the century. Although some authorities still placed their faith in such factors as the angle of the sun's rays or the influence of the moon, the search for the "exciting cause" focused more and more narrowly on the dangerous "miasma." Hypotheses about chemical poisons in the air enjoyed a general vogue in Europe, and the authority of Liebig was added to MacCulloch's earlier theory that most disease was caused by the chemical products of putrefaction.[13]

The miasma causing tropical fevers might originate, according

12. Henry R. Carter, *Yellow Fever, An Epidemiological and Historical Study of its Place of Origin* (Baltimore, 1931), p. 67; Bryson, *Principal Diseases*, p. 228.
13. J. Liebig, *Chemistry and Physics in Relation to Physiology and Pathology* (Philadelphia, [1852]), pp. 17–26.

to differing opinions, from uncultivated land, from swamps, from green wood, from rotting ships, timbers, from bilge water, or from a variety of other sources. The common element, however, was an association with decay (especially of vegetable matter), with heat, and with dampness. The new empirical data, however, made it possible to narrow the field somewhat. Swamps had always been associated with fevers, but Major Tulloch concluded from his statistics on military mortality that no such correlation applied in West Africa. Commissioner Madden came to the same conclusion, and both were right.[14] The plans of the Niger Expedition were nevertheless based on an inordinate fear of the swamps of the delta and an unwarranted confidence in the healthiness of the drier interior.

The search for the chemical properties of the fatal gas represented another line of effort. Excessive oxygen and excessive carbon dioxide in the air were both investigated. Just as the Niger Expedition was about to sail, attention turned to hydrogen sulfide as a third alternative. This possibility was brought to light by Sir William Burnett's effort to prevent corrosion of copper sheathing on ship's bottoms. He collected samples of water from the African coast and found they contained an unusual proportion of hydrogen sulfide. Professor J. F. Daniel of Kings' College, London, then advanced the hypothesis that this gas, known to be poisonous, was in fact the cause of African fevers. The suggestion was preposterous, and its failings were soon pointed out. Hydrogen sulfide smells like rotten eggs, and its symptoms as a poison are nothing like those of malaria.[15] Further investigation showed that the waters off the African coast were chemically identical with other sea water.

The flurry of chemical interest nevertheless led to an elaborate effort to prevent fever on the Niger Expedition. The steamers were equipped with mechanical ventilators and chemical air-purifiers capable of drying the air, passing it over charcoal, and filtering any small particles that might be in it.[16] In practice the apparatus turned out to be a bulky nuisance. The medical staff of the expedition conducted extensive chemical tests of both air and water, and they con-

14. PP, 1840, xxx [C. 228], p. 26; PP, 1842, xii (551), p. 416.

15. J. F. Daniel, "On the Waters of the African Coast," *Friend of Africa*, I, 18–23 (January, 1841), first published as a series of letters in *The Nautical Magazine* of January 1841. For the refutation see *Friend of Africa*, I, 213–14 (December 1841).

16. D. B. Reid, *Friend of Africa*, I, 44–47 and 65–73 (February, 1841).

cluded that the fever was caused by "a certain peculiarity of atmosphere . . . inappreciable by chemical agency."[17]

Other authorities, however, thought they knew enough about the nature of the gas to devise preventive measures. In 1831, James Boyle had proposed an elaborate scheme to protect Freetown from the swamps on the opposite side of the Sierra Leone River. This scheme included the formation on the Bullom shore of a kind of anti-malarial colony, densely settled by Africans. The settlers were to drain the land, plant paw-paw trees, keep the brush clear, and, in the wet season, maintain continuous fires in a range of clay kilns. The carbon dioxide of the fires would then purify the atmosphere before it crossed the water to Freetown.[18]

Still other preventive possibilities were implicit in the theory that the miasma was heavier than air, a belief already old but still strongly held. One of the more exotic projects was the suggestion of F. H. Rankin. Like Boyle, his object was to protect Freetown from the Bullom swamps, this time by building a wall along the Bullom shore, thirty feet high and about eighteen miles long. This measure would save the city from the "travelling miasma; creeping, as it does, assassin-like, close to the earth."[19]

Buxton also shared the belief that the miasma would not be found at any great distance above sea level. He based his planning for the Niger Expedition on the assumption that safe altitudes would be reached at about 400 feet. He was not only wrong, but better evidence was already available through careful work in medical topography. Even at the time the expedition was preparing to sail, T. Sterling, who had been financially involved in Laird's earlier effort, protested to the Colonial Office that real safety could only be found at altitudes higher than 4,000 feet. This figure was an accurate estimate of the upper range of *Anopheles gambiae* or *A. funestus* in West African conditions. Macgregor Laird himself had set the lower limit of safety at 3,000 feet in 1837 but raised it to 5,000 feet in 1842. Insofar as a solution to the problem of survival could be found through

17. William Allen and T. R. H. Thomson, *A Narrative of the Expedition to the River Niger in 1841,* 2 vols. (London, 1848), II, 165. See also J. O. M'William, *Medical History of the Expedition to the Niger during the Years 1841–42 . . .* (London, 1843), pp. 157–162.

18. Boyle, *Medico-Historical Account,* pp. 60–64.

19. F. H. Rankin, *The White Man's Grave: A Visit to Sierra Leone in 1834,* 2 vols. (London, 1836), pp. 147–48.

medical topography, Laird had found it. He suggested the formation of British settlements high on the slopes of Mount Cameroons and on the high mountains of Fernando Po, but his vision of dominating the mouths of the Niger from these two healthy hill stations was not acted upon.[20]

Broad studies of medical topography became an even more popular form of investigation after 1830 than they had been in the early decades of the century.[21] The published reports led off in many directions, some less useful than others. The very idea of medical topography contained strong undertones of the earlier belief that different diseases were peculiar to distinct geographical environments. The idea had no future in the history of medicine, but it led to the first investigations of climatology in West Africa. Investigators looked into the pattern of the rains, which apparently moved northward during the summer months and then receded to the south. The appearance of severe electrical storms just before the onset of the rainy season raised questions about possible relationships of electrical discharges and disease. The dry and dusty harmattan winds that blew down from the Sahara for a few weeks during the winter raised still further questions about the causes of climate, as well as the relation of climate to disease.[22] Incidentally and without notice, most of the writers on medical topography abandoned the glib environmental generalizations of the eighteenth century. Assumptions about the possible influence of heat or humidity on the human psyche were not so much forgotten as left out of the field of investigation. The new attitude was more narrowly empirical and more narrowly centered on the problem of disease.

The goal was still to find a healthy spot and to define the healthiest possible environment in general terms. The results were not par-

20. T. F. Buxton, *The Remedy: Being a Sequel to the African Slave Trade* (London, 1840), p. 67; T. Sterling, Memorandum of 3 March 1846. CO 2/22; M. Laird and R. A. K. Oldfield, *Narrative of an Expedition into the Interior of Africa by the River Niger in 1832-4*, 2 vols. (London, 1837), I, 299; M. Laird, Memorandum for the West Africa Committee, PP, 1842, xi (551), pp. 350-51.

21. The principal studies in this field were: Charles Stormont, *Essai sur la topographie médicale de la côte occidentale d'Afrique* . . . (Paris, 1822); Boyle, *Medico-Historical Account;* Thévenot, *Traité des maladies des européens;* Burton, "Observations"; W. F. Daniell, *Sketches of the Medical Topography and Native Diseases of the Gulf of Guinea* (London, 1849); Bryson, *Principal Diseases,* especially pp. 1–31.

22. For meteorology and climatology, see, in addition to the standard works on medical topography: R. R. Madden, Commissioner's Report, PP, 1842, xii (551), p. 412; A. Tulloch, PP, 1840, xxx [C. 228], p. 26; T. H. Hutchinson, *Narrative of the Niger, Tshadda, and Binuë Exploration* (London, 1855), pp. 31 and 81.

ticularly heartening. The very best of the investigations found that there was very little difference between one part of West Africa and another. Laird's solution of taking to the high mountains was all very well, but most of West Africa was not high enough. Real safety near the coast was in fact limited to the heights of Mount Cameroons and Fernando Po. Even the belief in a healthy interior was shown to be wrong by R. R. Madden's study of the mortality statistics of inland exploration, and the warning was repeated again after the experience of the Niger expedition.[23]

In such matters as these, however, the best of the empirical investigations had to compete with popular belief that not only survived but remained the dominant opinion. The myth of the healthy interior lived on into the twentieth century. Certain points on the coast also retained their good reputation, one decade after another. Gorée was one of these. Another was the Banana Islands, Smeathman's "tropical paradise" and the original goal for the Province of Freedom. The Bananas fitted exactly into the established picture of healthfulness—a heavily cultivated island, free of swamps, with some elevation, and enjoying the sea breeze.[24] Other coastal points enjoyed rapidly changing reputations, depending on the incidence of yellow fever epidemics or unusual publicity, and these changes had an important influence on strategic planning. Fernando Po, whose special reputation for lack of disease in the 1820's had been one source of the government's intention to make it their principal base, lost its good reputation during the early 1830's. Sierra Leone lost its bad one. By the mid-1840's, Sierra Leone and the Gold Coast were considered among the safest places on the whole coast, while the Oil Rivers were most widely feared.[25]

The familiar rules for personal conduct and personal hygiene also survived from earlier decades—often without empirical support.

23. R. R. Madden, Commissioner's Report, PP, 1842, xii (551), p. 415; T. R. H. Thomson, Evidence before the Hutt Committee, 23 May 1848, PP, 1847–1848, xxii (366), p. 129; Hutchinson, Narrative of the Niger, p. 192.

24. H. I. Ricketts, Narrative of the Ashantee War with a View of the Present State of Sierra Leone (London, 1831), pp. 212–13; Boyle, Medico-Historical Account, pp. 64–70; J. Rendall to Glenelg, 3 January 1839, CO 2/22.

25. See especially: R. M. Martin, History of the British Possessions in the Indian and Atlantic Oceans (London, 1837), p. 533; Rankin, White Man's Grave, pp. 164–79; Daniell, Sketches of Medical Topography, pp. 58–59; W. F. Daniell, "Some Observations on the Medical Topography, Climate, and Diseases of the Bights of Benin and Biafara, West Coast of Africa," Friend of the African, III, 105–8, 111–13, 138–40 (December 1845–February 1846), p. 106.

There was still a stress on moderation, with special beliefs about the proper hours for meals and the best place to sleep, avoidance of fatigue, damp, and the night air. The recommended quantity of clothing continued to increase. Flannel waist-belts were added to the older recommendation of flannel next to the skin. The hat formerly worn for protection against the sun now took on insulated padding.[26] But some of the new rules brought real improvements. After malaria and yellow fever, dysentery was the most serious threat. By 1841, the Niger Expedition ordered the men to boil all drinking water. The expedition of 1854 drank only water that had passed through the ship's boilers before being filtered. Mosquito nets also came into more common use, becoming standard equipment on the Niger, both in 1841 and 1854. While they certainly made the travellers more comfortable, in conditions of hyperendemic malaria, the most assiduous use of nets and protective clothing was only likely to delay infection. Those who travelled into the interior or lived on shore were certain to receive an infective mosquito bite within a few weeks or months. But rules of conduct, whether sensible or not, were psychologically necessary. Where death was both common and mysterious, it was essential to lay out an area of personal responsibility, so that each could consider "all men mortal but himself."[27]

The sailors of the anti-slavery squadron were in a much better position to protect themselves from infestation with malarial parasites. Alexander Bryson's detailed study of naval health records led to a new understanding of the empirical behavior of the disease and to a number of preventive reforms. He was able to establish the incubation period for malaria, so that the incidence of fever could be related systematically to the place it was contracted. It was found that the men came down with fever about two weeks after contact with the shore, gathering wood and water or chasing slavers up rivers and creeks in open boats. Thereafter, detached service was carefully controlled, and any commander who sent boats away overnight had to justify his action in writing to the Commander-in-Chief of the Station.

26. For the rules of conduct given in the General Orders of the Niger Expedition, see: M'William, *Medical History of the Expedition*, pp. 16–24. For a semi-official set of French rules for West Africa at the same period, see: Thévenot, *Traité des maladies des européens*, pp. 256–83.

27. The psychological function of these rules was remarked at the time. See: Madden, Commissioner's Report, PP, 1842, xii (551), pp. 533–34; "Reminiscences of the Gold Coast, Being Extracts from Notes Taken during a Tour of Service in 1847–8," *Colburn's United Service Magazine*, III, 587 (1850).

Bryson also found that malaria was rarely contracted more than a mile from shore, a correct estimate of the maximum range of the more common West African vectors. These discoveries were all passed on as orders and advice to individual commanders and ships' surgeons. Taken along with Bryson's orders for the control of epidemic yellow fever aboard ship, they clearly had an important influence on the improving health of the squadron.[28]

The development of regular quinine prophylaxis against malaria was still more important in reducing the mortality from malaria. The standard dosage of chinchona bark and wine continued in the *Instructions for Surgeons* reissued by the navy in 1835 and 1844, and the drug appears to have been more frequently used for prophylaxis as it came to be more popular for the cure of malaria. Really effective chinchona prophylaxis, however, had to wait for the development of more palatable and reliable chinchona derivatives, cheaply produced, and backed by medical authority. Quinine, isolated in 1820, was produced commercially in Britain from 1827 onward. By the early 1830's, the price was low enough to make general use possible.[29] By the later 1830's, quinine was gradually coming into popularity on the Coast as a superior substitute for bark, but the significant change came only with the Niger Expedition.

The medical officers of the Expedition were ordered to give the men bark and wine daily in the usual way and were allowed to substitute quinine if they thought necessary.[30] Some of them followed this advice, at least part of the time, and two of them were very favorably impressed with the results.[31] Dr. T. R. H. Thomson continued his experiments after the Expedition withdrew from the river. He found, among other things, that the quinine had not been used with sufficient regularity or in sufficient quantities. In place of the recommended dose of two or three grains, he switched to a routine daily intake of six to ten grains. He experimented on himself on this new basis and had no clinical symptoms of fever while he was in West Africa, even though he was ashore a great deal. When he re-

28. Bryson, *Principal Diseases,* 178; Frederick E. Forbes, *Six Months' Service in the African Blockade* (London, 1849), pp. 123–24.

29. P. F. Russell, *Man's Mastery of Malaria* (London, 1955), pp. 105–6 and 132–33.

30. General order, signed by H. D. Trotter, 16 June 1841, PP, 1842, xlviii [C. 472], p. 114.

31. M'William, *Medical History,* p. 188.

turned to England and stopped taking quinine, however, he came down with malaria.[32]

The train of thought which led Thomson to this discovery is an instructive example of the way in which deduction from false premises might lead to discoveries that were empirically effective. Thomson began by accepting the common practice of labeling the two different phases of malaria as intermittent and remittent fevers. The later phase, or intermittent, was already commonly treated with quinine. He further observed that people with intermittent fever never came down with remittent at the same time. He therefore concluded that intermittent fever had the power of controlling remittent fever, and quinine had the power of controlling intermittent. Might not quinine then have the power of controlling remittent as well?

Though Thomson was the first to publish his results in a prominent journal, other observers were reporting similar evidence. Dr. Madden showed in 1841 that boat companies on detached service, which were actually forced to take the prescribed bark and wine, emerged with significantly lower rates of morbidity and mortality.[33] Alexander Bryson's collection and collation of the reports from naval surgeons proved even more conclusively in 1847 that both bark and quinine, taken regularly, could provide moderately effective protection against fever, and he confirmed this finding in 1854.[34]

As a result, the Navy changed over to quinine as the usual prophylactic, and the new orders were issued extending its use by shore parties. At the end of 1848, the Director-General of the Medical Department of the Army sent a circular to West African Governors, ad-

32. T. R. H. Thomson, "On the Value of Quinine in African Remittent Fever," *The Lancet*, 1846 (I), 244–45 (28 February 1846).

33. A problem arises in trying to assess the statistics of sickness and death during the period when bark and wine was the official naval prophylaxis against fever. In spite of standing orders, the men disliked the taste of the medicine and many surgeons were lax in enforcing the treatment (C. Lloyd, *The Navy and the Slave Trade* [London, 1949], p. 137; A. Bryson, "Prophylactic Influence of Quinine," *Medical Times and Gazette*, VII [n.s.,] 6–7 [7 January 1854]). Madden's case in point was a raid against the slave barracoons in the Gallinas River east of Sierra Leone in November 1840. On this occasion, the treatment was enforced among a group of 130 officers and men who spent seven days in the river. Of those attacked by fever on the Gallinas raid, only 15 per cent died, as against a corresponding figure of 31 per cent on the Niger Expedition the following year. In spite of many unknown circumstances, the contrast between these rates of mortality suggests that the bark used on the Niger Expedition may have been of poor quality, that its use was not fully enforced, or that the treatment of the disease was in some other respect less effective than the measures taken at the Gallinas. (Madden, Commissioner's Report, PP, 1842, xii (551), p. 226).

34. Bryson, "Prophylactic Influence of Quinine," pp. 6–7.

vising the general use of quinine prophylaxis. The quinine habit was already spreading among Europeans on the Coast, even before this official notification. Early in 1848 it had already become common practice for Europeans on the Gold Coast to keep a bottle of quinine on the side table, to be taken at the slightest feeling of danger.[35]

But even yet the knowledge was fragile. No one understoood what quinine actually did to the human body. Some feared that it might have harmful side effects, and in the long run they were proved correct when quinine was found to be a contributing factor in blackwater fever. The final mark of success for quinine came only with the *Pleiad* expedition of 1854. With medical orders drafted by Bryson himself, and commanded by a medical man, Dr. W. B. Baikie, the expedition returned without a single fatality, and it was hailed as a medical triumph. Its startling contrast to the medical failure of 1841 helped to set the reputation of quinine in the public mind, both in Britain and on the African coast. Curiously enough, Baikie himself was not at first convinced. His early reports played down the role of quinine and gave special credit to his own care in selecting the proper season for entering the river.[36] The general and overwhelming impression, however, was that quinine prophylaxis had made the Niger usable as it had never been before, and many authorities were so struck by the burst of publicity, they gave Dr. Baikie credit for inventing the treatment.

The triumph of quinine was one part of the triumph of empiricism, but it was not alone among the important medical reforms of the 1840's. The abolition of dangerous forms of treatment was perhaps of equal importance, and it too drew on the experience of medical men in Africa itself. While copious bloodletting and strong doses of mercurial preparations remained the standard recommendation of the British medical world into the 1850's and beyond, medical practice on the Coast began to change as early as the 1830's. Following Boyle's attack in 1831 on the general bleeding of fever victims, the practice began to decline. By 1841, R. R. Madden found that only one out of eight doctors on the Coast was still making free use of

35. Bryson, *Principal Diseases*, pp. 218–19; Bryson, "Prophylactic Influence of Quinine"; Acting Lt.-Gov. Fitzpatrick to Earl Grey, 10 March 1850, PP, 1850, xxxvi [C. 1232], p. 95; "Reminiscences of the Gold Coast," p. 584.

36. A. Bryson, undated memorandum for the Chadda Expedition [c. 1853], IA, Calprof 1/9; W. B. Baikie, in *Reports of the British Association for the Advancement of Science*, XXVI, 106–7 (1856).

the lancet. Leeches and cupping were still in style, but local bleeding of this kind was more unpleasant than dangerous to the patient.[37]

Overdosage with mercury declined more slowly. Only one of eight medical men in West Africa had abandoned it by 1841, though the investigations of Dr. William Stevens in the Danish West Indies suggested it was dangerous. Dr. Madden's report reflected the state of affairs at the beginning of the 1840's. He was forthright in his condemnation of heavy bleeding but still deferential to the mercurial school in his condemnation of calomel. The Niger Expedition sailed with the needed reforms half accomplished. Only local bleeding was used on the expedition, but calomel to the point of salavation was still practiced. One can only guess that this treatment may have offset some of the benefits of quinine prophylaxis and helped to produce a higher death rate than might have been necessary.[38] During the 1840's the remaining popularity of mercury treatments gradually waned. Bryson condemned both mercury and excessive bleeding, and his authority helped to change the practice not only of the navy but of civilian doctors as well.[39] He was opposed, indeed, to all painful forms of treatment. Seamen would still die of fever, but at least they would be spared the additional agony of a "night-cap blister" covering the whole scalp.

The treatment of fever improved in positive ways as well. Quinine, which was adopted for treatment before it was popular for prophylaxis, came into general use during the 1830's. Five of Madden's eight medical informants recommended it as early as 1841, but only for "intermittents" or to replace the chinchona bark as a "tonic" at the stage of recuperation. It would have been more effective in larger quantities and at earlier stages of the disease. Further improvements came gradually between Boyle's hesitant acceptance in 1831 and Bryson's authoritative recommendation in 1847, and there were many byways of experimentation. Madden thought quinine might be most effective, if applied externally to the raw surface of a blister. Favorite remedies survived long after the 1840's, though often in conjunction with quinine. Hot sand, steam baths, and hot water might be tried experimentally, and Bryson himself allowed small doses of

---

37. R. R. Madden, Commission's Report, PP, 1842, xii (551), pp. 424–25.
38. Burton, "Observations," p. 346; Allen and Thomson, *A Narrative of the Expedition*, II, 162–63; M'William, *Medical History*, pp. 194–98.
39. Bryson, *Principal Diseases*, pp. xi–xii, 232–34.

strychnine or arsenic in cases that did not yield to quinine.[40] Experimentation went on, and empirical discoveries remained fragile knowledge, but the success of quinine as a prophylactic confirmed its reputation for treating fevers as well. It remained the principal anti-malarial drug for nearly a century.

Both the new evidence and the greater care in its interpretation led Europeans to reconsider some old beliefs about the tropics as a human environment. The basic assumption behind all colonial thought and policy was the belief that black men could live and work in hot countries, while white men could not. This belief also lay at the heart of Western thought about the African race—the one unquestioned "fact" about race difference. It was to remain dominant in the popular mind and even in official British thought, but the best of the new investigations raised doubts.

The demography of Sierra Leone posed a special problem and increased these doubts. Commissioners Wellington and Rowan had shown in 1826 that the population was far too low, given the constant immigration of liberated Africans. Whatever the errors in their calculations, they had raised the problem of African mortality in Africa; and the Sierra Leone population continued to puzzle later investigators. It grew from about 13,000 in 1826 to 45,000 by the mid-1840's and then levelled off at about that figure for the next quarter century. Meanwhile, more than 75,000 liberated Africans had been emancipated in Sierra Leone by 1845, and various commentators tried to explain what had become of them.[41]

The problem of African mortality was taken up from another angle by Commissioner Madden's investigation of 1841. His questionnaire addressed to officials and medical men asked about the general health of the Africans. The answers were mixed. Half thought that Africans were healthy, and half thought they were unhealthy. Nine

40. Bryson, *Principal Diseases*, pp. 244–46; Bryson, "Memorandum for the Chadda Expedition," IA, Calprof 1/9; Daniell, *Sketches of Medical Topography*, pp. 120–21; Boyle, *Medico-Historical Account*, pp. 114–15, 127–37, 188.

41. For demographic discussions at the time see: Chief Justice J. W. Jeffcott, PP, 1831–1832, xlvii (364), p. 5; R. R. Madden, Commissioner's Report, PP, 1842, xii (551), pp. 248–49; Macgregor Laird, Memorandum for the West Africa Committee, presented 11 July 1842, PP, 1842, xi (551), p. 570. For recent discussions of the same problem see: R. R. Kuczynski, *Demographic Survey of the British Colonial Empire, Volume I: West Africa* (London, 1948), pp. 95–150; N. A. Cox-George, *Finance and Development in West Africa. The Sierra Leone Experience* (London, 1961), pp. 112–21; and C. Fyfe, *A History of Sierra Leone* (London, 1962), pp. 182–84.

out of twelve answers gave the opinion that the African life span was shorter than that of Europeans.[42]

Other evidence took the form of mortality figures for African troops. A decade after the Government's 1829 decision to use only colored troops in West Africa, Major Tulloch's statistical survey of military mortality led to some unexpected conclusions. African soldiers, mainly recruited liberated Africans, had a low mortality from "fevers" as long as they served in Africa—only 2.4 per thousand per annum. But when men of the same origin were assigned to Jamaica, the corresponding figure rose to 8.2 per thousand per annum.[43] The facts were especially striking, because Jamaica was almost universally thought to have a much better "climate" than West Africa.

Negro Americans coming to Africa fared even worse. Those who settled in Liberia died at a frightening rate, especially if they had come from northern states. West Indians of African descent were also attacked by the African "climate." One group of West Indian missionary agents for the Baptist Missionary Society died even more rapidly than the Society's European agents. Some Africans were recruited for the Niger Expedition in Britain, and those who had been absent from Africa for some time appeared to have lost their allegedly racial immunity.[44] Still other investigations and impressions seemed to show that certain people of European descent had a degree of protection against the most serious forms of fever. Italians, Spaniards, Brazilians, Portuguese, and those from the south of France were all noted at various times as especially favored in the West African "climate."[45] (These people all came from areas that were malarial in the nineteenth century.)

If these reports had been put together systematically, they could have revealed something very close to the modern conception of tropical disease and tropical immunities. They were not put together, however, and they were not brought forward with sufficient publicity to shake the older beliefs in racial immunity; but they were enough to

---

42. PP, 1842, xii (551), *passim*.

43. Tulloch, PP, 1840, xxx [C. 288], pp. 16–17.

44. "Civilization of Africa," *Westminster Review*, XV, 518 (1831); J. Angus, Evidence to Lords' Committee on the Slave Trade, 14 May 1849, PP, (Lords) 1849, xxviii (32), p. 134; William Allen to Lord Stanley, 5 February 1843, PP, 1843, xlviii [C. 472], p. 138.

45. Boyle, *Medico-Historical Account*, pp. 121–22; Burton, "Observations," p. 307; Thévenot, *Traité des maladies des européens*, pp. 157–68.

shift the dominant opinion among those who had a special concern about West African health conditions. Major Tulloch argued, in his official army report, that continuous residence in Africa, and not race *per se,* was the factor most closely correlated with immunity to fevers. This conclusion could be associated with the older European understanding that a newcomer would be relatively safe after he had passed through the "seasoning sickness." The medical officials of the Niger Expedition agreed with this general line of analysis.[46]

But other conclusions were also possible, and some of them kept to the racial explanations of African disease. Prichard, for example, used some of these data to refine his theory about the origins of race. He was concerned to prove that racial differences came from adaptations to different climates, and he thought racial change could take place in only a few generations. Rather than accept the apparent immunity of Negroes as non-racial, he argued that even a relatively short absence from Africa had the power to change their race.[47] Prichard's voice was the authoritative voice of British anthropology, and his analysis fitted both the old preconceptions and a new emphasis on racial explanations. The anti-racist implications of the new data fell on barren ground.

Instead, the real triumph of empiricism was in solving the problem of survival. The most important breakthrough of all was not to come until the first decade of the twentieth century, but the combination of quinine therapy, better precautionary measures, and the abolition of dangerous treatments was enough to make a real difference. The best statistics for West African mortality are those of the African squadron of the Royal Navy. Mortality per thousand mean strength dropped from 65 per annum during the period 1825–45 to 22 per annum in the period 1858–67, and the sharpest decline centered in the mid-1840's.[48]

Death rates on shore were much higher than these in any period, but such statistical information as we have indicates a similar improvement with a similar timing. As to timing, officials and other ob-

46. Tulloch, PP, 1840, xxx [C. 288], pp. 16–17; William Allen to Lord Stanley, 5 February 1843, PP, 1843, xlviii [C. 472], p. 138; M'William, *Medical History,* pp. 179–80.

47. J. C. Prichard, *Natural History of Man,* 4th ed., 2 vols. (London, 1855), II, 650.

48. The average annual mortality from all causes was still 58 per thousand during the period 1840–1842. By 1846–1848, it had already dropped to 27 per thousand (Bryson, *Principal Diseases,* pp. 177–78; PP, 1850, xxiv (35), appendix, p. 211; PP, 1867–1868, lxiv (158), p. 7).

servers in all three of the British coastal holdings reported a very marked "improvement of the climate" in the later 1840's and early 1850's, and this in spite of the yellow fever epidemic at Sierra Leone in 1847.[49] Some suggestion of the probable magnitude of the change between the early and late nineteenth century is found in the two surveys most nearly covering statistically viable groups of Europeans. Between 1819 and 1836, the annual average death rate per thousand mean strength of European troops on the West African coast was 483 for enlisted men and 209 for officers. Between 1881 and 1897, the annual average death rate for officials was 76 on the Gold Coast and 53 in Lagos.[50] Since further medical reforms after 1850 and before the 1880's were not comparable in importance to those of the 1840's, it is fair to assume that quinine prophylaxis and the abolition of dangerous treatments reduced European mortality in West Africa by at least half—possibly much more.

These medical reforms helped to close an epoch. The image of Africa as the "white man's grave" lived on in the British popular mind, but the improvement over the recent past was understood well enough in official and missionary circles to reduce sharply the most serious impediment to any African activity. Europeans could not yet go to West Africa with the same confidence they might feel in embarking for the West Indies or India, but the price in human life was much lower. They could go there, as Mrs. Jellyby put it, "with precaution."

49. [Elizabeth Melville], A Residence in Sierra Leone (London, 1849), p. 77; Benjamin Pine, Annual Report for Sierra Leone, 1847, PP, 1847–1848, xlvi [C. 1005], p. 196; N. W. Macdonald, Evidence before Lords' Slave Trade Committee, 14 May 1849, PP, 1849 (Lords), xxxviii (32), p. 123; J. Bannerman to Earl Grey, 7 April 1851, PP, 1851, xxxiv [C. 1421], p. 198; S. J. Hill, Annual Report for the Gold Coast, 1851, PP, 1852, xxxi [C. 1539], p. 186; J. L. Wilson, Western Africa: its History, Condition, and Prospects (New York, 1856), pp. 511–14; three opinions from the Gambia quoted in Kuczynski, Demographic Survey, I, 386. The impact of these reports was felt in high government circles, and their importance was mentioned in Parliament, see: Earl of Aberdeen, Lords, 22 February 1848, 3 H 96, c. 1039.

50. PP, 1840, xxx [C. 228], pp. 7 and 24; Kuczynski, Demographic Survey, I, 535–36.

15

THE RACISTS

AND

THEIR OPPONENTS

The three decades ending in 1859 with the publication of Darwin's *Origin of Species,* were a period of basic reorientation in British biology. Evolution was already in the air and in the works of some scientists. Only Darwin's general hypothesis was missing; but, lacking the Darwinian revolution, many older forms of biological thought flourished alongside the new. Physical anthropology (more commonly called ethnology in this period) was caught up in the general ferment of the biological sciences, but in ways that were to be disastrous for its future development. Edwards' *Caractères physiologique des races humaines* (1829) marked the beginning of a new flowering for pseudo-scientific racism. Between Edwards' publication and Darwin's, the groundwork was laid for the racial doctrines which were to dominate Western thought about non-Western peoples for a half century or more.

The Darwinian revolution was to cut off many of the meanderings of early nineteenth-century biology, but it allowed the racist error to stand. While it neither confirmed nor denied the pre-Darwinian racial theories, its consequences were to be far more disastrous

to the supporters of Christian and anti-racist monogenesis than to
their opponents. For Darwinians, both polygenesis and monogenesis
were beside the point, but racists could use the theory of natural selection to "prove" that human varieties must be vastly different from
one another. For monogenists, not only was the scientific basis for
their position swept away; its other support in the authority of
Christian revelation was no more valid for Darwinians than other
aspects of the Christian tradition—when that tradition was con-
fronted by scientific truth.

Meanwhile, in the last pre-Darwinian decades, as the racist position
grew progressively stronger, the change was mainly one of degree:
where earlier writers had held that race was *an* important influence on human culture, the new generation saw race as *the* crucial
determinant, not only of culture but of human character and of all
history. Hundreds of variant theories were to appear in the mood of
this new emphasis. Some would claim the rigor of historical law, conceived in detail and projected into the future. Others were content to
use the fact of race as a key to understanding the present condition of
man. In either case, the basic theories were followed in turn by countless specific applications, special formulations, calls to action, warn-
ings of danger, and racio-political policies adopted by governments.

In time, the new racism was to become the most important cluster
of ideas in British imperial theory, but that time was not yet. Prichard
still dominated British anthropological thought into the 1850's, just
as humanitarianism still dominated at the seat of political power. In
addition, Negroes dropped from their old central place in the scientific literature of race. Racial differences, seen in black and white,
were the natural place to begin, but more minute racial variations
now claimed the attention of scientists. Even so, the new emphasis
on race inevitably came to affect European attitudes toward the
Africans.

The rising public interest in biology extended to the study of race.
The new ethnological societies helped to promote that interest, and
the recognition of ethnology by the British Association in 1847 was
a sign of success. In the 1840's and 1850's, the major literary quarterlies gave the same kind of attention to racial questions they had
once given to geographical exploration.

The intellectual atmosphere of ethnology was nevertheless pre-
Darwinian, still working on the old hypotheses, still pushing along

lines of investigation set earlier in the century. One of these earlier directions of racial theory had been the association of race and language, already followed by some anthropologists to the point of using language as one basis for racial classifications. It was a point of some importance, since it increased the tendency to confuse race and culture. If language could become a racial trait, then other aspects of culture might be added, even though they had nothing whatever to do with the physical nature of man. The tendency was logical enough in its pre-Darwinian setting. Orthodox Christians still thought in terms of a world only some six thousand years old. All human diversity, therefore—both racial and cultural—must have arisen in that relatively short period since Adam and Eve left the garden. The anthropologists had some data on the speed of linguistic change, say from Latin to Italian, and the pace of change had not been very great over two thousand years. Given the existing differences in physical race, it was possible to assume (for lack of better data) that the pace of physical change might be much greater. Thus Prichard himself suggested that purely physical traits might be merely transitory, while language differences were "perhaps much more ancient distinctions than the varieties of form and colour."[1]

The primacy of linguistic traits could be justified in other ways as well. According to one ethnologist, "Language distinguishes man from the inferior animals. The communication of his inward feelings, the expression of his thoughts by means of words, is common to man, in all the different stages of physical, mental, and social development. From his language we can perceive the structure and disposition of his mind, his prevailing passions and tendencies: in language the changes and revolutions which the mind of the nation has undergone have left indelible traces. . . ."[2]

Linguistic differences were taken up still more readily by the polygenists. Holding, as they did, that God had created each race separately, they could also believe that he had endowed each with an appropriate language. Hence, Edwards and his school used linguistic evidence as the key to migrations and subsequent racial mixture. Since Edwards was principally interested in Europe, he had to depend

---

1. J. C. Prichard, "Abstract of a Comparative Review of Philological and Physical Researches as Applied to the History of the Human Species," *Reports of the British Association for the Advancement of Science,* II, 529–44 (1832), p. 544.

2. E. Diffenbach, "The Study of Ethnology," *Journal of the Ethnological Society,* I, 15–26 (1848), pp. 20–21.

largely on linguistic evidence: physical differences among Europeans were relatively small, and data about physical race in the distant past were hard to come by.

Along with the shift toward language as a criterion of race classification, there was a further shift toward head shape and away from skin color. Continental ethnologists led this tendency. They had done so since the beginning—from Camper's now-discredited "facial angle," through the early development of phrenology, and more recently in Edwards' insistence on the primacy of head shape. Phrenology, with its hope of discerning the inner nature of the human mind by examining its outer covering, was the crucial mediating influence, even though most ethnologists rejected the specific dicta of phrenological theory. They turned instead to other forms of craniometry. The most influential of these was the cephalic index, first announced in 1840 by Anders Retzius of Stockholm. By measuring the relation between the length and width of the skull, Retzius established the familiar classification into brachycephalic and dolichocephalic, but his full craniometric system was still more complex. He combined the cephalic index with measurements of the face, the height, and the jugular breadth of the head to produce a four-fold system of numerical classification. This system gradually came into general use on the Continent during the 1840's, and somewhat later in England. Retzius was thus the effective founder of craniometry, but he had no wish to distinguish race by physical criteria alone. Like other ethnologists of his time, he too accepted language as a racial trait.[3]

Meanwhile, phrenology went its own way as an influential but separate study. As it spread to England and America it moved beyond its original purpose as a guide to individual psychology. George Combe violated Gall's warning against applying the system to groups of people and tried to analyze the character of entire races. According to his analysis of African skulls, they showed a higher stage of development than those of American Indians or Australian aborigines, but lower than those of Europeans. Specifically, African skulls showed that, "The organs of Philoprogenitiveness and Concentrativeness are largely developed; the former of which produces love of

3. A. C. Haddon, *History of Anthropology,* 2nd ed. (London, 1934), pp. 20–21; E. W. Count (Ed.), *This is Race* (New York, 1950), p. 707; E. W. Count, "The Evolution of the Race Idea in Modern Western Culture during the period of the Pre-Darwinian Nineteenth Century," *Transactions of the New York Academy of Sciences,* VIII (2nd series), 139–65 (February, 1946), p. 151.

Figure 15. An Ashanti war captain.
(From Bowdich, *Mission from Cape Coast to Ashantee.*)

Figure 16. "A Caboceer of Ashantee equipt for War."
(From Dupuis, *Journal of Residence in Ashantee.*)

Discussion of Figures 15 through 23

The image of Africa was presented to English readers of the early nineteenth century in a literal as well as a figurative sense. The illustrations of travel books, in particular, could carry the sense of the romantic beauty of African scenery and people, or else they could carry the message of African savagery.

The different treatment of illustrative material was especially striking in the first two reports from Ashanti by Bowdich and Dupuis. Both, for example, published illustrations of Ashanti soldiers. Bowdich's soldier showed a rather picturesque barbarism (*Fig. 15*), while Dupuis leaned much further toward the image of a savage Africa (*Fig. 16*). Bowdich's illustrations of Ashanti architecture were exotic, but remarkably close to the canons of British taste at a period when Georgian was giving way to the first stirrings of the Gothic revival (*Fig. 17*). Dupuis' illustrations of Ashanti priests were equally clear in their intent to show graphically the bloodthirsty character of African "paganism" (*Fig. 18*). Neither author, however, was absolutely consistent in the point of view of his illustrations. Both Bowdich and Dupuis showed Ashanti festivals that were more "barbarous" than "savage" (*Figs. 19 and 20*).

With the growth of pseudo-scientific racism, much the same kind of bias could be introduced in the portrayal of facial features. In this respect there were three alternatives. One was to show a more or less accurate rendition of negroid features, without exaggeration and without modification to make them appear more European (*Fig. 21*). But even an anthropologist such as Prichard chose his illustrations with care, so as to emphasize the inter-relations of race and culture. He published a pair of portraits, showing the less civilized man of Mandara with exaggerated negroid traits, while the more "civilized" type of Bornu could have been a European who merely happened to have a black skin (*Fig. 22*). Nor was this point left to the reader's imagination. After describing the Hausa people as "acute, intelligent, and industrious," Prichard included a portrait of a single individual (*Fig. 23*), taken in London, and pointed out that, "the countenance, if the complexion were white instead of black, would have nothing unlike the European." (J. C. Prichard, *The Natural History of Man*, I, 296.)

Figure 17. A Courtyard in Kumasi. The seated figures
are playing Warri, the traditional West African board game. (From Bowdich.)

Figure 18. "Priests or Magicians of Ashantee invoking the National deities." (From Dupuis.)

Figure 19. "The First Day of the Yam Custom" (detail showing three British visitors with the Asantehene). (From Bowdich.)

Figure 20. "The Close of the Adai Custom." (From Dupuis.)

Figure 21. King Gezo of Dahomey in 1850.
(From Forbes, *Dahomey and the Dahomans*.)

Figure 22. African racial types from Mandara (*left*)
and Bornu (*right*). (From Prichard, *The Natural History of Man.*)

Figure 23. "A Native of Hausa."
(From Prichard, *The Natural History of Man.*)

children, and the latter that concentration of mind which is favorable to settled and sedentary employments. The organs of Veneration and Hope are also considerable in size. The greatest deficiencies lie in Conscientiousness, Cautiousness, Ideality, and Reflection."[4]

We need hardly be surprised that this description fitted the traditional concept of the "Negro character," since Combe backed his phrenological conclusions by citing the appropriate passages from Leyden and Murray's *Historical Account of Dicovery and Travels in Africa.* It might appear to Combe that "science" could now "confirm" the findings of the travellers to Africa, but it is equally clear in retrospect that Combe started with the data of the travellers and caused phrenology to say the same. Furthermore, new generations of travellers would now be doubly prepared. They would know in advance the findings of science and those of past travellers. The circular flow of repetitive error was thus reinforced.

Phrenology was still more important indirectly, through its influence on prominent American anthropologists. Partly through Combe's influence, Samuel George Morton, a Philadelphia physician and professor of anatomy, became interested in collecting and measuring skulls. In 1839 he published *Crania Americana,* which compared American Indian, "Caucasian," "Malay," Negro, and "Mongolian" skulls. The study was supplemented with the help of George Robins Gliddon, a former United States Vice-Consul in Cairo, and *Crania Aegyptiaca* appeared in 1844 with still more measurements of African skulls.[5]

Morton was more interested in the size, than in the shape of the skull. He measured cranial capacity in cubic inches by filling each skull with white pepper seeds and then measuring the volume of the seeds. His published findings showed a range of mean capacity from 87 cubic inches for "Caucasians" to 78 cubic inches for Negroes. In fact, his measurements had no statistical valadity (even if the capacity of the skull were a genuine measure of intellect): his sample of Negro skulls consisted of only 20 from Negro Americans and 9 from Liberia.[6]

4. George Combe, *A System of Phrenology* (New York, 1845), p. 433. This edition was based on the fourth English edition, London, 1836.

5. S. G. Morton *Crania Americana* (Philadelphia, 1839) and *Crania Aegyptiaca* (Philadelphia, 1844); William Stanton, *The Leopard's Spots: Scientific Attitudes Toward Race in America, 1815–1859* (Chicago, 1960), pp. 24–32 and 45–54.

6. Morton, *Crania Americana,* pp. 253 and 260–61.

Morton's measurement of human intelligence by pepper seeds was, nevertheless, enormously influential. It seemed to give mathematical precision to the old belief in a scale of human races. It was, therefore, taken up in the American South and widely publicized as a pro-slavery argument. British anthropologists received it as a serious contribution to their science, and it seemed to have the support of anatomical studies in England itself. A Dr. Caldwell reported to the British Association in 1841 that the African race "bore anatomically a nearer resemblance to the higher Quadrumana than to the highest varieties of his own species."[7]

Caldwell's anatomy was simply mistaken, but comparative anatomy was not yet sufficiently developed to bring an immediate correction. In spite of real progress on the frontiers of science, there was still no adequate way to prevent empirical error from creeping in —and, once published, from enjoying the generally higher prestige of science as a whole. As late as 1831, for example, it was possible to publish respectably a multi-volume work in which orang-outangs and chimpanzees were classified as human and set in a regular hierarchy along with the other races of man.[8] Thus old errors could survive, while new ones were sometimes being added.

At times, old errors, once exposed, were revitalized. Polygenesis enjoyed a brief revival on this account during the 1850's. The incontrovertible argument for monogenesis had been the fact that all human races can breed together and produce fertile offspring: by definition, they belonged to one species.[9] The data supporting this position were absolutely correct; but data were not yet carefully checked, and pseudo-data could still be invented to prove the opposite. In this case, Robert Knox advanced the "fact" that mulattoes might be fertile for a generation or so, but after that, one or the other of the original, "pure" races would predominate: a cross-bred race could not survive in competition with "pure" races. (He revived, in short, the century-old pseudo-data of Long.) The claim was plainly contrary to centuries of experience in the West Indies and elsewhere, but it was widely believed. Edwin Norris accepted Knox's data on this point and "corrected" the fourth and posthumous edition

8. Thomas Hope, *An Essay on the Origin and Prospects of Man,* 3 vols. (London, 1831), II, 391–97.

7. *Reports of the British Association,* XI, 75 (1841).

9. J. C. Prichard, *Natural History of Man,* 3rd ed., 2 vols. (London, 1848), I, 7–24.

of Prichard's *Natural History*. Paul Broca in France took the same data from Knox and used it to restate the case for polygenesis.[10]

An argument for polygenesis as late as the 1850's was not so much mistaken as beside the point. Evolutionary ideas had made the old quarrel irrelevant and raised new issues in its place. Robert Knox, for example, chose not to use his newly invented data about human hybridity in a polygenist sense: he was already an evolutionist. According to his view, there had been one creation, in which all existing species were implicit, but not present. They evolved later according to a great original plan. First came "animals lowest on the scale, acquatic chiefly; then the mollusca and shellfish; then fishes; next birds, then quadrupeds, and, lastly, man." What Knox lacked and Darwin supplied was a notion of how this might have taken place. For Knox it was simply caused by "continuous generation." His data came mainly from embryology, where he recognized the principle later represented by the phrase, "phylogeny recapitulates ontogeny."[11] As for the origins of human races, Knox held that, however they may have evolved, they could be considered permanent, "for at least a term of years which history does not yet enable us to determine."[12]

Most British anthropologists, however, accepted monogenesis for the reasons Prichard had earlier laid down. They then went on to other problems. Race classification was one of these, since the new criteria suggested new possibilities in place of the familiar divisions by skin color. Prichard had, indeed, pointed out that skin color would yield no clear divisions but only imperceptible gradations from one race to the next. R. G. Latham tried to straighten out matters by depending still more heavily on the factor of language. As a starting point, he accepted Cuvier's three-fold system, rechristening the races as Mongolidae, Atlantidae (African), and Lapetidae (European), but the result only multiplied the confusion between cultural and physical characteristics. His Atlantidae, for example, included not only Negro Africans but all people who spoke Semitic languages. Thus Arabs, Jews, Berbers, and Egyptians—clearly non-Negro in physical type—

10. Robert Knox, *Races of Man: a Fragment*, 2nd ed. (London, 1862), pp. 64–66 and 89–90; Edwin Norris in J. C. Prichard, *Natural History of Man*, 4th ed., 2 vols. (London, 1855), I, xviii; P. Broca, *On the Phenomena of Hybridity in Genus Homo* (London, 1864), pp. 61–71.

11. Knox, *Races of Man*, pp. 171–76.

12. Knox, *Races of Man*, p. 448.

were removed from the racial group of the other light-skinned peoples. Latham was also inconsistent. Though he knew the Malgache spoke a language related to Malay, he classified them as Atlantidae on grounds of physical appearance.[13]

In the hands of non-scholarly writers, the confusion between physical and cultural criteria reached the point of absurdity. Combe, the phrenologist, claimed that the Negro people of the Western Sudan were not really Negroes at all. They were physically like other Negro peoples, but their "state of comparative civilization," as reported by Clapperton, showed they had reached heights impossible for the "inferior" Negro race. In this case, the stereotype of Negro inferiority was strong enough to counteract the custom of dividing mankind according to physical appearance.[14] For other writers, the image of the ugly Negro had a similar result. A military officer who served on the Gold Coast argued that the Fante could not be "pure Ethiopian" in race because they were a strong and handsome people.[15] A missionary to the Gambia claimed the Mandinka must be a mixed race because they lacked the "flat nose and thick lips" of the stereotype.[16]

With some scholars, the concept of race as a physical fact dwindled to the point of disappearance. Carl Gustav Carus in Germany used a classification that was largely cultural, though he tried to support his conclusions by reference to Morton's tables of cranial measurement. He divided mankind into four groups. First there were the "day people" of Europe, North Africa, Arabia, and India, who had achieved the highest civilizations. At a lower level were the "eastern twilight people" of East Asia and the "western twilight people" of the Americas, whose progress was more limited. Last of all were the "night people" of Africa, Australia, and New Guinea, who were held to be the natural slaves of the others.[17]

These new classifications implied a basic shift in the concept of race, but the shift was not seriously questioned or even discussed. Scholarly debate centered instead on racial theories with clear politi-

13. R. G. Latham, *Natural History of the Varieties of Man* (London, 1850), esp. p. 14. For still another new system of classification see P. A. Browne, *The Classification of Mankind, by the Hair and Wool of their Heads* (Philadelphia, 1852).

14. Combe, *System of Phrenology*, p. 421. See also Hope, *Origin and Prospects of Man*, II, 400–401 for a similar re-classification.

15. "Reminiscences of the Gold Coast, Being Extracts from Notes taken during a Tour of Service in 1847–8," *Colburn's United Service Magazine*, 1850 (III), 72.

16. R. M. Macbriar, *Sketches of a Missionary's Travels in Egypt, Syria, Western Africa, &c., &c.* (London, 1839), p. 246.

17. C. G. Carus, *Ueber ungleiche Befähigung der verschiedenen Menschheitsstämme für höhere geistige Entwicklung* (Leipzig, 1849), esp. pp. 17–25 and 32–35.

cal implications, and the focal issue of the 1840's and 1850's was American Negro slavery. This controversy made a curious contrast to the earlier British discussion of slave emancipation in the colonies. Racial theory had hardly entered the British decision of 1833. The pro-slavery forces at that time argued their case as one of economic necessity, dropping the claim that slavery was good for the Negroes themselves; but the racial justification for slavery reappeared in America during the 1830's.

It was precisely at this time that American abolitionists imported the whole paraphernalia of the British anti-slavery movement. With its "peculiar institution" thus called to account, the American South looked to its defenses. Most southerners had believed all along that their slaves were an inferior race, but they now felt called upon to prove that slavery was the natural and proper condition for Negroes. As Christians, they preferred the Biblical curse on the sons of Ham to scientific racial arguments which seemed to contradict the Bible; but the possibility of buttressing the case for Negro inferiority had its attractions, if only for a minority. In the 1830's, there was still a dearth of recent works in the tradition of pseudo-scientific racism. The first move was therefore to revive the racists of the later eighteenth century. J. H. Guenebault of South Carolina, for example, went to Julien Joseph Virey's *Histoire naturelle du genre humaine,* first published in 1800 and incorporating all of the polygenetic anti-African arguments of the previous decades—back to Edward Long and the others whose theories had been worked over in the French and English debates about slavery in the 1790's. Guenebault translated and selected the anti-African sections from Virey's work and published the result as *The Natural History of the Negro Race.* The book was read in England as well as America, and the older group of racist pro-slavery arguments took a new lease on life.[18]

But these arguments were no longer in tune with the recent findings of science. During the 1840's, some of the American supporters of slavery began to look for newer scientific arguments. George Combe's effort to popularize phrenology in America provided one source which merged with S. G. Morton's work on cranial capacities.

18. J. J. Virey, *Histoire naturelle du genre humaine,* 2 vols. (Paris, 1800); J. H. Guenebault, *The Natural History of the Negro Race* (Charleston, S.C., 1837). For the American controversy over race and slavery see: Stanton, *The Leopard's Spots;* W. S. Jenkins, *Pro-Slavery Thought in the Old South* (Chapel Hill, 1935); E. Lurie, "Louis Agassiz and the Races of Man," *Isis,* XLV, 227–42 (September, 1954); J. C. Furnas, *The Road to Harpers Ferry* (New York, 1959).

A new group of American polygenists received the scientific benediction of Louis Agassiz, who had immigrated from Switzerland in 1846. From Britain they drew in the new pseudo-scientific racism of Robert Knox, whose *Races of Man* (1850) was immediately given an American edition. It was soon joined by newer and equally "scientific" racist publications of the Americans themselves. The culminating production was that of Dr. Josiah Clark Nott, one of the most respected physicians in the South, and G. R. Gliddon, who had helped Morton collect skulls from Egypt. Their principal publications were two: *Types of Mankind* in 1854 and *The Indigenous Races of the Earth* in 1857. Both were thoroughly scientific in tone, drawing widely on the recent work of European anthropologists. For the popular audience and those who preferred literary evidence, John Campbell collected all the anti-African authorities he could find—from Herodotus to Robert Knox and Thomas Carlyle—and put together *Negro-Mania* to prove that Africans had never produced a civilization, nor a single individual of outstanding ability.[19]

American polygenetic ethnology never became the most popular defense of slavery, even in the United States. Its denial of revealed religion was too much of a handicap. Nor was it generally accepted in the dominant circles of British ethnology.[20] But Nott and Gliddon's *Types of Mankind* was published in England in 1854, where it was seriously reviewed and sometimes favorably received. Its principal role in England was to add one more voice to the growing chorus of pseudo-scientific racists, which included by 1855 Carus of Germany, Gobineau of France, and Robert Knox in Britain itself. In the trans-Atlantic exchange of ideas, Britain gave the anti-slavery crusade to America in the 1830's and received back the American racism of the 1850's.

Even earlier, American experience had added another and different aspect to British racial thought. From the first settlement of the Americas, European immigrants and travellers noticed that the Indians appeared to die out. The demographic pattern—clear enough in retrospect—was one of differential mortality similar to the "white man's grave" on the Guinea Coast. Only now the non-Europeans

---

19. J. Campbell, *"Negro-Mania" Being an Examination of the Falsely Assumed Equality Between the Various Races of Men; Demonstrated by the Investigations of Champollion, Wilkinson and Others, together with a Concluding Chapter, Presenting a Comparative Statement of the Condition of the Negroes in the West Indies Before and Since Emancipation* (Philadelphia, 1851).

20. See Richard Cull, "On Recent Progress in Ethnology," *Journal of the Ethnological Society*, IV, 297–316 (1856).

rather than the Europeans were the victims. It can be easily explained in the light of modern knowledge. The Indians of the Americas, the Australians, the Polynesians, and, indeed, any of the various peoples who were cut off from the major Eurasian-African land mass for centuries, had lost contact with the diseases or strains of disease common to the rest of the world. In some cases, they developed new diseases of their own, such as syphilis, but the exchange of disease on the re-establishment of contact was unequal. The Europeans were able to survive in the new environment, but isolated non-Europeans were less well prepared to combat the new diseases brought from Europe and Africa. Within a century after 1492, the Caribbean lowlands of tropical America were depopulated. In the tropical highlands and temperate North America the Indians survived, but only after a prolonged decline of population before demographic recovery could begin.

From the first, the Europeans sought to explain the death of the Indians. For Las Casas, it was caused by the cruelty and immorality of the Spanish settlers. Seventeenth-century British commentators also blamed Spanish cruelty for the death of the Arawaks, but they preferred other explanations for the decline of the North American Indians. The most common theories followed a line of thought advanced by Daniel Denton as early as 1670. The extinction of the aborigines was the work of Providence, acting in the interests of the English nation: "where the English come to settle, a Divine Hand makes way for them by removing or cutting off the *Indians,* either by Wars one with the other, or by some raging mortal Disease."[21]

During the course of the eighteenth century, British settlers in North America took up variations on this theme, shifting away from the initial emphasis on God's favor to the English nation toward an allied theory of Divine intervention in the cause of civilization. The aborigines were seen as "savages," whose death made room for the "civilization" of the westward-moving settlers and confirmed the law of human progress.[22]

Neither the problem nor its explanation attracted much British attention in the eighteenth century, but new waves of emigration to the settlement colonies in the early nineteenth century raised the issue more forcefully, especially in regard to Canada and Australia. The new settlement colonies were administered more tightly from

21. D. Denton, *A Brief Description of New York* . . . (London, 1670), p. 7.
22. R. H. Pearce, *The Savages of America: A Study of the Indian and the Idea of Civilization* (Baltimore, 1953), pp. 42–49.

London than the lost thirteen of North America. The disappearance of the aborigines was now seen as a metropolitan problem, and reports of the missionaries brought it to the attention of British humanitarians. Thomas Fowell Buxton took it up in Parliament. Under his chairmanship, a Select Committee on the Aborigines sat through three sessions, from 1835 to 1837. The hearings were accompanied by a flood of books and pamphlets and abundant notice in the press (with an incidental result in the foundation of the Aborigines Protection Society and later of the Ethnological Society). British scientists were attracted to the problem of aboriginal mortality. Prichard stated an ecological variant of the eighteenth-century American theory—when contact occurred between agricultural and pastoral peoples, the pastoralists died out, as though by divine law from "the time when the first shepherd fell by the hand of the first tiller of the soil."[23] Racial explanations, however, were much more popular. The importance of race was already widely discussed. The exterminated people were all of "the colored races," while the exterminators always appeared to be European. It seemed obvious that some natural law of race relations was at work, that the extinction of the non-Europeans was part of the natural evolution of the world.[24] William C. Wells had long before published an evolutionary theory of the origin of race. The new theories of racial evolution were now much more widely publicized.

The publicity, both of the Committee's hearings and the theorizing that followed, profoundly influenced British colonial theory and practice during the middle decades of the nineteenth century. At one extreme it was argued that the death of the aborigines proved the inferiority of the "colored races." Let them therefore die as the laws of progress command! As a middle course, humanitarian settlers sometimes urged that the "natives" be removed to distant reserves for their own protection—incidentally leaving good agricultural land open for white settlement. At the other extreme, some missionaries wished to restrict settlement by Europeans. If missionaries, and only missionaries, were allowed to visit the aborigines, they argued, "demoralization" at the hands of the settlers could be stopped.

23. J. C. Prichard, *Ethnological Extracts* (London, Spottiswoode, n.d.), p. 3.
24. For a sample of these discussions see: PP, 1836, vii (538); PP, 1837, vii (425); Saxe Bannister, *Humane Policy; or Justice to the Aborigines of New Settlements . . .* (London, 1830); H. Merivale, *Lectures on Colonisation and Colonies*, 2 vols. (London, 1841–1842), esp. II, 202–217; William MacCann, *Two Thousand Mile Ride through the Argentine Provinces*, 2 vols. (London, 1853), esp. I, 253–70; and the publications of the Aborigines Protection Society.

West Africa was largely absolved from the direct influence of these discussions, but some elements filtered in to become suggestions for African policy. Most observers realized that differential mortality in West Africa ran against the Europeans, not against the Africans. A few, however, were so impressed by the world-wide disappearance of the aborigines, they were unable to conceive of West Africa as an exception to so universal a "law." The exact nature of the law, however, was in dispute. Some saw it as a cultural law, in which the savages fell away before the civilized. In this sense, it was predicted as early as 1822 that the newly acquired civilization of the Sierra Leoneans would make them the inevitable conquerors of Africa.[25] But if the law were understood to be a racial law, then it was possible to argue that contact with the Europeans was already demoralizing the people of Sierra Leone and preparing for their extinction—that all Africans, indeed, were destined for inevitable disappearance.[26] The only practical result of such misapplied theory was the beginning of a long series of suggestions that Africans must be kept from drinking spirits on account of their "racial weakness." For the time being, it was only suggestion, though in the later nineteenth century it became the official policy of the British government.[27]

The more immediate and far more important consequence for West Africa was indirect. It lay in the realm of ideas, where the aborigines debate strengthened evolutionary racism and led it in new directions. A few Continental historians had already looked to racial determinism as the key to history—as, indeed, had the eighteenth-century American theorists who saw their triumph over "savagery" as the triumph of progress. During the 1840's and 1850's, British theorists whose background lay in moral, rather than natural, philosophy began to borrow the racial thought of the scientists. Under a strong impression from the "facts" of aboriginal extinction, they too began to set up racial theories of history.

Thomas Arnold put forward one of the earliest of these, and one of the most influential, if only because of the prominence of its author. At his inaugural lecture as Regius Professor of History at Oxford in December 1841, he resurrected the ancient idea of a mov-

25. *Quarterly Review*, XXVIII, 175–77 (October, 1822).
26. J. Howison, *European Colonies in Various Parts of the World, Viewed in Their Social, Moral, and Physical Condition*, 2 vols. (London, 1834), I, 99; *Westminster Review*, XXV, 185 (July 1836); MacCann, *Argentine Provinces*, I, 257.
27. See, for example: Paul Read, *Lord John Russell, Sir Thomas Fowell Buxton, and the Niger Expedition* (London, 1840), p. 40; *Blackwood's Magazine*, XLIX, 112 (1840); F. E. Forbes, *Dahomey and the Dahomans*, 2 vols. (London, 1851), I, 38.

ing focus of civilization—now set in terms of race. In Arnold's view, the force of world history came from a series of creative races, each of which made its maximum contribution and then sank into oblivion, leaving the heritage of civilization to a greater successor. What the Greeks gave to the Romans, the Romans passed in turn to the Germanic race; and of that race the greatest nation was England. For Bishop Berkeley, a century earlier, the process had been similar—if non-racial—and it would continue at least one more step.

> Westward the course of empire takes its way;
> The first four Acts already past,
> A fifth shall close the Drama with the Day;
> Time's noblest offspring is the last.

Not so for Arnold—England's achievement was not merely the latest stage in history, it was the last. No great race remained to carry on. The alternative for other peoples was clear: "they either receive the impression of foreign elements so completely that their own individual character is absorbed, and they take their whole being from without; or being incapable of taking in higher elements, they dwindle away when brought into the presence of a more powerful life, and become at last extinct altogether."[28]

After Arnold's death, W. R. Greg took up the speculation in the *Westminster Review,* and with more direct application to the future of Africa. He admitted that some races were indeed becoming extinct, but the Negro race appeared to be a striking exception. North American census figures showed that Negroes could survive and multiply, not only away from their tropical home but in contact with Europeans. Greg held a low opinion of African intellectual ability; but he thought Negroes were racially endowed with an imitative quality. They could therefore assimilate what the West had to offer. Europeans also had their racial faults, and it was in this context that Greg laid down his famous contrast between their "vehement, energetic, proud, tenacious, and revengeful" character set against the natural Christian submissiveness of the Africans. Human progress would still be possible, once European achievements were grafted onto African stock. Greg believed that, "the future progress of mankind will present an aspect rather moral than intellectual; that, to the advance in the material and mental civilisation which the world

---

28. T. Arnold, *Introductory Lectures on Modern History* (New York, 1842), pp. 46–47.

owes to the classic and Teutonic races, will now be added improvement in those mild and happier virtues which Christianity has so long and so fruitlessly enjoined; that the seed, which eighteen centuries ago was sown by the way side, or on the rock or amid thorns, may now bear an ample harvest in more kindly and congenial soil."[29]

Continental theorists of the 1840's also took up the theme of racially determined history, and often with more elaboration than the English essays. Gustav Klemm's *Allegemeine Cultur-Geschichte der Menschheit* began to appear in 1843 and ran to ten volumes in the decade that followed. Klemm distinguished between "active" and "passive" races. Each type had characteristics suitable to a particular phase of human progress. The passive races made the first steps toward civilization, but they soon lost creativity. More active races then took up the burden of achievement. Persians, Arabs, Greeks, and Romans each made their contribution, until the pinnacle was finally reached by the German race of northern Europe.[30]

The theme of achievement by a lineal succession of great races might also be modified into a form of counterpoint. Baron Christian de Bunsen, the Prussian Ambassador to Britain, took the view that civilization was the joint achievement of two "great races," the Japhetic (that is, the speakers of Indo-European languages) and the Semitic, each of which had influenced the other throughout history.[31] Neither Klemm nor De Bunsen, however, were thoroughgoing racists. Klemm was mainly interested in culture, and in very nearly the modern sense of the term.[32] De Bunsen was mainly interested in language. The use of racial interpretations was, for them, merely a fashionable supplement to an argument that was essentially nonracist.

A thoroughly racial theory of history, however, was not far behind. The first important proponent in Great Britain was Dr. Robert Knox, the real founder of British racism and one of the key figures in the general Western movement toward a dogmatic pseudo-scientific racism. Knox's importance has often been underrated, perhaps

29. [W. R. Greg], "Dr. Arnold," *Westminster Review*, XXX, 7 (January 1843).

30. G. Klemm, *Allegemeine Cultur-Geschichte der Menschheit*, 10 parts (Leipzig, 1843–1852), esp. I, 195–205.

31. C. C. J. Bunsen, "On the Results of Recent Egyptian Researches in Reference to Asiatic and African Ethnology, and the Classification of Languages," *Reports of the British Association*, XVII, 254–99 (1847).

32. R. H. Lowie, *The History of Ethnological Theory* (New York, 1937), pp. 11–14.

on account of his professional career. In his youth he had shown great promise as an anatomist. After military service in Europe during the Napoleonic Wars, he kept his commission as an army surgeon and served in South Africa from 1817 to 1820. While there, he became interested in the anatomy of the various South African races and began thinking about the role of race in history. On his return he studied briefly in Paris with Cuvier and was further impressed by the racial theories of French writers such as Geoffroy de Saint-Hilaire.

On his return to Edinburgh, he established a school of anatomy and was soon recognized as one of the outstanding British authorities. Then, in 1828, his chance of continuing an orthodox scientific career was destroyed. At that time there were no regular legal channels for obtaining anatomical specimens, and it was the usual practice of anatomists to purchase them from grave robbers. William Burke and William Hare who supplied Knox, however, were discovered to have used more direct methods. Knox was not personally implicated in the murders, but the scandal ruined both his school and his reputation. Barred from professional work, he became a popular lecturer on scientific subjects and was forced to live by his pen rather than his practice.[33]

The nature of his new audience had an important influence on the style and content of Knox's later writing. His *Races of Man* was first presented in lecture form in 1846, and the published version retained the oratorical style of the lecture platform. Knox also leaned slightly toward charlatanism, ready and able to serve the ordinary man's desire to know the full implications of the new biology. He called his system "transcendental anatomy," implying a rather nebulous extension beyond the range of empirical data. His conclusions were presented without qualification, without question, and without solid evidence. In this way he reached a wider audience than most scientists could hope to reach, and his work was also accepted by some other scientists. Darwin, for example, was to cite from it with approval.

Knox left no doubt about the key to understanding human affairs: "Race is everything: literature, science, art—in a word, civilization depends on it."[34] On account of his rambling style, it was not always precisely clear how the influence of race made itself felt, but the

---

33. H. Lonsdale, *A Sketch of the Life and Writings of Robert Knox, the Anatomist* (London, 1870) is the only biography, written partly to clear Knox's name of the continuing scandal.
34. Knox, *Races of Man*, v.

history of the world was seen as an evolutionary struggle between races—especially between the light and the dark races. The dark-skinned peoples were supposed to have developed first in the course of human evolution, but having reached their maximum achievement they had become stagnant. The later, light-skinned peoples were destined to achieve much more, and in the course of their achievement they would wage a war to the death against the rest, until the dark races became extinct.

According to Knox, the factor of race was crucial within Europe as well. The people of the great race were, for him the "Saxons." The Semites were not even considered to be members of the white race, and the Greeks and Italians were "weak races" whose achievements in the classical world must have come from race mixture with the "Celtic, Gothic, and Saxon." The *Pax Romana* had, furthermore, brought peace to Europe at the price of stultifying the struggle of the races, which alone was the source of human creativity. It was only after Rome fell that the Europeans were able to resume their antagonisms and advance on the road to progress.[35]

These ideas in milder form were already common, but Knox's treatment of race and empire was more original. He conceded a very important role to climatic environment. Europeans could flourish only in Europe. Overseas, the power of Europe could only be sustained by constant immigration or by the kind of military dominance Britain maintained in India. "A *real native* permanent American, or Australian race of pure Saxon blood, is a dream which can never be realized."[36] The future of the Europeans in the tropical world was still more in doubt. Knox was fully aware that the aborigines might well die out in America and Australia, but the Europeans died in Africa. The natural enemy was therefore the race that could survive. "Look at the Negro, so well known to you, and say, need I describe him? Is he shaped like any white person? Is the anatomy of his frame, of his muscles, or organs like ours? Does he walk like us, think like us, act like us? Not in the least. What an innate hatred the Saxon has for him and how I have laughed at the mock philanthropy of England! . . . and yet this despised race drove the warlike French from St. Domingo, and the issue of the struggle with them in Jamaica might be doubtful."[37]

35. Knox, *Races of Man*. The theory as a whole is summarized on pp. 588–600.
36. Knox, *Races of Man*, p. 51.
37. Knox, *Races of Man*, pp. 243–44.

Here was a new note in British racial thought. Earlier generations had sometimes despised the Africans, sometimes pitied them, but never feared them. Yet, for Knox: "If there be a dark race destined to contend with the fair races of man for a portion of the earth, given to man as an inheritance, it is the Negro. The tropical regions of the earth seem peculiarly to belong to him; his energy is considerable: aided by the tropical sun, he repels the white invader. From St. Domingo he drove out the Celt; from Jamaica he will expel the Saxon; and the expulsion of the Lusitanian from Brazil, by the Negro, is merely a matter of time."[38]

Nor was the African threat merely the Negro ability to survive in the tropics. Knox had served in South Africa at a period when a European victory in the frontier wars was not quite a foregone conclusion. Perhaps for this reason, he stressed the military power of the African race, a threat that was the more serious because the Africans were, in his opinion, innately incapable of attaining "civilization." His policy for the West Indies—suggested in hyperbole—was to expel the fierce Negroes and bring in more docile and feeble Chinese and Indians: "Over these the Saxon and Celt might lord it, as we do in India, with a few European bayonets, levying taxes and land-rent; holding a monopoly of trade; furnishing them with salt at fifty times its value; but we cannot do this with the true Negro."[39]

As for the future of Africa itself, Knox left the question open— but with the suggestion that the Africans might well be able to de- fend themselves indefinitely on their home ground.

Knox's voice was clearly that of a minority, and he carried the idea of race struggle further even than his fellow racists; but he was not alone. The older, non-evolutionary variant of the racial myth was also gaining strength during the 1840's. Only a year before *The Races of Man*, Thomas Carlyle had published his "Occasional Dis- course on the Nigger Question" in *Fraser's Magazine*. Carlyle's spe- cial concern was the West Indies, and his racism was teleological rather than evolutionary. For him, Africans were not inferior merely by chance or for the time being. They had been created inferior *in order* to serve their European masters: "That, you may depend on it, my obscure Black friends, is and was always the Law of the World, for you and for all men: To *be* servants, the more foolish of us to

38. Knox, *Races of Man*, p. 456.
39. Knox, *Races of Man*, p. 268. See also p. 246.

the more wise; and only sorrow, futility and disappointment will betide both, till both in some approximate degree get to conform to the same."[40]

Carlyle's point of view represented the heart of the pro-slavery racism found in the American South and other slave-holding societies, but Knox's evolutionary racism gained popularity through the 1850's. When Disraeli argued in 1852 against the wisdom of having emancipated the West Indian slaves, he did so in Knoxian terms: "In the structure, the decay, and the development of the various families of man, the vicissitudes of history find their main solution. All is race."[41]

Eighteen fifty-four was the great year for racist publications. Nott and Gliddon accepted Knox and proclaimed that human progress came from a "war of races." Bulwer Lytton, later to become Secretary of State for Colonies, presented his own racial interpretation of history. In France, Count de Gobineau began publication of his *Essai sur l'inégalité des races humaines,* the most famous and perhaps the most influential of all racist works in the nineteenth century, and de Gobineau based his theory solidly on the groundwork laid during the previous decade—on Knox, Morton, and Carus.[42]

The impact of these theorists was already felt outside the scientific circle immediately concerned with raciology. The change was especially marked in the prominent literary reviews. The *Edinburgh Review,* with a long liberal and anti-slavery record, attacked Earl Grey's colonial policy in 1853 on grounds that Grey had disregarded innate racial differences. The reviewer rested his case on Knox's ideas and on an extreme belief in the inevitability of aboriginal extinction. A year later another reviewer repeated Knox's special fear that the Africans, alone of the "dark races," would avoid their "natural fate" and defy European power. The *Westminster* praised the work of Nott and Gliddon and hailed Knox's *Races of Man* as a "singular work" which "explains much heretofore most obscure." By the later 1850's, Heinrich Barth, the least prejudiced, least culture bound of all the travellers to Africa accepted the teachings of European "sci-

40. [T. Carlyle], "Occasional Discourse on the Nigger Question," *Fraser's Magazine,* XL, 670–79 (December, 1849), p. 677.

41. B. Disraeli, *Lord George Bentinck: A Political Biography,* 10th ed. (London, 1881), p. 239. See also p. 234.

42. J. C. Nott and G. R. Gliddon, *Types of Mankind* (London, 1854), p. 53; E. Bulwer Lytton, Speech to the Leeds Mechanics Institute, 25 January 1854, in *Speeches of Edward Lord Lytton,* 2 vols. (London, 1874), I, 172–89; Arthur, Comte de Gobineau, *Essai sur l'inégalité des races humaines,* 4 vols. (Paris, 1853–55).

ence"—that language was a racial trait, and race was an important determinant of African culture. Even so, the acceptance of racism was not universal. The Ethnological Society still held out for potential equality and condemned the religious unorthodoxy of Nott and Gliddon. An important shift in scientific opinion had nevertheless begun.[43]

Much of this shift was in the realm of general theory rather than specific attitudes toward Africans. It is much more difficult to gauge the opinions of the small and often tacit group of Europeans who either served in West Africa or had an important role in forming West African policy. It is, however, clear that the most ferocious racist opinion came either from white West Indians, whose experience was formed in a slave-holding society, or else from theorists whose actual contact with Africans was very small. The general pattern of racist opinion was, in short, very nearly what it had been since the later eighteenth century. Just as the slave dealers of the earlier period had inclined to think of Africans as men like themselves, the new generation of legitimate traders and colonial officials were more liberal than the English at home. Sir George Stephen noticed this fact in 1849. While he recognized that there was a good deal of anti-Negro sentiment among "good society" in Britain, "yet men whom business or colonial connection has brought into familiar intercourse with the black or coloured races, know well that the educated among them are not inferior to whites in any of those qualities which acquire esteem for the gentleman or confidence for the merchant."[44]

Dr. Madden's investigation of 1841 provides a modicum of quantitative evidence in support of this generalization. Among the questions addressed to medical and administrative officers, one read: "Is there any peculiarity in . . . [the Africans'] . . . physical structure that would justify the opinion of their being a distinct, or of their mental capacity that would justify their being considered an inferior race?"

Of the nine clear answers, only two held the Africans to be inherently inferior. Two, including George Maclean, the President of the Gold Coast Council, gave the opinion of present inferiority, but

43. *Edinburgh Review*, XCVIII, 79–80 and 95 (July 1853), and C, 199 (July 1854); *Westminster Review*, LXV, 199–204, 209 (1856); H. Barth, "A General Historical Description of the State of Human Society in Northern Central Africa," *Journal of the Royal Geographical Society*, XXX, 112–28 (1860); Cull, "On Recent Progress in Ethnology."

44. Sir George Stephen, *The Niger Trade Considered in Connexion with the African Blockade* (London, 1849), pp. 63–64.

potential equality. The other five answered in favor of equality.[45] A
second series of questions on the learning ability of African children
was put to a group of nine, mainly missionaries and teachers. Of
those answering, only Maclean held that Africans had less learning
capacity than white children would have done in similar circumstances.[46]

While Madden's survey cannot be taken seriously as an opinion
questionnaire of unquestioned reliability, its results are generally
consonant with the impression given by other West African reports.
There was plenty of cultural arrogance on the Coast, plenty of plain
xenophobia about Africa and the Africans, but relatively little serious
racism of the kind expressed by a theorist like Knox. The balance of
opinion on the Coast appears to have become gradually less sanguine
about the racial status of the Africans, but the change in attitude
came very slowly in comparison with the more rapid rise of racism
at home. It was only in the 1850's and later that a new generation of
officials began to arrive, already imbued with the new fashion of
theoretical racism.

In Britain itself, the vast majority of the educated public appears
to have accepted at least some aspects of the new racial doctrine, if
only as a vague feeling that science supported the common xenophobic prejudice. The range of European opinion, however, was very
much wider than the range of opinion among Europeans in Africa.
Coastal opinion was kept more uniform by the fact that all observers
had a common experience in dealing with Africans. By contrast, few
Europeans in Europe had intimate contact with African visitors.
There was plenty of room for imagination or theoretical belief to
distort whatever empirical information they might have. A single
individual might combine several diverse images of "the African."
De Gobineau, for example, described the general character of the
Africa race in terms more malevolent than the most vitriolic of the
reports from Africa. Yet at other times he recognized that individual
Africans deviated widely from his own stereotype. "A good number

45. PP, 1842, xii (551), pp. 99, 101, 104, 106, 111, 118, 223, 354, 356, and 359.
46. PP, 1842, xii (551), pp. 88–89, 90–96, 219–20, 342, 345–46, and 348–50.
Neither group of answers is large enough to be a statistically valid sample, but the first
set seems to have included most of the medical men on the Coast, while the second
included the leading missionaries of all denominations. Thus the results have more
validity than the small size of the sample would indicate. On the other hand, Madden
was far from being an impartial investigator, and the published results of his questionnaire may reflect his own anti-racist point of view. The original questionnaires and
answers are to be found in CO 267/171, 172, and 173.

of black chiefs surpass, in the force and abundance of their ideas, in the power of their minds, and in the intensity of their active faculties, the common level which our peasants, or even our bourgeois of ordinary education and endowment, can attain."[47]

One tendency of British thought was especially marked. As scholars began to use racial explanations for all sorts of social phenomena, less sophisticated commentators also introduced the factor of race. In the days of the Sierra Leone Company, the Africans or the Nova Scotians had served as a useful scapegoat when things went wrong in Africa. Later on, the alleged racial traits of the "natives" made it even easier to blame them for European failures. This tendency often carried commonplace British attitudes through curious and irrational channels. By the 1840's or 1850's, for example, all rational assessments of the British failures on the Coast picked the "climate" as the single factor most seriously limiting any and all European activity. At another and less conscious level of analysis, a subtle shift took place. The missionary image of African savagery was set in the public mind, and the opposition of a fierce people was added to that of a fierce "climate."[48] This tendency appeared especially in the retrospective assessment of the Niger failure. After a decade, the public had forgotten the details and remembered only that something had gone wrong. If, after such expense and sacrifice, the Africans were not civilized, it was easy to assume they were uncivilizable.[49]

A similar tendency to implicate the Africans ran as a minor strand through the British debate about the failure of the anti-slave-trade blockade. In the later 1840's it occurred again to explain the "failure" of West Indian slave emancipation. The ruin of the West Indian plantations was loudly proclaimed after 1846, partly because of a change in the British sugar duties and partly because of a general financial panic in 1847. The true cause of the crisis was not well understood at the time, and it was too complex for easy popular explanation; but everyone "knew" that Negroes were inherently lazy, and it was simple enough to blame the ex-slaves. In this atmosphere,

47. Arthur, Comte de Gobineau, *Essai sur l'inégalité des races humaines,* 2nd ed., 2 vols. (Paris, 1884), I, 214–15, 185–86.

48. See, for example: A. B. B., "Introduction," to R. and J. Lander, *Journal of an Expedition to Explore the Course and Termination of the Niger . . . ,* 2 vols. (New York, 1858).

49. For a contemporary discussion of the psychology of this transfer from climate to people, see B. Cruickshank, *Eighteen Years on the Gold Coast of Africa, Including an Account of the Native Tribes, and Their Intercourse with Europeans,* 2 vols. (London, 1853), I, 8.

Disraeli suggested that slavery might well be reimposed, and Carlyle's "Nigger Question" gave a plausible racist solution to the whole problem.[50]

The Africans nevertheless had their champions after the 1830's, but the defense was gradually weakening. The old magic of the anti-slavery cause no longer brought an automatic emotional response. For one thing, the humanitarians had promised too much, too soon: as 1850 approached, the West Indies were not prosperous, and West Africa was not "civilized." Newer causes were more exciting. A generation whose parents had been roused to erase the evil of the slave trade, was stirred in its turn by the new hope for perpetual peace through free trade. The immense effort required in 1850 to muster a Parliamentary majority merely to preserve the anti-slavery squadron was symptomatic of the general trend of opinion.[51]

The case presented by the pro African writers was also intellectually weak—no weaker, perhaps, than it had been in the past, but less convincing in the new intellectual atmosphere of the 1840's or 1850's. The strongest argument, for the humanitarians themselves, was that of religion, and Richard Watson's classic statement of 1824 was reprinted and paraphrased for decades afterward. But Watson was explicitly opposed to science and its teachings. As the prestige of science increased—as the old Evangelical fervor dwindled away into mere Victorian respectability—a strict interpretation of the Bible no longer carried the weight it once had done.

Humanitarian writers were also trapped by their own dislike of African culture as it was, and by their prejudice in favor of their own physical type. An occasional humanitarian traveller might admit that Africans could be, in their own way, as handsome as Europeans, but the view was rare.[52] Many works, overtly in defense of the Africans, gave way to cultural or racial prejudice on almost every point short of the minimum claims of "spiritual equality."[53] Edward Binns, for example, attacked African culture in terms as violent as those of the

50. B. Disraeli, Commons, 28 July 1846, 3 H 88, cc. 165–66.
51. See Thomas, Lord Denman, *Uncle Tom's Cabin, Bleak House, Slavery and Slave Trade* (London, 1853), p. 8.
52. See, for example, F. H. Rankin, *The White Man's Grave: A Visit to Sierra Leone in 1834*, 2 vols. (London, 1836), II, 50–52.
53. See, for example, B. L., "Sierra Leone," *Westminster Review*, XXV, 176–77 (July 1836); W. B. K., "On the Varieties of the Human Race," *The Colonial Magazine*, IV, 83–87, 179–88, 360–69, 484–91 and V, 37 (January–May, 1841), p. 86; W. and R. Chambers (Eds.), "Intelligent Negroes," *Chambers's Miscellany of Useful and Entertaining Tracts*, Vol. VII (Edinburgh, 1845), p. 32; C. P. W., *The Natives of Africa* (London, [1853]), p. 7.

racists. He believed that most Africans were cannibals, and he characterized "the African" as "suspicious, fickle, fierce, libidinous, cruel, cunning, treacherous, blood-thirsty, in his uncivilized state."[54] Binns gave away another argument to the pseudo-scientists by adopting phrenology and trying to prove by its techniques that Africans were fully equal to whites in their natural abilities.[55]

The defenders of the Africans were, in fact, almost always inept in discussing the "scientific" aspects of race. They used literary authority much more effectively. Blumenbach's list of "noble Negroes," as extended by Abbé Grégoire, continued to grow until it reached its apogee in Wilson Armistead's *Tribute to the Negro* (1848). Armistead's proofs of Negro equality ran to more than five hundred close-packed pages, and he soon replaced Grégoire as the standard mine for pro-Negro arguments. By 1856, Edward Blyden of Liberia was using the list of "noble Negroes" to answer the racists of Europe.[56] But even here there was a weakness, which Carus and then Gobineau were quick to point out. The list of "noble Negroes" was made up almost entirely of Africans who had made good in the West or under a very strong influence from Western culture. It was, indeed, originally drawn up to prove that Africans could attain "civilization." Now the racists pointed out that it merely proved Africans were inferior, since it showed they had the ability to imitate but not the creative drive to make a civilization of their own.[57] On this point, as on many others, the cultural chauvinism of the pro-Negro group rebounded to the aid of racism.

The crucial weakness of the anti-racist case in the early nineteenth century was the failure to distinguish between race and culture. It not only weakened the public arguments of those who wished to stem the rising tide of racism; it also led serious scholars of good will into an acceptance of racial doctrines. Prichard's attempt (and ultimate failure) to defend the racial equality of mankind through the theory

54. Edward Binns, "Prodromus Toward a Philosophical Inquiry into the Intellectual Powers of the Negro," *Simmonds's Colonial Magazine*, I, 464–70 and II, 48–59, 154–84 (April–July, 1844), I, 467.
55. Binns, "Intellectual Powers of the Negro," II, 159–60, 183–84.
56. For lists or biographies of eminent Negroes, published in this period, see: Binns, "Intellectual Powers of the Negro," II, 48–59; Chambers, "Intelligent Negroes;" W. Armistead, *A Tribute to the Negro* (Manchester, 1848), p. 120–43 and 191–564; H. G. Adams, *God's Image in Ebony* (London, 1854); E. W. Blyden, *A Voice from Bleeding Africa* (Liberia, 1856).
57. Gobineau, *L'inégalité des races* (1884), I, 74.

of monogenesis illustrates the way this crucial error led nineteenth-century science into the racist myth. Prichard admitted, to begin with, that African culture was a barbarism to be deplored. He also accepted the supposition of other ethnologists that race and culture were intimately connected. On the basis of these two assumptions, the Africans were necessarily regarded as an inferior race—at present. Prichard tried to save the Christian tradition of racial equality by adding a time element. The equality of all races existed, but it was potential, not actual. That was enough, if one accepted Prichard's assumption that physical characteristics would change rapidly with a change in culture.[58] On this specific point, he was not only wrong in the light of modern anthropology; the error could be demonstrated before his own death. Morton showed in 1844 that the Egyptian skeletons associated with the earliest phases of Egyptian civilization were physically like those of modern men. Hence: "The physical or organic characters which distinguish the several races of man, are as old as the oldest records of our species."[59] Morton's data were, of course, correct, though neither he nor Prichard understood that the "oldest records of our species" were very new indeed measured against the scale of time usually needed to produce a radical change of racial type. Nevertheless, any scientist who accepted Prichard's assumptions and Morton's data would have to conclude that the African peoples were not only inferior at present. They were permanently so. The intellectual foundation of racial egalitarianism was thus destroyed, and it was not to be recovered until scientists could start over again with new assumptions.

In spite of this erosion of its basic ideology, humanitarianism was still the philosophy in office throughout the 1840's. Both the ideology and the political influence of the humanitarians were secure at least until the end of the Russell Government in 1852. The rise of the new pseudo-scientific racism, however, pointed to a new frame of thought that was to dominate the second half of the century. Meanwhile, there was merely a crack in the pre-Darwinian world view. The forms and meanings of African life were still investigated, and the British plans for the future of Africa were still laid, in the light of the older tradition.

58. J. C. Prichard, *Researches into the Physical History of Man,* 4th ed., 5 vols. (London, 1851), II, 340–46; Prichard, *Natural History of Man* (1855), I, 97–101.
59. Morton, *Crania Aegyptiaca,* p. 66.

16

LANGUAGE, CULTURE,

AND

HISTORY

The literary tradition in African studies altered slowly as the mid-century approached, with nothing in the offing comparable to the Darwinian revolution which hung over biological sciences. If any revolutionary change had taken place, it was the eighteenth-century shift from an emphasis on static analysis of society to the nineteenth-century emphasis on historical or evolutionary analysis.[1] This new attitude, however, was firmly in office by the 1830's, when the great works of Von Ranke, Michelet, and Macaulay began to appear. It gained some further impetus from the romantic movement of the early nineteenth century, but that was all.

Genuine innovation in the social studies, however, continued at another point, where historical knowledge and analysis could be linked with data not commonly taken into account by historians. The racists from Edwards through Knox and Gobineau brought physical anthropology into historical explanations. Karl Marx joined history and classical economics. Gustav Klemm combined history and eth-

---

1. A. O. Lovejoy, *The Great Chain of Being* (Cambridge, Mass., 1936), pp. 242–87.

nography in a more thorough and detailed presentation than had been common in the past, but, for all his talk of the need to create a "culture history" and study mankind's changing way of life, rather than the deeds of kings, his basic assumptions were those of the eighteenth-century moral philosophers. Klemm looked, as they had done, for the earliest stages of man, frozen, as it were, in the present-day life of the Eskimos or South American Indians.

Klemm's work and that of other historical ethnographers nevertheless brought about a slightly different attitude toward the data about African culture. The examples from Africa were more detailed than ever before, and Klemm used Ashanti for a case study of the "second stage" of human development. The general assessment of cultural stages also began to change in small ways. Where the common belief of the early nineteenth century had set pastoralism at a second stage, above mere hunting and below sedentary agriculture, Klemm and some of his contemporaries tended to promote it to a place one stage higher than agriculture. The exact reason for the change was rarely explicit, but it was clearly associated with admiration for the military strength of mounted warriors, and seems to have gained something from the social superiority of European cavalry. In any event, it raised the status of certain African cultures, such as the pastoral southern Bantu or the Fulbe of West Africa. Even the sedentary African cultures were now more clearly marked out at a level superior to the American Indians or Polynesians, the most admired of the eighteenth-century "noble savages."[2] But these small alterations in assigned status were a minor matter. For most Europeans, all "barbarous" societies were seen across a widening gap from the civilization of Europe, even though Europeans were more willing than before to extend the scope of their studies to the far side of the cultural gulf and take greater account of the "primitive" condition of man.

The new histories and discussions of early man raised some new problems and exposed old problems which had been passed over. One point of increasing interest was an implicit conflict with the Christian tradition: even non-scientific histories of culture could have some dangerous implications. According to the usual understanding of

2. G. Klemm, *Allegemeine Cultur-Geschichte der Menschheit,* 10 parts (Leipzig, 1843–1852), esp. I, 20–23. See also H. Merivale, *Lectures on Colonisation and Colonies,* 2 vols. (London, 1841–1842), II, 155–57; *The Colonial Intelligencer,* II, 132–33 (1848).

Genesis, Adam and Eve had not been savages. They were thought of as endowed from the beginning with a reasonably "advanced" culture. The new picture of mankind advancing only very slowly during centuries of cultural evolution could not be squared with the common opinion. The usual impression was, indeed, based on conjecture rather than scripture—the Bible has very little ethnographic information about the Garden of Eden—but it was firmly believed.

Another point of difficulty was the question of cultural diffusion or independent invention. The assumption that human society advances toward civilization through a fixed progression of stages might be taken to imply that all stages were necessary—even that each society must invent by itself all the techniques required for advance from one stage to the next. Traditional Christian historiography had rarely dealt explicitly with the problem—had not even been especially conscious that it was a problem—but Christian writers took for granted the fact that "religious truth" was one cultural trait which had diffused from a single center. By implication, they had often assumed that all cultural change was the product of similar diffusion.

These problems and their implications for Africa were taken up in 1844 by the Reverend D. J. East. He accepted the idea of stages in human progress. This idea was, in fact, implicit in the Biblical story and in most of the Christian historical tradition. The creation, the fall of Adam, the coming of Christ, and the Last Judgment are all marks along a road of spiritual progress. But East was also an uncompromising diffusionist. For him, the first stage of progress was merely that period when religious truth had been the sole possession of the family of Abraham. In a second stage, the Greek philosophers gained some elements of truth through natural reason. The third stage began when "the Everlasting Word was made flesh" through the coming of Christ. At this point the completed message was available for general diffusion to all mankind, and mankind could not pass on to the fourth stage until all had heard it. When this had happened, history would enter a higher stage. Christian conduct would be perfected on earth, and the agents of this perfection would be the Africans, who, as natural Christians, would teach Christian humility to the Asians and Europeans, until at last the world would know peace and Christian unity.[3]

3. D. J. East, *Western Africa; Its Condition, and Christianity the Means of its Recovery* (London, 1844), pp. 107–8.

Other Christian writers chose to meet the threat of new and unorthodox theories of society and history in other ways. One of the most elaborate defenses was William Cooke Taylor's *Natural History of Society,* published in 1841. He denied that man could have evolved, either physically from the apes, as Lamarck had suggested, or culturally from savagery, as the moral philosophers claimed. He denied, furthermore, that man in the savage state was innocent and good, and had later become evil—a view he attributed to Rousseau. He denied the whole of the racist doctrine and concluded, "that the capacity of becoming civilized belongs to the whole human race—that civilization is natural to man—that barbarism is not 'a state of nature,' and that there is no *prima facie* evidence for assuming it to be the original condition of man."[4]

For Taylor, man had originally been endowed by God with a knowledge of both agriculture and mineralogy. But the world had changed since then. Some men had slipped downward into barbarism (and here Taylor reintroduced the strain of pessimism so common in early Christian historiography), while others had known progress. Thus the idea of progress could be retained, and Taylor went further and proclaimed progress in social life as the dominant mark of "civilization." It was an ingenious theory, since it retained the nineteenth-century feeling of cultural superiority over the "degraded" part of mankind, while denying both racism and the usual view of historical evolution. The condition he assigned to savages and barbarians, moreover, was no better than that ascribed to them by the racist writers. They were considered physically weak, unable to visualize mentally what was not physically present, unable to think in terms of means and ends, unable to count beyond a very few numbers—often no further than three.[5]

Other Christian commentators held similar opinions, but made a distinction between savages and barbarians. Rufus Anderson, an American missionary theorist, held that barbarians, like the East Indians, suffered mainly from "plenitude of error—the unrestrained accumulations and perversions of depraved intellect for three thousand years." Savages, on the other hand, had the opposite failing, "For, the savage has few ideas, sees only the objects just about him,

---

4. W. Cooke Taylor, *The Natural History of Society in the Barbarous and Civilized State: an Essay Towards Discovering the Origin and Course of Human Improvement,* 2 vols. (New York, 1841), I, 17–30. First edition London, 1840.
5. Taylor, *Natural History,* esp. I, 17–46 and 210–300.

perceives nothing of the relations of things, and occupies his thoughts
only about his physical experiences and wants."[6]

Meanwhile, new data were accumulating, which might provide the
basis for accepting or rejecting these broader theories. While the
contribution of general ethnography was slight, linguistic research
pushed rapidly forward from the 1830's onward, supported by the
dual need of ethnologists, with their emphasis on linguistic traits, and
missionaries, with their need to know African languages in order to
reach the Africans. So many vocabularies were available by 1840 that
Edwin Norris was able to compile a small multilingual dictionary for
the use of the Niger Expedition. In it, he gave more than fifteen hundred English words, with their equivalents in Hausa, Ibo, Yoruba,
Fulfulde (the language of the Fulani), Mandinka, Bambara, Fante,
and Wolof.[7] It was not complete in all these languages, but it represented a continuation of the Senegal Company's earlier effort to prepare a multilingual dictionary of African languages.[8] By 1847, R. G.
Latham had available some fourteen vocabularies of Akan languages,
eleven of various Ibo dialects, and eight of Yoruba, among others.[9]

While these vocabularies were used with confidence—and often
with too much confidence—by the linguists in Europe, they were
nearly useless for missionary purposes. Comparative word lists, made
hurriedly and without a uniform orthography, were far from a usable
knowledge of a language. By 1840, the Church Missionary Society had
come to realize that much of its earlier linguistic work would have to
be scrapped and a new start made. Missionary societies now had
enough field staff to allow specialized linguistic research, and European linguists were beginning to develop a distinct discipline and
method. When Baron C. C. J. de Bunsen, himself a linguist, became
Prussian Ambassador to London in 1841, he played a mediating role

6. Rufus Anderson, *The Theory of Missions to the Heathen* (Boston, 1845), p. 13.
7. E. Norris, *Outline of a Vocabulary of a Few of the Principal Languages of
Western and Central Africa: Compiled for the use of the Niger Expedition* (London,
1841).
8. This work contained about two thousand words in the seven most important
languages of the Senegambia. It was published in: *Mémoires de la Société Ethnologique*, II (2), 205–67 (1845).
9. R. G. Latham, "On the Present State and Recent Progress of Ethnographical
Philology," *Reports of the British Association for the Advancement of Science*, XVII,
154–229 (1847). As a guide to linguistic material available at this time, see: J. S.
Vater, *Litteratur der Grammatiken, Lexika und Wörtersammlungen aller Sprachen der
Erde*, 2nd ed. (Berlin, 1847); revised and enlarged by B. Jülg. See also R. N. Cust,
A Sketch of the Modern Languages of Africa, 2 vols. (London, 1883), I, 23–38.

between the new school of scientific linguistics in Germany and the practical needs of the English missionary societies. It was through his efforts that the CMS introduced a uniform orthography in 1848; and K. R. Lepsius of Berlin produced an improved system for them in 1854.

Anglo-German missionary cooperation in Africa was already an established tradition, and the CMS in particular employed German trained linguists. The Reverend J. F. Schön accompanied the Niger Expedition and worked with Ibo and Hausa. His successor, S. W. Koelle, became a full-time linguist attached to the CMS staff in Sierra Leone, where he studied Vai and Kanuri. Other missionaries in Sierra Leone worked with Bullom, Susu, Sherbro, and Temne; and the studies of Yoruba published by the Reverend Samuel Crowther were the first in English by an African scholar studying an African language. Other missionary societies took up the languages appropriate to their own work, such as Efik studies by the Presbyterians in Calabar, and Akan studies by Basel missionaries and Wesleyans on the Gold Coast.[10]

The high point of these missionary linguistic studies was Koelle's *Polyglotta Africana,* the first really trustworthy comparative vocabulary of African languages. From his base in Sierra Leone, Koelle collected the equivalents of about 300 words and phrases in 160 different African languages. His informants were mainly liberated Africans, but he carefully recorded the length of their absence from their home country and thus established a standard of reliability. Koelle feared that the work would suffer from the fact that it was purely lexical, but it was an important step forward. With all languages in the collection recorded by a single trained observer, using a single system of orthography, vocabulary comparisons could be made on a sound basis.[11]

West African languages posed a special problem for linguists in Europe, who tried to depend on data gathered by other people. Most of these languages are tonal, a fact which Europeans were slow both to recognize and to record. Even those who recognized the importance

10. J. F. Ade Ajayi, "Christian Missions and the Making of Nigeria 1841–1891 " (Unpublished Ph.D. thesis, London, 1958), pp. 302ff.; H. Halleur, *A.B.C. darium der Ashanti-Sprache* (Basel, 1845); R. Brookings, *Nucleus of a Grammar of the Fanti Language: With a Vocabulary* (London, 1843).
11. S. W. Koelle, *Polyglotta Africana, or a Comparative Vocabulary of Nearly 300 Words and Phrases in more than 100 Distinct African Languages* (London, 1854).

of tonal variations had no easy way of describing them to a European audience. The Reverend J. Raban could only note in his Yoruba vocabulary of 1831 that certain words were "uttered with a depressed voice," though Samuel Crowther distinguished the three Yoruba tones in his vocabulary of 1843. The discovery of tonality in other languages was much slower. Riis devoted more than one hundred pages to a grammatical analysis of Twi without any obvious recognition of tone; and Koelle made no attempt to indicate tone in the *Polyglotta Africana,* though he was conscious that some of the languages included were tonal.[12]

It is clear that many of the pejorative judgments of African languages throughout the nineteenth century were based on an ignorance of tonal differences. Where the grammatical context or even the meaning of a word depended on tone, the Europeans were quick to assume that the language was "primitive," because it seemed to them to lack grammatical regularity.

However weak their empirical base in African languages, linguistic studies in Europe were developing along the lines already taken by anthropology. One effort was to arrange languages on an absolute scale of value, not unlike the Great Chain of Being. In another direction, linguists were trying to arrive at an evolutionary theory of language. A third effort was to discover the familial relations between similar languages, showing, for example, whether related languages were parent and offspring or collateral descendants from a common ancestor language.

The influence of biological thought is obvious. Even a humanitarian like Thomas Hodgkin believed that a "natural history of language" would be found to parallel the "natural history of man." Hodgkin accepted language as a genuine racial trait—believing that men of one race were physically unable to pronounce correctly the words used by another. Some of the pseudo-scientific racists went much further. Guenebault tried a kind of phonetic phrenology, arguing that people who could not pronounce the sound of the letter "R" were "pusillanimous," while those who used this sound frequently were brave. For Gobineau, linguistic theory and racial theory were identi-

12. J. Raban, *Vocabulary of Eyo, or Aku, a Dialect of Western Africa,* 2 parts (London, 1831); S. Crowther, *Vocabulary of the Yoruba Language* (London, 1843), pp. 1–5; H. N. Riis, *Grammatical Outlines of the Oji Language, with Special Reference to the Akwapim Dialect together with a Collection of Proverbs* (Basel, 1854).

cal: "The hierarchy of language corresponds rigorously to the hierarchy of races."[13]

Even the theorists who opposed the new racism pictured an evolution of language following the same course as cultural evolution. Cooke Taylor, for example, sketched a theory of linguistic development parallel to his Christian view of culture history. In this view, God gave language to man in the Garden of Eden. After the fall of Adam, some languages had advanced, while others became degenerate. The degraded languages were thought to "err both in excess and defect." They had too many suffixes and affixes, too many synonyms, and yet too few objects or concepts for which there were any words at all. Baron de Bunsen took a similar view, presenting the linguistic aspect in much greater detail. For him, the original language was monosyllabic, like Chinese. It might degenerate, but, if it progressed, it passed through a series of stages. At a second and higher level, it would develop suffixes, affixes, and compound words. At the third and highest level, words would be inflected to show additional meanings and grammatical relations.[14]

It was against this background of developing theory that authorities on African languages passed their judgments. Since African languages were neither monosyllabic, nor yet so inflectional as Latin, they might be placed half-way up the ascending scale—and this would agree with the usual African place on the "scale of civilization." Latham and the most respected English authorities tended toward this view, but others disagreed. It was equally possible to place African languages on the descending scale. Guenebault, for example, believed African languages were "degenerate" and described them as they should have been in his theory—monosyllabic and, of course, without the "R" sound.[15]

13. T. Hodgkin, "On the Importance of Studying and Preserving the Languages Spoken by uncivilized Nations, with the View of Elucidating the Physical History of Man," *London and Edinburgh Philosophical Magazine*, VII, 27–36, 94–106 (July–August 1835); J. H. Guenebault, *The Natural History of the Negro Race* (Charleston, S.C., 1837); Arthur, Comte de Gobineau, *Essai sur l'inégalité des races humaines*, 2nd ed., 2 vols. (Paris, 1884), I, 187–214. Quotation from p. 213.

14. Cooke Taylor, *Natural History*, I, 37; C. C. J. de Bunsen, "On the Results of Recent Egyptian Researches in Reference to Asiatic and African Ethnology, and the Classification of Languages," *Reports of the British Association*, XVII, 254–99 (1847), pp. 265–90.

15. Latham, "Recent Progress of Ethnographical Philology," p. 217; Guenebault, *Natural History*, p. 34.

Still other authorities (often unconsciously) adopted Latin as the standard of linguistic perfection. The strongly tonal languages, which were also the most difficult for Europeans to learn, were thus placed lowest on the scale of value. Bantu languages were generally preferred, partly because they were less tonal and easier to learn, and partly because they were highly inflected. Hausa was also esteemed, for similar reasons. Schön, the first Hausa scholar, became the founder of a pro-Hausa tradition which was to have a long history.[16] Given these attitudes, it was only natural that some of the missionary linguists who prepared the first grammars should try to "improve" the African languages, bringing them closer to the "laws of construction," meaning the rules of Latin grammar.[17]

In other respects, however, the linguistic reputation of the West Africans improved as a result of better knowledge. The belief that all African societies were non-literate was shaken in 1849 by the rediscovery of the Vai syllabary, which was well publicized by the discoverer, Lt. Forbes of the Navy. Koelle immediately set out from Sierra Leone to the Vai country (in present-day Liberia) to make a further study, and CMS had a set of Vai syllables cast in type for printing the language.[18]

Linguistic studies also led to a new appreciation of African literature. It was a common European myth that Africans had no memory of the past, no tradition, and no literature. As early as 1828, Baron Roger had published a selection of Wolof fables from Senegal, but oral literature was more frequently taken down and translated after 1840. Riis recorded 268 Twi proverbs and published them with a translation and commentary. Koelle prepared a book of Kanuri material, including proverbs, fables, stories, and historical accounts, mainly to serve as an introductory reader for missionary students

16. J. F. Schön in *Journals of the Rev. James Frederick Schön and Mr. Samuel Crowther, who with the Sanction of Her Majesty's Government Accompanied the Expedition up the Niger in 1841* (London, 1842), pp. 119–20; J. L. Wilson, "Comparative Vocabularies of Some of the Principal Negro Dialects of Africa," *Journal of the American Oriental Society*, I, 317–82 (New York, 1851); J. L. Wilson, *Western Africa: Its History, Condition, and Prospects* (New York, 1856), pp. 455 and 457–61.

17. R. M. Macbriar, *Mandingo Grammar* (London, 1837), p. vi.

18. F. E. Forbes, *Dahomey and the Dahomans*, 2 vols. (London, 1851), I, 196; S. W. Koelle, *Outlines of a Grammar of the Vei Language* (London, 1854), pp. 1–8; S. W. Koelle, *Narrative of an Expedition into the Vy Country of West Africa* (London, 1849). In fact, the Mum language of the Cameroons also had a system of notation, and it was common to write several African languages in Arabic script. The independent invention of a system of notation was therefore as unnecessary in much of Africa as it was for Europe itself.

of the language. O. E. Vidal studied Yoruba proverbs, both as a form of literature to be appreciated for its esthetic merit and for the sake of understanding the Yoruba system of values. French researchers in Algeria also began to throw some light on the Arabic literature of the Western Sudan. Cherbonneau published a brief account of Ahmad Baba and sixteen other literary figures from Timbuctu. These authors who appreciated African literature also tried to counteract the dominant cultural arrogance of their time by showing that Africa had a cultural tradition of its own, and one worthy of notice. In this they failed. Their works were obscurely published, and the unfavorable image of African letters was already too firmly set in the public mind to be easily changed.[19]

The study of African language could also be used as one possible key to early African history, hence to an understanding of the way in which African culture came to be as it was. Relationships between different African languages were accepted as evidence about earlier contact between different African peoples, and linguistic relations between African and non-African languages were used to provide clues to historic relations between Africa and the outside world. Linguistic evidence had already been used for historical purposes in Europe, notably by ethnological historians like W. F. Edwards. Any attempt to reach similar conclusions about Africa, however, necessarily had to wait for an accurate classification of African languages.

A new attempt was possible with the new data of the 1840's; but linguistic classification, like race classification, required accepted criteria, and no such criteria existed. The earliest classifications depended mainly on a superficial comparison of vocabularies, but the new scientific school of Grimm, Humboldt, Bopp, and de Bunsen, among others, demanded something more. They demanded systematic structural comparisons, being suspicious of chance analogy and the intrusion of loan-words. Even the new West African data were not sufficient to meet this standard. Classifiers therefore continued to rely on lexical affinities, even when, as in Koelle's case, the author realized

19. See J. Howison, *European Colonies in Various Parts of the World, Viewed in their Social, Moral, and Physical Conditions,* 2 vols. (London, 1834), I, 91–97 for the usual negative opinion. See also: Riis, *Grammatical Outlines,* pp. 110–36; S. W. Koelle, *African Native Literature* (London, 1854); O. E. Vidal, "Introductory Remarks," in S. Crowther, *Vocabulary of the Yòruba Language,* 2nd ed. (London, 1852), pp. 17–38; Baron Roger, *Fables sénégalaises, recueilliés de l'ouolof et mises en vers français* (Paris, 1828); A. Cherbonneau, "Essai sur la litterature arabe du Soudan," *Annuaire de la Société Archaeologique de Constantine,* II, 1–48 (1854–1855).

that this classification would be criticized.[20] Others were less careful. Prichard combined linguistic and racial characteristics, while Latham used analogies of grammatical structure at one point, and vocabulary at another.

Latham was, indeed, the most industrious of the English classifiers of West African languages. He published his original classification in 1844 and modified it later in 1846, 1847, 1850, and 1858. His underlying scheme consisted of a five-fold division, placing a large central African language group alongside Coptic, Hottentot, Berber, and "Kaffrarian" (meaning the group now called Bantu). In fact, his large central African group extended as far east as the Nile and beyond, and took in languages as diverse as Somali, Nubian, Hausa, and Dinka, grouping them with languages of the Guinea Coast and the Western Sudan. His sub-divisions within this larger division were more nearly accurate. He identified the large Mandingo group, the Akan languages, and picked out an Ibo-Ashanti sub-family, which approximately parallels the present-day Kwa sub-family, stretching from southern Sierra Leone along the coast through Western Nigeria.[21]

In later revisions, Latham altered this classification, sometimes toward greater accuracy and sometimes not. By 1846, he had come (quite correctly) to suspect an affinity between Coptic, Berber, and the Semitic languages. By 1847 he began to believe that all African languages might well be related to one another, and related to Semitic as well. He may someday be proven correct, but it was only a guess. Finally, in 1858, he become so confused between the lexical and structural forms of classification that he stopped classifying altogether. Instead, he insisted that African languages could not be put into language families. They stretched out as an indefinite series, each related to its neighbors, but in several different ways.

Both Koelle and Wilhelm Bleek drew up classifications of African languages based on a single criterion. For Bleek, it was grammatical

    20. Bunsen, "Recent Egyptian Researches," p. 255; Koelle, *Polyglotta Africana,* p. iv.
    21. R. G. Latham, "On the Ethnography of Africa as Determined by its Languages," *Reports of the British Association,* XIV, 79–80 (1844); "Contributions to the study of the Languages of Africa," *Proceedings of the Philological Society,* II, 218–22 (2 February 1846); "Recent Progress of Ethnographical Philology," pp. 222–29; *Natural History of the Varieties of Man* (London, 1850), pp. 471–86; "On Certain Classes in African Philology; Especially the Mandingo, Kouri, Nufi, and Fula Groups," *Transactions of the Philological Society for 1885,* pp. 107–22. Cf. J. H. Greenberg, *Studies in African Linguistic Classification* (New Haven, 1955).

structure; but his general scheme was no more accurate than Latham's had been, and he had little to say in detail about West African languages.[22] Koelle had the advantage of using lexical comparisons, for which there were more published data, and for which he could gather large quantities of data himself. Koelle, therefore, became the pioneer classifier of West African languages, laying the base on which others were to build, even though they were to modify much of his work.[23]

Koelle himself stayed clear of broad historical conclusions based on his linguistic data, but others were less cautious. As early as 1839, R. M. Macbriar, a Wesleyan missionary in the Gambia, believed he had discovered a linguistic relationship between Fulfulde and the Bantu languages. He concluded that neither the Fulbe nor the Bantu-speaking peoples were "true Negroes." They must therefore be related peoples who had entered Africa together and then separated, as the Fulbe moved off toward Cape Verde and the Bantu toward the Cape of Good Hope.[24] This suggestion was an early version of the "Hamite myth," by which later racist historians transformed the Bantu language group into a racial group with "Hamite blood" and thus distinct from the "true Negroes" of West Africa.

Somewhat later, O. E. Vidal, working with CMS research from Sierra Leone, believed he had found a similar connection between the neighboring and related languages of the Temne, Bullom, and Sherbro, and the Bantu family.[25] In 1855, Bleek, who had by then

22. W. H. I. Bleek, *De Nominum Generibus Linguarum Africae Australis, Copticae, Semiticarum Aliarumque Sexualium* (Bonn, 1851), esp. p. 59.

23. His work may be compared with the recent and authoritative classification of J. H. Greenberg. Koelle's "North-West Atlantic" language family is substantially the same as Greenberg's "West Atlantic" without Fulfulde and Wolof, which Koelle left unclassified. Greenberg's "Mandingo" compares with Koelle's "North-Western High-Sudan." Greenberg's "Kwa" is nearly the same as Koelle's "Upper-Guinea Languages," though Koelle left Ashanti unclassified and made the Nupe group and the Edo-Ibo group separate language families. Greenberg's "Gur" approximates Koelle's "North-Eastern High Sudan." Koelle left Hausa unclassified, with proper caution, since it is a distant relative of the Semitic languages. Kanuri and related languages, which Koelle called "Central African," became Greenberg's "Central Saharan."

Koelle placed all of the above language families in a larger West African group, separate from another major grouping of "South African" languages, recognized by initial inflection. He included in this grouping both the Bantu language family and the languages later called Semi-Bantu. It corresponds closely, therefore, to the group Greenberg calls the "Central Group" of the "Niger-Congo Language Family." (Koelle, *Polyglotta Africana*, pp. 1–13; Greenberg, *African Linguistic Classification*.)

24. R. M. Macbriar, *Sketches of a Missionary's Travels in Egypt, Syria, Western Africa, &c., &c.* (London, 1839), pp. 242–43.

25. Personal communication from Dr. P. E. H. Hair. See *Church Missionary Intelligencer*, III, 115–20 (May, 1852).

conducted linguistic research on Fernando Po, combined the Vidal and Macbriar hypotheses and added Wolof and the Akan languages to the group supposed to have Bantu affinities. He concluded on linguistic grounds that all of these West African peoples must have migrated northward from the Cape and, indeed, that the cradle of African life must be in the country of the Xhosa and the Hottentots of the far south.[26] His underlying data contained a germ of truth. Most West African languages are now recognized as members of the same Niger-Congo language family to which the Bantu languages also belong. The probable direction of the migration, however, was from north to south, and not the reverse.

The broad historical theories of the professional linguists merged with those of non-professional commentators, who were still concerned with the problem of explaining the causes of African "barbarism." The older static forms of analysis were still important, but the balance was shifting toward historical explanations on one hand and racial explanations on the other. Humanitarians continued to prefer historical and diffusionist theories. If they could show that African culture had been formed by diffusion from centers in southwestern Asia, they could also show the possibility of more cultural diffusion from Europe. The elementary principle was expressed in the couplet:

> "Let *us* not the Negro Slave despise,
> *Just such our sires* appeared in Caesar's eyes."[27]

Travellers to West Africa continued to turn up evidence, both spurious and genuine, indicating an earlier contact with the east. In the light of culture theories suggesting possible "degeneration" from an earlier, higher stage of development, it was natural to interpret West African religion as a "corrupted" version of Zoroastrianism or a "degraded" form of the religion of ancient Egypt.[28]

The most elaborate new exposition of this kind came from Brodie

26. W. H. Bleek, "On the Languages of Western and Southern Africa," *Transactions of the Philological Society of London* (1855), pp. 40–50.

27. W. Armistead, *A Tribute to the Negro* (Manchester, 1848), p. 31. See also: T. Fowell Buxton, *The African Slave Trade*, 2nd ed. (London, 1839), p. xiv; "On the Practicality of Civilizing Aboriginal Populations," *Ethnological Abstracts* (London, Spottiswoode, [1840?]).

28. W. Allen and T. R. H. Thomson, *A Narrative of the Expedition to the River Niger in 1841*, 2 vols. (London, 1848), II, 378–401; W. F. Daniell, *Sketches of the Medical Topography and Native Diseases of the Gulf of Guinea* (London, 1849), pp. 26–36, 90–91, and 99.

Cruickshank. He began with the basic assumption that all races of men are roughly equal in their abilities, but the human endowment includes original sin—"the corrupt tendency of the human heart, . . . to which white men and black are equally subject."[29] Therefore, all human societies contained both the seeds of progress and the seeds of degeneration. Cruickshank also held that acquired characteristics were heritable.[30] Therefore, progress would beget further progress, but the movement either upwards or downwards would be relatively slow and society at any stage would be relatively stable.

Cruickshank accepted the usual stages of progress—for those societies which had made progress. That is, they began as isolated hunting and gathering families, then moved to organized hunting in larger groups, then to agriculture, and so on. West African society had reached the agricultural stage, and it was not a pleasant state of society. At that stage the strong were able to subordinate the weak: "Physical strength we take to be the foundation of all power in a barbarous state, and injustice the foundation of all property."[31] But there were, for Cruickshank, limits set by a limited productivity. He held that inequalities of status, wealth, and power, are necessarily small in poor societies, since the whole society is too close to subsistence to support a real aristocracy.

But, for Cruickshank, a further question was crucial: had this stage been reached in Africa by independent development or by degeneration from a higher state of progress elsewhere? He found some evidence for either view. Degeneration was suggested by certain parallels between Gold Coast customs and those of ancient Egypt, though the Egyptian traits appeared to be "corrupted by the uncertain light of tradition." On the other hand, he recognized the possibility that the human mind might be nearly the same everywhere. In that case, even isolated societies might be expected to invent such traits independently as they entered the agricultural stage.[32] Cruickshank leaned toward the diffusionist position, but he left room for the other possibility.

He believed, in any event, that the agricultural stage in West

29. B. Cruickshank, *Eighteen Years on the Gold Coast of Africa, Including an Account of the Native Tribes, and Their Intercourse with Europeans*, 2 vols. (London, 1853), II, 2.

30. Cruickshank, *Eighteen Years*, II, 57–58.

31. Cruickshank, *Eighteen Years*, I, 291.

32. Cruickshank, *Eighteen Years*, I, 6–7; II, 256.

Africa had been reached at least some centuries before the birth of Christ. From that time till the coming of the European slave trade in the later fifteenth century, West African society had neither advanced toward a higher stage, nor had it regressed. The only significant historical change had been the introduction of the trans-Sahara slave trade, and its principal influence south of the forest had been to drive refugees down from the northern savannas and force them to league together in stronger states like Ashanti.[33]

Maritime contact with the Europeans, however, had brought progressive debasement, caused by the slave trade. Cruickshank recognized that the Africans themselves lived in a slave-holding society, but he also saw important differences between the African institution and the plantation slavery of tropical America. He believed that the nature of slavery changed with the different stages of human progress. At the earliest stages, it was a natural labor system, but it was also relatively mild. The lot of the slave was not very different from that of his master. As society progressed, however, the position of the slave became increasingly miserable. It reached its nadir with the commercial stage. West Africa's misfortune was that Europeans, having reached this stage, introduced the worst possible form of slavery through the slave trade. With it came greed. It destroyed the precarious hold of morality in African society, turning each man and each tribe against his neighbor.[34] In the future, however, Cruickshank believed African society could turn upward again. With the guidance of Christianity and new influences from Europe, it would ultimately reach the same degree of civilization attainable by mankind anywhere.

Cruickshank's sketch of African history was a long step forward. By discarding racial factors and crude environmentalism, he achieved a point of departure essentially similar to that used by historians of Africa a century later. His conclusions were based more on speculation than on evidence, but many of his hypotheses, dressed in the language of modern social science, would be tenable today. His basic social theory was the common coin of his time, but eighteen years of experience in Africa allowed him to cut through the worst of the cultural chauvinism. This combination of direct observation and a thorough grounding in European social theory was very rare. Few of

33. Cruickshank, *Eighteen Years*, II, 298–99.
34. Cruickshank, *Eighteen Years*, II, 300–310.

Cruickshank's fellow merchants or government officials had either the education or inclination for scholarship, and scholars who stayed in Europe had to depend on data of uncertain validity.

Most commentators rested their explanations of Africa on the older forms of static analysis—when, indeed, they did not adopt a thoroughgoing racism. African "barbarism" was attributed to some combination of race, climate, and the slave trade. The commander of the Niger Expedition, for example, allowed for all three of these causes, with emphasis on the pernicious consequences of tropical exuberance. In spite of fifty-years' worth of new information about Africa, his contrast between the challenge of a hard climate and ease of life in Africa reads as though nothing had been learned since the 1770's.

> With the negro . . . his climate superinduces a repugnance to exertion; he places his whole happiness in the idea of repose:—His necessities are few, and nature hardly requires solicitation to supply them, but heaps her treasures around in abundance, like trees in the Mahomedan Paradise, that require not the trouble of stretching forth the hand to pluck fruit from the bending branches. . . . The negro may therefore be characterized as having means of gratification exceeding his wants, and the white man as having wants exceeding such means of gratification as are supplied to him by nature.[35]

Even older forms of analysis were present on the fringes of European thought and comment. The ancient belief in a divine curse occasionally made an appearance. The standard version held that Africans had been cursed as the sons of Ham: this could be used to argue for permanent subordination to the Europeans. A missionary version held the curse to be only temporary: this could be used as a call for greater effort to spread the "reign of Christ" and cancel the ancient dispensation.[36] According to still another version, the Africans themselves believed they had been cursed by God, and they explained their own "inferiority" in this way.[37]

A newer line of suggestion followed from the high mortality of Europeans in Africa. One hypothesis explained the slave trade itself as the result of differential mortality. Europeans could not live as plantation managers in West Africa, but they could survive more successfully in the West Indies. Therefore they took African slaves to the West Indies, and Africa was barbarized while tropical America

---

35. Allen and Thomson, *A Narrative of the Expedition,* II, 420.
36. East, *Western Africa,* p. 2.
37. Howison, *European Colonies,* I, 152–53.

became rich.[38] According to another version, the principal influence of high mortality was to discourage trade and hence cultural diffusion. Thus African society had been forced to develop in isolation.[39]

The direct influence of the tropical climate still attracted some share of the blame, and in ways still derived from Montesquieu. Commissioner Madden endowed the Africans with all the usual "southern vices," and he pointed out an unnoticed implication. Sexuality was a southern trait, and sexuality led to polygyny. Polygyny, in turn, kept women in a low status, and (since Millar's time) a low status for women was known to mark a lower stage of social progress. Therefore, by implication, climatically induced sexuality somehow retarded progress.[40]

Other new factors began to attract some attention. One of these was diet. An authority on the matter claimed that: "No race of man, it might be safely asserted, ever acquired a respectable amount of civilization that had not some cereal for a portion of its food."[41]

Another was ecology. John Howison contrasted the personality type of the Moors of Mauritania and the Wolof of Senegal. The first were "tall, athletic, and active, and ferocious in temper and inclined to warfare." These characteristics were supposed to come from their life of plunder and hunting on desert and steppe. The Wolof, on the other hand, were sedentary farmers. In personality they were therefore: "mild in temper, and of a serene and placid disposition: not being harassed by any particular idea connected with their mode of life, they deliver themselves up without reserve to the impressions of the moment, and are lovers of society, hospitable, inclined to pleasure, and averse to mental exertion, but withal timid, indolent, deficient in steadiness, and destitute of foresight."[42]

Howison's theory smacks more of the standard stereotypes than empirical observation, and other theories were even more fantastic. Edward Phillips set forth a rainfall theory to explain the savagery of Africans in the forest zone: "The inhabitants of these central districts are perpetually driven about as the rains shift their geographical position, and, in consequence, a roaming and predatory

---

38. Variants of this reasoning were very common. As an example, see: William Howitt, *Colonization and Christianity* (London, 1838), pp. 501–2.
39. R. R. Madden, Commissioner's Report, PP, 1842, xii (551), p. 432.
40. PP, 1842, xii (551), pp. 430–32.
41. J. Crawfurd, *Reports of the British Association*, XXVIII, 149 (1858).
42. Howison, *European Colonies*, I, 53.

life is the inevitable birthright of those nations which occupy the central regions of Africa."[43] This completely imaginary forest nomadism was held to breed war, raids, and counter-raids, so that the Africans of the rain-forest were natural slave hunters.

With a more accurate empirical base, the same could be said of the desert. As W. D. Cooley put it:

> The Desert, if it is not absolutely the root of the evil, has, at least, been from the earliest times the great nursery of slave hunters. The demoralization of the towns on the southern borders of the desert has been pointed out; and if the vast extent be considered of the region in which man has no riches but slaves, no enjoyment but slaves, no article of trade but slaves, and where the hearts of the wandering thousands are closed against pity by the galling misery of life, it will be difficult to resist the conviction that the solid buttress on which slavery rests in Africa, is—The Desert.[44]

But the desert had its defenders. James Richardson, the desert explorer, attacked Cooley's opinion and took up the cause of the Tuaregs in particular: "In deserts and mountains we find always freemen. . . ." The Tuaregs were such free men. They worked at any commerce that happened to cross their territory, but the roots of slavery were found in the luxurious and soft life of the Maghrib. Desert people were merely its agents.[45]

The desert was also the route of Islamic penetration, and the role of Islam in West African history could be variously interpreted. After Clapperton, no well read European any longer believed the Western Sudan was ruled by North Africans. A fuller understanding of Sudanese history came with Cooley's pioneer history in 1841 and especially with the publication of Barth's travels in 1857–58. European attitudes also changed. The humanitarians, whose intellectual ancestors had generally approved of Islamic influence, now went into opposition. The government in Sierra Leone, which had once welcomed Muslim visitors, began in the 1830's to distrust them, and there was occasional panic fear of a Muslim rebellion.[46] Other officials suspected that Islam was merely a religion of "outward ob-

43. Edward Phillips, *Simmonds's Colonial Magazine*, X, 3 (January, 1847).

44. W. D. Cooley, *The Negroland of the Arabs Examined and Explained* (London, 1841), p. 139.

45. J. Richardson, *Travels in the Great Desert of the Sahara*, 2 vols. (London, 1848), pp. xxvi–xxviii.

46. PP, 1842, xii (551), pp. 247, 370–71; Christopher Fyfe, *A History of Sierra Leone* (London, 1962), pp. 186–87 and 215.

servances" requiring no "exertion of the mind."[47] Missionaries hinted that a kind of Gresham's Law of religion was at work, and conversion to Islam might be a bar to the influence of Christianity.

The "civilizing force" once attributed to Islam was also called into question, and some claimed that Islam was the real cause of African backwardness. The point could be argued on historical grounds—that the spread of Islam into North Africa in the eighth century had cut off contact between Europe and Africa. Thus it had excluded the civilizing force of Christianity. Other writers admitted that the trans-Sahara trade should have been a progressive influence, but it was rendered ineffective by the sins of the "Arab" slave traders. As one put it: "Moreover, the religion they bring, though superior to the Paganism they find, is not a *civilizing* religion; it is very good for conquering, but very bad for improving the conquered."[48]

Many of the travellers, and especially those who used the northern approaches, countered with pro-Islamic arguments. They were better informed than earlier writers of this opinion, and they put their case more forcefully. James Richardson in particular believed that Islam had brought more civilization to Africa than Europe had done. He pointed to the degree of literacy in the desert towns of Ghat and Ghadames, which was higher than that of England. His further warning was almost unique in its time: "Let us then take care how we arrogate to ourselves the right and fact of civilizing the world."[49]

Traditional African polytheism was blamed even more often than Islam for the failings of West African society. All travellers, and especially the missionaries, were opposed to "paganism," but few understood it. Some claimed that West Africa had no religion at all—"no regular system of mythology, and no received and defined mode of belief."[50] Others believed that Africans worshipped the devil—quite literally, the same devil known to Western belief—and they were seemingly unable to conceive of a theological system distinct from the religions of southwestern Asia.[51] The "fetish," a material

47. William Allen to Lord Stanley, 5 February 1843, PP, 1843, xlviii [C. 472], p. 3.
48. "Expedition to the Niger," *Edinburgh Review,* LXXII, 460 (January, 1841). See also Saxe Bannister, *Humane Policy; or Justice to the Aborigines of New Settlements* . . . (London, 1830), pp. 2–3.
49. J. Richardson, *Travels in the Sahara,* I, xxxvi.
50. Howison, *European Colonies,* I, 75.
51. See, as a particular example: W. Fox, *A Brief History of the Wesleyan Missions on the Western Coast of Africa* (London, 1851), p. 250.

object endowed with certain spiritual powers, was almost universally misconstrued. It was generally believed that the "worship" of such objects was the beginning and end of African "superstition," and some missionaries thought the "fetish" was simply any object chosen at random.[52] A few missionaries, however, recognized that African polytheism was a genuine religion, and a very few tried to acquire a systematic understanding of the beliefs they sought to replace.[53]

All missionaries and lay commentators, however, had a general concept of African religion, whether based on study or on mere supposition. For some, probably in the minority, it appeared as a neutral force—merely the absence of religious truth. For most, it was something more, a positive evil depressing society below the moral level attainable by unaided natural reason. Cruickshank stated this position in theological terms. For him, the idols of the Fante represented the "worst passions of our nature" in deified form, and thus aggravated the natural depravity of man.[54] Most of the missionaries were less precise, but no less firm, in the belief that somehow "paganism" caused "barbarism."

African political systems were also occasionally given some share of the blame. They were understood to be "despotisms" and despotism was understood to be inimical to progress. A deeper understanding of African political systems was apparently less common that it had been in the past, though occasional travellers paid some attention. J. L. Wilson, an American missionary, put Dahomey and Ashanti on a par in size and power with the second-rate kingdoms of Europe—perhaps on account of republican prejudice. He reported, quite accurately, that: "The form of government every where is nominal monarchy, but, when closely scrutinized, it shows much more of the popular or patriarchal element than the monarchic."[55]

Most African rulers were stigmatized as "blood-thirsty tyrants," yet the most accurate reporting showed a different picture. Cruickshank's report on his government mission to Abomey in 1848 portrayed Gezo of Dahomey in terms unusually free of cultural bias:

52. See, in particular: William Allen to Lord Stanley, 5 February 1843, PP, 1843, xlviii [C. 472], p. 136; *Journal of Civilization*, 3 July 1841, p. 133. Cf. Geoffrey Parrinder, *West African Religion*, 2nd ed. (London, 1961).
53. For example: J. Beecham, *Ashantee and the Gold Coast* (London, 1841), pp. 170–256.
54. Cruickshank, *Eighteen Years*, II, 257. See also Beecham, *Ashantee*, pp. 250 ff.
55. Wilson, *Western Africa*, p. 31.

I left him with the conviction on my mind, that he is a man of superior intellect, and endowed with an extraordinary capacity for government. Surrounded by the adulation of his people, which amounts to adoration, he nevertheless maintains a degree of modesty and equanimity in his deportment which is truly astonishing. His police, fiscal and judicial arrangements, excited my admiration, and are worthy of a people much further advanced in the scale of civilization. The nature of his government renders him dependent upon the efficiency and fidelity of his troops, and the manner in which he maintains them bespeaks the skillful commander. With power in his hands the most despotic, he is yet served with love rather than fear, and no aspersion has ever been cast upon appeals made to his justice. To strangers he is hospitable and kind; to his subjects, equitable and generous. Impressed with the dignity of his station, he maintains great frugality and temperance in his personal habits, and rarely gives way to sudden ebullitions of anger. His mind is active and inquiring, and he betrays a laudable anxiety to be made acquainted with the laws, manners, and customs of foreign nations. Like all uneducated Africans, he is strongly attached to the customs of his fathers, and regards with much suspicion any attempted innovation. . . .[56]

Aside from Cruickshank and a few others, there were remarkably few who made an effort to understand the internal workings of African politics or to deal with the recent history of the various African states. Barth contributed greatly to an understanding to the political life of the Fulani emirates and of Bornu, and J. L. Wilson tried to analyze the decline of the three great kingdoms of the forest and forest edge—Dahomey, Oyo, and Benin.[57] Otherwise, investigation of the rapidly changing African scene seems to have been overshadowed by the assumption that Africa was stagnant and devoid of change.

Most discussion of African internal affairs turned instead to the distinctions between differing African peoples—distinctions which were normally viewed as a permanent and static part of the nature of things. The superiority of the interior was now an article of faith and the point of departure for further discussion. Prichard lent his scientific authority and gave the idea certain racial overtones:

We may further remark, and perhaps this observation is fully as important as that of any other connected fact or coincidence, that physical qualities of particular races of Africans are evidently related to their moral or social condition, and to the degrees of barbarism or civilization under which they

56. Cruickshank, Report of 9 November 1848, PP, 1849 (Lords), xxviii (32), Appendix, p. 187.
57. Wilson, *Western Africa*, pp. 189–91.

exist. The tribes in whose prevalent conformation the Negro type is discernible in an exaggerated degree, are, uniformly in the lowest stage of human society; they are either ferocious savages, or stupid, sensual, and indolent—such as the Papels, Bulloms, and other rude hordes on the coast of Western Guinea, and many tribes near the Slave Coast, and in the Bight of Benin, countries where the slave-trade has been carried on to the greatest extent, and has exercised its usual baneful influence. On the other hand, whenever we hear of a Negro state, the inhabitants of which have attained any considerable degree of improvement in their social condition, we constantly find that their physical characters deviate considerably from the strongly-marked or exaggerated type of the Negro. The Ashanti, Sulima, the Dahomans, are exemplifications of this remark. The Negroes of Guber [Gobir] and Hausa, where a considerable degree of civilization has long existed, are perhaps the finest race of genuine Negroes in the whole continent, unless the Iolofs [Wolofs] are to be excepted.[58]

Latham concurred in principle and drew a division between interior and coastal peoples. His "Western Negro Atlantidae" included all coastal peoples from the Wolof of the lower Senegal to the Ibo of eastern Nigeria, including some of the peoples Prichard had admired. His "Central Negro Atlantidae," on the other hand, ran from Yoruba on the west, through Nupe and Hausa to Bagirmi on the east. With the exception of the Yoruba, all these people lived well inland.[59] The classification makes no sense in either linguistic or physical terms, but it does make sense in geographical terms. The people of the interior became a separate race, ostensibly because of their location.

The Europeans engaged in Niger exploration had a more concrete reason for preferring inland peoples. The Niger expeditions usually met a hostile reception from the trading towns of the delta, which were fearful of losing their monopoly over the commerce of the interior. Once beyond the delta, however, the Africans were more friendly, and especially so near the confluence of the Niger and Benue, where the danger of Fulani raids made the Europeans welcome as possible allies. In these circumstances, it is hardly surprising that coastal traders were put down as "vicious" and the inland Africans praised for their politeness.[60] The new reports merged easily with presuppositions dating back to the time of Swedenborg.

58. J. C. Prichard, *Researches into the Physical History of Man,* 4th ed., 5 vols. (London, 1851), II, 338.
59. Latham, *Natural History,* pp. 471–86.
60. See C. C. Ifemesia, "British Enterprise on the Niger, 1830–1869 " (Unpublished Ph.D. thesis, London, 1959).

Individual rating scales for West African "tribes" usually followed the coastal-interior dichotomy, placing either the Mandinka or
the Fulbe at the top and one of the coastal peoples at the bottom,
but there was endless room for individual opinion. One might have
the Ashanti at the bottom, on grounds that they were "uncivilized,
conceited, bloodthirsty, insolent, superstitious, and untrustworthy,"
while another would place the Ashanti quite high and save the bottom slot for either Dahomey or the Ibo.[61] Ashanti gradually lost
ground, however, to the Fante, who were more closely associated
with the British posts after Maclean's administration. The Yoruba
reputation rose markedly, while that of Dahomey remained low.
The Kru people of Liberia kept a good reputation, since they served
as sailors on British ships; while other peoples in the vicinity of
Sierra Leone gradually lost out in favor of the liberated Africans,
whose rapid acculturation brought them into a new era of good re-
pute from the mid-1830's onward into the 1850's. Among the various
groups represented in Sierra Leone, the Ibo began to lose their old
reputation for savagery and to gain a new one for commercial enterprise. As one official put it: "the Eboes of Freetown are the most
intelligent and the most parsimonious race in the whole country;
they will go anywhere and everywhere for money."[62]
An occasional author tried to account for these "racial" differences
within West Africa. Daniell thought that climate and soil might explain the differences between the Ijaw people of Bonny in the Niger
delta and the Efik of the more elevated sandstone region around the
mouth of the Cross River.[63] Rankin tried to distinguish between West
Indians of African descent and West Africans by claiming the slave
trade had been racially selective: "The slaves who find their way
from the West India plantations to England are totally unlike the
free natives of Africa: they are, with few exceptions, specimens of
the lowest grade of mankind, and are taken from certain tribes despised by their black neighbours. Amongst the more intellectual and

61. [Jane Marcet], *History of Africa* (London, 1830), pp. 168–74; W. B. K., "On
the Varieties of the Human Race," *Colonial Magazine*, V, 37–40 (January–May,
1841); R. G. Latham, *The Ethnology of the British Colonies and Dependencies*
(London, 1851), pp. 34 and 62.
62. Logan Hook, Evidence before the West Africa Committee, 8 July 1842, PP,
1842, xi (451), p. 535.
63. W. F. Daniell, "On the Natives of Old Callebar, West Coast of Africa,"
Journal of the Ethnological Society, I, 210–27 (1848), pp. 212–13.

more cultivated [in Africa], as noble features, as lofty an expression, as fine a countenance is discovered as Europe could offer."[64]

Rankin's impression was simply mistaken, but the slightly non-Negroid appearance of the Fulbe people posed a problem for anthropologists and historians alike. Europeans had been in occasional contact with some of the Fulbe in the Senegambia from the earliest voyages to West Africa. In the eighteenth and nineteenth centuries a new interest was roused by the foundation of a series of Fulbe-dominated states from Futa Toro and Futa Jallon in the west to the Sokoto Fulani in the east. By the 1830's, the reputed Fulbe superiority rested on three different grounds. Some of them were pastoral in an era when pastoralism was valued above sedentary agriculture. As the founders of new states, they appeared to be a conquering people. Their Europeanoid features suggested, in an era of incipient racism, that they might be racially superior as well.

The question of Fulbe origins and their role in West African history therefore came to be the historical question which aroused the most general interest, especially in France. A variety of different theories were advanced. Fulbe origins were traced to a group of Persians who were supposed to have come to Morocco with Hercules. Another fanciful hypothesis identified them with the Carthaginians and suggested possible contacts with the ancient Britons. Still others traced Fulbe migrations from Bornu, Arabia, or even made them the original inhabitants of West Africa. The most elaborate theory was published in France by Gustave d'Eichthal, who traced hypothetical Fulbe migrations from Malaya to Madagascar to Merowe to Darfur and finally to West Africa. It was not universally accepted, but it has a certain importance as another precursor of the "Hamite" myth, similar to the hypothesis already suggested by Macbriar. By assigning the Fulbe a very long migration route, they could be given the role of cultural bearers for all of Africa. Racists with a very low opinion of Negro capabilities could explain any "higher" trait in Africa by introducing the Fulbe, or later the "Hamites." D'Eichthal himself used his theory in this sense, claiming the "noble negroes" of pro-African literature were not Negroes at all, but Fulbe.[65]

64. F. H. Rankin, *The White Man's Grave: A Visit to Sierra Leone in 1834,* 2 vols. (London, 1836), II, 10–11.

65. G. d'Eichthal, "Histoire de origine des Foulahs ou Fellans," *Mémoires de la Société Ethnologique,* I (2), 1–296 (1841), esp. p. 118. For other speculations on

Barth tried to bring studies of the Fulbe problem into closer touch with reality. Among other things, he pointed to three pieces of evidence still recognized as valid. Fulfulde is a West Atlantic language, related to Wolof and other languages spoken in the immediate hinterland of Cape Verde. Secondly, Fulbe social structure has certain similarities to Wolof social structure, again indicating a cradle near the lower Senegal. Third, traditional history throughout the Western Sudan clearly indicated Fulbe emigrants coming from the west, not the east. But this evidence raised a further problem. It was the general assumption that race, language, and culture were closely related. The Fulbe were related in language and culture to the Wolof but were racially distinct. Barth explained these facts, and the peopling of West Africa generally, by a two-stream theory. One stream of intrusive population was held to be of Berber origin and to come from the region of Libya: these people would be light in color. Another stream was black in color and originated in southern Arabia. Once the two reached the Western Sudan they met and mingled for centuries, but the race mixture was never quite complete. One remnant was the Fulbe as a stabilized mixed race. Others were to be found here and there throughout the western Sudan, where some social classes and other groupings were lighter in color than their neighbors.[66]

Scholars have not yet reached full agreement on the question of Fulbe origins, but some aspects of Barth's hypothesis are still tenable. His important contribution, however, was not the precise hypotheses he laid down. It was his method of working with a combination of ethnographic, linguistic, and documentary evidence to solve the problems of early African history. Some of Barth's views, such as his racist preconceptions, would no longer be considered valid, but the questions he posed and the way he went about answering them were closer to the methods of the 1960's than to those of the 1830's.

Fulbe origins see: Marcet, *History of Africa*, pp. 167–68; T. J. Hutchinson, *Narrative of the Niger, Tshadda, & Binuë Exploration* (London, 1855), pp. 66–67 and 75–76; *Journal of Civilization*, 3 July 1841, p. 133; Macbriar, *Missionary Travels*, pp. 239–41; A. Raffenel, *Voyage dans l'Afrique occidentale exécuté en 1843 et 1844* (Paris, 1846), esp. pp. 106 and 262–66; P. D. Boilat, *Esquisses sénégalaises* (Paris, 1853), pp. 384–413; L. H. Hecquard, *Voyage sur la côte et dans l'Intérieur de l'Afrique occidentale* (Paris, 1853).

66. H. Barth, *Travels and Discoveries in North and Central Africa*, 5 vols. (London, 1857–1858), IV, 146–56; Barth, "A General Historical Description of the State of Human Society in Northern Central Africa," *Journal of the Royal Geographical Society*, XXX, 112–28 (1860), pp. 115–19.

Alongside the scholarly interest in establishing the racial status of various West African peoples, there was a further interest in assessing the place of West Africans as a whole—especially in relation to other African peoples. Bunsen arranged all African peoples in a hierarchy, according to linguistic criteria. As a result of Bantu inflections, he placed the Bantu-speakers high on the list. The Bantu languages were even identified as "Japhetic" (that is, European) ; but they were a much degraded form of Japhetic, and they had been subject to still further degeneration until certain branches had become Hottentot and finally the language of the Bushmen.[67] Morton in 1839 had made a similar distinction, dividing the Negro race within Africa into three sub-groups—Negro (which would include West Africans), "Caffrarian" (meaning the Bantu-speakers), and Hottentots—and he placed them in that order, West Africans at the top and southern Africans at the bottom.[68] He was followed by Nott and Gliddon, who placed the West Africans lower on the scale than the Nubians, Ethiopians, and Fulbe, but higher than the Bantu-speakers, Hottentots, and Bushmen.[69] The consensus thus placed the West Africans quite high on the scale of African life—though for reasons that were quite mistaken—while maintaining a wider gap than ever between Africans and Europeans.

In all, British thought about African culture and history in these decades raised more new questions than it answered. The best of the new scholarship marked a new beginning, perhaps *the* beginning, of scholarly knowledge about West Africa. But the availability of relatively good analysis was not enough to override the mass of incorrect information and conjecture. The missionary press, the pamphlets, or the polemics of debate about African questions were read by far more people than read the works of the scholars. Nor could the careful attention to the many influences forming African society—the kind of attention given by a scholar like Barth—have the popular appeal of the simple explanation of the world given by a pseudo-scientist like Knox. The understanding of African culture, even in educated circles, therefore, continued very much as it had been in the early decades of the century, but it was now much less accurate than the best understanding available.

67. Bunsen, "Recent Egyptian Research," pp. 297–99.
68. S. G. Morton, *Crania Americana* (Philadelphia, 1839), pp. 6–7.
69. J. C. Nott and R. G. Gliddon, *Types of Mankind* (London, 1854), pp. 182–90 and 209.

17

CULTURE CONTACT

AND

CONVERSION

> I lay great stress upon African com-
> merce, *more* upon the cultivation of
> the soil, but *most* of all upon the
> elevation of the native mind.
> T. F. Buxton, *The Remedy*

The Niger Expedition was mainly based on a body of ideas which grew up during the early part of the century. Further experience in Africa, however, brought new ideas and modified old ones. New trends in Western thought brought new emphases. The idea that civilization meant Westernization enjoyed a special vogue in the mid-nineteenth century—and not only in regard to Africa. E. G. Wakefield was incensed at the neo-barbarism of the North American frontiersmen, and his projects for Australia and New Zealand were contrived to avoid a similar decline of standards. Thomas Babington Macaulay's famous "Minute" on Indian education in 1835 was a clear call to Anglicize and snuff out the "barbarous" traditions of the East. D. F. Sarmiento's classic, *Facundo— civilización y barbarie,* was a similar call to wipe out the barbarism of the Argentine *gauchos.* Elsewhere in Latin America, the remnants of Indian culture were meeting opposition. The Mexican *reforma* in the time of Benito Juárez attacked a dual enemy: the corporate powers of the church and the corporate forms of Indian village life.

In both cases, the cause was that of "civilization," meaning the industrial civilization of contemporary Europe and North America. The dominant British attitude toward Africa became more conversionist than ever. The Niger Expedition itself was a large-scale public effort to convert barbarians to Western ways. The middle decades of the century represent, indeed, the height of conversionist sentiment. The dominant tone of the early century had been insular, almost isolationist, concerned at most with the British position in Western Europe. After the great cost of the wars against Napoleon, the British were inclined to be parsimonious about expensive charities at a distance. The missionary movement was growing, but, before 1830, it was a faint shadow of what it would become. After 1870, on the other hand, the idea of conversion declined. Humanitarian motives found new manifestations. In that great age of imperialism racism became dominant in European thought. Few believed that any "lower race" could actually reach the heights of Western achievement. Their salvation would have to be achieved in some other way; but meanwhile they were entitled, in their inferiority, to the paternal protection of a Western power. The idea of trusteeship gradually replaced that of conversion.

The conversionist sentiment of the mid-century and trusteeship at the end were two ways of assessing the proper goals for non-Western peoples. They were, in turn, associated with distinct political aims in British imperial theory at these two periods. To become, in any full sense, the trustee of the "lower races" required the annexation of their territory. To convert them to the Western way of life implied informal influence, but it avoided the burden of direct administration.[1] Both policies demanded more intense overseas activity than was called for early in the century, and the new call for action after 1830 was reinforced by a growing net of British trade and investment in the tropical world. Between 1816–20 and 1838–42, the increased value of British exports to tropical and sub-tropical lands exceeded the total increase in British exports.[2]

West Africa was still peripheral to Britain's commercial interests, but the potential commerce of West Africa could hardly be ignored;

1. For the mid-century British tendency to keep the African empire informal, see R. Robinson and J. Gallagher, *Africa and the Victorians* (London, 1961), pp. 1–52.
2. A. Imlah, *Economic Elements in the Pax Britannica* (Cambridge, Mass., 1958), p. 130.

and West Africa had a special claim to the British conscience on account of the slave trade. Even among the opponents of the Niger Expedition only a minority believed that Britain should avoid all forms of activity in West Africa. The rest favored British action, but they wanted some other kind of action. The failure and withdrawal of 1842 was not, therefore, a withdrawal from West Africa, but merely the withdrawal of one particular scheme. The continued missionary effort and the Parliamentary Committee of 1842 confirm, in different ways, the continued private and public intention to convert West Africa from barbarism to civilization and commerce with the world.

Problems arising from the contact of two cultures were widely discussed, but seldom with great depth of understanding. The increasing emphasis on racial factors tended to turn the discussion aside. The Aborigines Committee, for example, were deeply concerned with the impact of European settlers on societies technically less proficient. The public and the scholars, however, saw mainly the racial aspect and ignored the cultural, social, and psychological implications of the evidence.

Increasing cultural chauvinism had a similar effect. Contact between the West and the aborigines was consistently set in terms of relations between superiors and inferiors. Assuming their own superiority, the Europeans believed that Africans must have a strong sense of inferiority. (If anything, West African rulers tended to underestimate the technical prowess and resources of their alien visitors.)

Commentators could, nevertheless, draw two opposite conclusions from the superior-inferior relationship. According to John Howison, it was a bar to culture change: "The general adherence of the negroes to their own customs is, in my opinion, to be chiefly attributed to the conviction that prevails amongst them that they are a peculiar and distinct race of beings, and that they have nothing in common with white men, and are unfitted to partake of their interests, avocations, and pleasures."[3]

In the more authoritative opinion of Herman Merivale, the reverse might well be the case: "the strong impression of the superiority of the whites as a different race, which leads the savage to despair of

3. J. Howison, *European Colonies in Various Parts of the World, Viewed in their Social, Moral and Physical Condition*, 2 vols. (London, 1834), I, 152–53.

raising himself out of his abject condition in respect to material or intellectual advancement, seems, if his sentiments be properly studied and directed, rather to have the tendency of disposing him to welcome instruction in those doctrines which point out that the diversity of gifts in this world is consistent with the equality of all under one common Father."[4]

Brodie Cruickshank, on the other hand, had actual experience of Afro-European relations on the Gold Coast and probed deeper into their psychological complexity:

> The native, keenly alive to his interests, supple and fawning, readily acknowledged the superiority of the white man in words, and hailed him, without any scruples of pride, as his master. But he had, and ever has had, a reservation in his mind which limits the signification of the term to his own construction of it, and has no more intention of giving implicit obedience, if he can help himself, when his pleasure and profit appear to him to be compromised, than if he had never entered into any undertaking upon the subject. Neither would he wish to shake himself free from the necessity of obedience. His object is to endeavour, on all occasions, to magnify the sacrifice which he is making to gratify your wishes, not so much from a determination not to obey them, as to obtain some bribe or concession for his obedience.
>
> A service of this description, appears to have been the nature of the dependence of the African upon the European on the Gold Coast from their earliest intercourse. It had certainly given rise to an incessant struggle, productive of every species of artifice on both sides, in the attempt of one party to extend their power and influence, and of the other to obtain new privileges. The relation in which they stood to each other never, in fact, appears to have been clearly defined or understood. Indeed, it is possible neither party wished it to be so, as any certainty upon the point would lessen the probability of advantages which might possibly turn up in the chapter of accidents.[5]

Still another kind of conclusion about culture contact followed from the evidence before the Aborigines Committee. It was clear that aborigines in the settlement colonies had not profited from the presence and example of the Europeans. Standish Motte was commissioned by the Aborigines Protection Society to prepare an outline of protective legislation that might be introduced in these colonies.

---

4. H. Merivale, *Lectures on Colonisation and Colonies,* 2 vols. (London, 1841–1842), II, 184. See also *Colonial Intelligencer,* II, 68 (1848); Sir George Stephen, *The Niger Trade Considered in Connexion with the African Blockade* (London, 1849), pp. 57–58.

5. Brodie Cruickshank, *Eighteen Years on the Gold Coast of Africa, Including an Account of the Native Tribes, and Their Intercourse with Europeans,* 2 vols. (London, 1853), I, 28–29.

He seized on the theoretical proposition that human societies might follow either the path of progress or the path of retrogression. It seemed to him that contact across a wide gap of cultural difference might carry the "untutored savage" downward rather than upward toward civilization: "Can it be wondered at that such a being becomes contaminated—that he becomes physically diseased, morally debased, and losing the simple and noble attributes of his native character, forgets the virtues of his race and clothes himself in the vices of civilized society?"[6]

He concluded that the problem could be met only after detailed study of each individual case. Correct action could only follow a, "consideration of, the moral, physical, and political condition of each nation and class of aborigines, the locality and nature of the soil they inhabit, its climate, productions, and capabilities; in fact, all the circumstances making a physiological, or political distinction, between the various aboriginal races of man now existing and a geographical and political difference between the countries they inhabit."[7]

In spite of occasional suggestions that civilization would drive the West Africans down the path toward extinction,[8] British commentators were not seriously worried about demoralization in that region. They were much more impressed by the fact that West African cultures had shown a peculiar staying power in the face of long contact with "civilization." Neither "legitimate trade" nor missionary teaching had produced much result by the 1840's. The failing could be explained in various ways—high European mortality, continued slave trade, incorrect methods—but it was clear that acculturation would be more difficult and more complex than earlier generations had thought.[9]

Yet the liberated Africans of Sierra Leone had taken to Christianity and civilization readily enough. So too had the ex-slaves of the West Indies. Perhaps people needed to pass through some form of cultural shock or uprooting from their own society. It was suggested that,

6. S. Motte, *Outline of a System of Legislation for Securing the Protection of the Aboriginal Inhabitants of all Countries Colonized by Great Britain* (London, 1840), pp. 7–8.

7. Motte, *System of Legislation*, pp. 11–12.

8. Howison, *European Colonies*, I, 99.

9. See, for example, H. V. Huntley, *Seven Years' Service on the Slave Coast of Western Africa*, 2 vols. (London, 1850), esp. I, 88; "Western Africa," *Westminster Review*, LVI, 6–12 (October, 1851).

"demoralization is one of the processes through which barbarism has to pass before it becomes susceptible to improvement as revolutions are considered the ordeals through which anarchy is brought into civil order."[10] Variations on this theme were used to justify large-scale African emigration to the West Indies. Workers sent to America on long-term contracts would ultimately return to Africa bringing civilization with them.[11] Lord John Russell laid down the official Government position in 1840: "It appears to H. M.'s Govt that on the one hand, men of African birth who have been trained in civilization and instructed in Christianity in Jamaica, or Barbados would be the best teachers of the Negro race in Africa itself:—on the other hand the miserable subjects of an African chief might acquire in Jamaica, Trinidad, or Guiana, competent means, the knowledge of true Religion and the arts of Social Life."[12]

The more common reaction of the conversionists was to concede that African "barbarism" was a "natural" condition. It could be changed only with "artificial" stimulation from the outside. For the actual program of stimulation, they usually fell back on a broad spectrum of action drawn from the older theories of acculturation. The civilizing effect of direct discipline was more often mentioned,[13] but the usual program called for a combination of British law, trade and economic development, religious and secular education.[14] Under each of these headings, there was a further elaboration of theory and suggestion.

Within the missionary movement, a special set of problems centered on the relationship of religious conversion to cultural change. Some of these were old questions—could people take on the Christian

10. R. R. Madden to Lord Edward Howard (Private), 1 August 1841, CO 267/170, f. 94. This is not Madden's view, but one he cited as opposed to his own.
11. Macgregor Laird, Evidence before West Africa Committee, 15 June 1842, PP, 1842, xi (551), p. 331; Colonial Gazette, 2 February 1842, p. 65; G. W. Hope, Commons, 25 February 1845, 3 H 77, c. 1192; J. L. Wilson, Western Africa: its History, Condition, and Prospects (New York, 1856), pp. 420–21.
12. Lord John Russell to R. R. Madden, 26 November 1840, CO 267/170. This position was accepted by the next Government as well. See Lord Stanley to Macdonald, 6 February 1843, PP, 1843, xxxiv [C. 438], p. 3.
13. See Grey to Winniett, 20 January 1849, CO 402/2; S. J. Hill to Newcastle, 15 April 1853, PP, 1852–1853, lxii [C. 1693], p. 198.
14. For some specific programs see: Saxe Bannister, Humane Policy; or Justice to the Aborigines of New Settlements . . . (London, 1830); Report of the Aborigines Committee, PP, 1837, vii (425), esp. pp. 82–84; T. F. Buxton, The Remedy: Being a Sequel to the African Slave Trade (London, 1840); Ethnological Extracts (London, Spottiswoode, [1840?]), pp. 4–10; Cruickshank, Eighteen Years, I, 7–11.

religion before they had become civilized? If Christianity required a change of culture, which should come first, conversion or civilization? These questions obviously affected missionary methods, and to provide answers required reference to broader theories of culture. If, for example, the aborigines inevitably became extinct on contact with "civilization," then missionaries bearing the Gospel also bore the cup of hemlock.

The missionary leadership caught this implication and took special pains to deny it in their evidence to the Aborigines Committee. Their general position was to hold that contact with lay settlers was almost always demoralizing, while missionary work alone could save the aborigines from their fate. Only a previous indoctrination with Christianity and the ways of Western civilization could prepare them for the impact of European settlement.[15] Furthermore, in their view, Christianity and civilization were inseparable. This position could be supported by reference to a special Christian culture theory. If the savage state were thought to grow from the untrammeled operation of original sin, the fault could only be corrected by the "doctrines of man's fallen state through sin, redemption by Christ, renovation by the power of the Holy Ghost, and the great and awful sanction of an eternal judgment." Christian theology combined with Christian moral teachings would make men "honest, sober, industrious, orderly, humble, self-denying, philanthropic, and beneficent." These, indeed, were held to be the qualities of civilized men.[16]

While the missionary leadership stressed the efficacy of spiritual means, the Parliamentary Committee emphasized the secular benefits that would follow conversion. It recommended religious instruction, pointing out that "savages are dangerous neighbours and unprofitable customers."[17] By giving the argument a further twist, the civilizing and Christianizing mission could become an economic mission as well. In the words of one publicist, it would produce: "a tide of wealth poured into Europe, such as the strongest imagination can scarcely grasp; and that, too, purchased, not with the blood and tears of the

15. See evidence of Messrs. Ellis, Coates, and Beecham, representing the three principal missionary societies, PP, 1836, vii (538).

16. Evidence of Dandeson Coates, Secretary of CMS, PP, 1836, vii (538), p. 516. See also D. J. East, *Western Africa; Its Condition, and Christianity the Means of Its Recovery* (London, 1844), pp. 219–308.

17. Report of the Aborigines Committee, PP, 1837, vii (425), p. 45 ff.

miserable, but by the moral elevation and happiness of countless tribes."[18]

The dominant attitude among the supporters of the missions was especially well illustrated by the outpouring of works on missionary theory in 1842. The immediate occasion was an inter-denominational competition offering a prize for the best work "On the Duty, Privilege, and Encouragement of Christians to Send the Gospel to the Heathen." Forty-eight essays were submitted, and five were published.[19] The winning essay by The Reverend Dr. John Harris recognized that spiritual benefits were to be expected, both for the missionary and the convert, but it too laid special emphasis on the material results. Missions could erase "habitual idleness, one of the most profilic evils of savage life."[20] For Harris, and for many others, the equation was not merely, Christianity equals civilization. It was: Christianity equals civilization, which equals production for the world market.[21]

This attitude, however, was not universal among missionary theorists. In 1845, Rufus Anderson in America published a volume on mission theory, which became one of the most influential works of its kind. Anderson (being a New Englander) insisted that New England enjoyed the most perfect form of society the world had ever known and had, in Christianity, the most perfect religion; but the two were separable. They must, indeed, be kept quite separate in missionary work. Religion was, for Anderson, only one aspect of culture. It was the missionary's job to teach this, and this alone, to the heathen. In the longer run, Christianity would inevitably lead to civilization, but the missionaries had only to do with the spiritual goals. Anderson also insisted on a sharp distinction between the proper functions of a missionary and those of a pastor. It was the missionary's task to make converts and establish a congregation. Once this much had been accomplished, he must move on to new fields,

18. W. Howitt, *Colonization and Christianity* (London, 1838), pp. 504–5.

19. John Harris, *The Great Commission* (London, 1842); R. W. Hamilton, *Missions: their Authority, Scope, and Encouragement* (London, 1842); John Macfarlane, *The Jubilee of the World: An Essay on Christian Missions* (Glasgow, 1842); J. B. Melson, *'Who is my Neighbour?' An Essay on Christian Missions* (London, 1842); B. W. Noel, *Christian Missions to Heathen Nations* (London, 1842).

20. Harris, *The Great Commission*, p. 208.

21. See Harris, *The Great Commission*, pp. 187–241.

leaving the pastor to guide and improve the moral and spiritual state of the flock.[22]

A similar distinction between religion and general culture was occasionally made in other contexts, and its implications in the mid-century intellectual setting could be very far-reaching indeed. The racists could use it as an argument for denying racial equality without denying the universality of Christianity. Gobineau, for example, argued that Christian civilization could never be transmitted to a racially inferior people, but Christianity could be—its universality came from the spiritual equality of another world, not of this. Thus: "The savage Galla may remain a Galla and yet become a believer as perfect, one of the elect as pure, as the most holy prelate of Europe. That is the striking superiority of Christianity, which derives from its principal characteristic of Grace."[23]

Here was a new twist to the old belief that Africans were natural Christians. Gobineau went on to say that Africans were inferior, and Christianity was a religion naturally suited to inferior peoples, just as it was especially suited to the poor and humble of Europe.

Christian paternalism, which was to flourish later in the century, was already implied by Gobineau's proposition. If it were assumed that Africans were racially inferior, and yet spiritually equal and capable of receiving the Christian message, the moral duty of the superior race was clear. It was to take up the "white man's burden" and exercise a trust over the spiritual and material welfare of people whose racial status was equivalent to that of minors. Such people could never attain the heights of Western civilization: it was better for them not to try. They might receive all the spiritual blessings of Christianity and still remain within their own culture. Charles Dickens suggested as much. He opposed the conversionist aims of the Niger Expedition, but he favored missionary work. He merely believed that it was better to reach "the black man through the black man" than to use European missionaries, since the black man "can only be successfully approached by a studied reference to the current of his own opinions and customs instead of ours."[24] This sentiment

22. Rufus Anderson, *The Theory of Missions to the Heathen* (Boston, 1845). See also J. F. A. Ajayi, "Henry Venn and the Policy of Development," *Journal of the Historical Society of Nigeria*, I, 311–42 (December, 1959).

23. Arthur, comte de Gobineau, *Essai sur l'inégalité des races humaines*, 2nd ed., 2 vols. (Paris, 1884), I, 66–67.

24. C. Dickens, "The Niger Expedition," in *Miscellaneous Papers* (London, 1908), esp. p. 124. First published in *Household Words*, 19 August 1848.

might seem to suggest cultural relativism, but Dickens and his generation measured culture by Western values. The implication is that of Christian paternalism or trusteeship.

As a matter of practical mission policy, the role of African missionaries and the future possibility of an African church had been pressing questions since the 1820's. The handling of the problem was intimately related to the incipient conflict between Christian paternalism and full cultural conversion. The CMS began toying with the idea of converting Africa by "native agency" as soon as the full toll of European mortality was apparent. The Fourah Bay Institution was founded in 1827 near Freetown in order to train teachers and missionaries for an African church. Other missionary societies also employed educated Africans and West Indians in positions of equality or near equality with their European co-workers. The ultimate aim was not clearly stated, but the implication was clear enough: African Christendom would sooner or later become a part of the Church, whether institutionally independent or linked with the mother church in Britain.

The idea of using "native agency" persisted throughout the period of high missionary mortality,[25] but the status of African missionaries was always a matter of uncertainty. Many field missionaries doubted the ability of their African subordinates. The Rev. J. F. Schön, for example, thought that West Indians had too high notions of their own importance. His attitude toward African missionary agents was both paternalistic and suspicious.[26] For Schön and other field missionaries, "native agency" was not expected to produce an independent native clergy—not, at least, for a very long time to come.

Meanwhile, the Church Missionary Society in England considered the question of "native agency" and an African church during the 1840's and ultimately arrived at a firm policy. The key figure in the Society was Henry Venn, son of one of the Clapham group and a secretary of CMS from 1841 onwards. Venn occasionally vacillated in his attitude toward an African clergy. His instructions for the Yoruba mission in 1844 set lower pay for African than for European

25. Charles Buxton (Ed.), *Memoirs of Sir Thomas Fowell Buxton, Baronet* (London, 1848), p. 554; CMS Committee, "Preface" to *Journals of the Rev. James Frederick Schon and Mr. Samuel Crowther, who with the Sanction of Her Majesty's Government Accompanied the Expedition up the Niger in 1841* (London, 1842), pp. vi ff.; J. M. Trew, *Africa Wasted by Britain and Restored by Native Agency* (London, 1843).
26. J. F. Schön, in *Journals of Schon and Crowther*, pp. 62–63 and 95–97.

missionaries—partly to keep them near the material level of their fellow countrymen, and partly from fear of promoting "self-indulgence." Again in 1851 he had some doubts about the wisdom of providing equal education for African pastors.[27] His final opinion, however, was firm. It was to aim for the goal of a self-supporting, self-governing, and self-propagating African church. In these aims, Venn was directly influenced by Rufus Anderson. He urged the missionaries to control their natural desire to stay on as pastors, and he tried to keep them moving to new fields once a congregation had been founded.[28] Venn held the CMS to the goal of full conversion during his secretaryship, but they too turned toward paternalism later in the century.[29]

Even with a firm goal, many questions remained. How soon, and how nearly, could an African church be created with full African control and full equality? What was the transitional role of the missionary? In particular, what were his responsibilities for temporal leadership over his flock? Individual missionaries answered these questions for themselves in many different ways, and some passed over from the mere preaching of the gospel to other activities: as long as the goal was complete conversion to Western civilization, something more than the gospel seemed to be required. The Rev. T. B. Freeman ran an experimental plantation for a time on the Gold Coast.[30] The Wesleyan-sponsored "Institution for Benefitting the Foulah Tribe," with its agricultural settlement at MacCarthy's Island in the Gambia, was created for material as well as spiritual ends, even though its explicit policy was Christianity first and civilization second, and control rested with the missionaries rather than the lay technicians of civilization.[31]

More extreme projects called for genuine theocracy. The Rev. R. W. Macbriar, for example, had a scheme for forming liberated

27. William Knight, *The Missionary Secretariat of Henry Venn, B.D.* (London, 1880), p. 306; Venn to Townsend, Gollmer and Crowther, 22 October and 25 October 1844, CMSA, CA 2/L1.

28. *Proceedings of the Church Missionary Society,* 1849–1850, p. lxiii; *Church Missionary Intelligencer,* I, 147–50 (November 1849); Henry Venn, CMS Committee Minutes on the Native Pastorate, printed in Knight, *Missionary Secretariat,* pp. 305–7.

29. See J. F. Ade Ajayi, "Christian Missions and the Making of Nigeria, 1841–1891" (Unpublished Ph.D. thesis, University of London, 1958).

30. PP, 1852–1853, lxii [C. 1693], pp. 200 ff.

31. William Fox, *A Brief History of the Wesleyan Missions on the Western Coast of Africa* (London, 1851), pp. 345, 444–45, 497–99, 506, 599.

Africans into a Christian community. Each family was to receive a plot of land to be farmed under strict regulation. Labor would be compulsory. Church-going would be compulsory. "Industrial education" for the children would be compulsory. Morality legislation would regulate the forms of dress and even the distribution of tasks between the sexes. Liquor, tobacco, sport, and Sunday work would all be prohibited. The ideal of a puritan theocracy, long dead as a possibility in England, could still be revived as a plan for Africa.[32]

Education, however, was the non-spiritual task which occupied the greatest part of the missionary effort. During the 1840's educational policy was also caught between the opposing tendencies of full conversion and trusteeship. Earlier education had been a near monopoly of the missionary societies, and it was strictly assimilationist. In spite of occasional protests against a literary education for Africans, there had been no easy way to avoid it. Missionary societies needed native agents and, if possible, African ministers with the full training of a European missionary. Business and government needed clerks, agents, and officials: Europeans were both expensive and short-lived. On this question the merchants and the missionaries saw eye to eye, and merchant houses occasionally asked the government to help with more and better education for Africans.[33]

At the same time, opinion on the Coast had often disapproved of educated Africans. They were supposed to be uppity, aggressive, undisciplined, and dishonest, lacking the good qualities of the Europeans and "bush Africans" alike. For many visitors, they were objects of fun—humorous caricatures of "civilized" men. This unfavorable image undoubtedly reflected certain aspects of reality. The educated Africans had been shaken loose from their social moorings in traditional society, without gaining a secure acceptance or a complete conversion to the Western way of life. They valued Western education very highly—their critics said too highly—but this was only natural when education was the road to advancement and prestige on the Coast. The fragment of Western society in Sierra Leone and the smaller posts was one of extreme social mobility, both for Africans and Europeans. For Europeans, service on the Coast in government or trade often brought high prestige or pay in return for brav-

32. R. M. Macbrair, *Sketches of a Missionary's Travels in Egypt, Syria, Western Africa, &c., &c.* (London, 1839), pp. 328 ff.
33. Hutton and Nicholls to J. Stephen, 23 March 1843, CO 96/2.

ing the dangers of the "climate." Men who had themselves recently moved upward in society tended to be all the more resentful of the pushiness of Africans trying to do the same. Those who looked on Africans as their inferior dependents especially disliked the kind of education that was calculated to give them feelings of equality.

Literary education was increasingly criticized, with a persistent demand for instruction in the agricultural and mechanical arts. In fact, both the criticism and the demand might shelter distinctly different points of view. Some men believed that, as education spread more broadly, it would produce an over supply of potential clerks and officials; and most children would find themselves ill prepared for other occupations. This group, therefore, called for the addition of technical education to the existing literary system. Other reformers, however, wanted to do away with the existing system for all African children, and substitute labor indoctrination. This second kind of demand rose not from a desire to make education useful, but from a xenophobic resentment of the educated Africans; and it was often justified on grounds that were frankly racist—that Africans were innately incapable of undertaking an education fitted for Europeans.[34]

Projects for educational reform could thus be turned to many purposes. One kind of plan was presented by Edward Nicholls in 1842. He called for a system of elementary schools in each British post, with selection of the best students to continue at a Normal School on Ascension Island, and a second selection of the very best to continue their higher education in England. The industrial aspect would be satisfied by apprenticing certain students in trades, and every school was to have an experimental farm. But even industrial training was to be limited. Africans were to be taught how to repair, but now how to manufacture the industrial products of England. Nicholls added: "I am clearly of the opinion that confining the Natives of Africa to the production of the raw materials of their native land with which it so richly abounds, is the most advantageous employ-

34. See, for example: R. R. Madden, Commissioner's Report, PP, 1842, xii (551), pp. 17, 430; J. Miller, Memorandum on Sierra Leone Schools, 1 February 1841, PP, 1842, xii (551), pp. 383–90; J. F. Schön, Evidence before West Africa Committee, 29 June 1842, PP, 1842, xi (551), p. 461; J. Duncan, Travels in Western Africa, 2 vols. (London, 1847), I, 36–37 and 42–43; [E. Melville], A Residence in Sierra Leone (London, 1849), p. 253; N. W. Macdonald, Evidence before Lords' Slave Trade Committee, 14 May 1849, PP (Lords), 1849, xxviii (32), p. 117; T. E. Poole, Life, Scenery, and Customs in Sierra Leone and the Gambia, 2 vols. (London, 1850), II, 8–11.

ment both for that and this country (at least) for a very long time to come."[35]

Other complaints against educational assimilation came from the West Indies especially during the 1840's. As a result, Earl Grey launched a general investigation of educational policy for the tropical colonies. The Committee of Council on Education were asked to report on "the mode in which . . . Industrial Schools for the coloured races may be conducted in the colonies, so as to combine intellectual and industrial education, and to render the labour of the children available towards meeting some part of the expense of their education." The terms of reference thus set industrial education as the desired goal. The Committee made three further assumptions on its own. It assumed that Negroes, as a race, had different mental capacities from Europeans. It assumed that tropical exuberance necessitated special training in order to free the people from "habits of listless contentment with the almost spontaneous gifts of a tropical climate." It assumed that people of African descent would only aspire to posts in "the humbler machinery of local affairs."

These assumptions led naturally to a plan of education designed for social and racial inferiors. It was to consist first of religious instruction, then of agriculture for boys and domestic science for girls, and the whole scheme was to be governed by the need to provide a docile and uncomplaining working class. The children were to be taught "habits of self-control and moral discipline." They were to be instructed in "the mutual interests of the mother-country and her dependencies; the rational basis of their connection, and the domestic and social duties of the coloured races." Their education in economics and politics was to include "the relation of wages, capital, and labour, and the influence of local and general government on personal security, independence, and order."[36]

This report was prepared with first consideration for the West Indian colonies, but it was circulated to the Governors of the West African dependencies. In 1847 and the following years, there was a spate of government correspondence on education policy. Governor Norman Macdonald of Sierra Leone took up the full doctrine. He centered his attack on Freetown Grammar School and the Fourah

35. Memorandum of 20 July 1842, enclosed with Nicholls to Canning, 28 June 1845, FO 82/616, f. 277.

36. Schuttleworth to Hawes, 9 January 1847. Printed version to be found in Miscellaneous Pamphlets, Vol. I, Colonial Office Library.

Bay Institution, demanding a change to a kind of education "more adapted to the mental energies and capabilities of the native population of the colony."[37] In this he failed. Men of African descent were too well established in the West African posts to tolerate an attack on their most advanced educational institutions. (Three of them, John Carr and William Fergusson in Sierra Leone, and James Bannerman in the Gold Coast, had acted as governor before the time of Macdonald's complaint.) For that matter, Earl Grey and most of the influential men in African affairs had never intended "industrial education" to be more than a supplement to the literary education of the elite.[38]

Of all the earlier devices for acculturation, "legitimate trade" was the only continuous rival to the plans for direct training. By the 1840's, it had become so much a catch phrase with an assumed meaning, commentators no longer took the trouble to explain precisely how it was to work. This was deceptive, since the meaning of the term was actually changing slowly through time. Five quite different values were now attached to "legitimate trade," though they were often confused with one another.[39] One was the value of trade for its own sake, the stimulation of the mental powers supposed to come from commercial dealings. A second was the old belief in trade as the necessary basis for an efficient division of labor. A third was its function as an avenue of cultural diffusion, promoting "civilization" by showing the barbarians the advanced technology of the West. Fourth, trade (and especially free trade of the Cobdenite variety) was supposed to promote international peace and friendly relations between peoples. Finally, there was MacQueen's more specific claim that African rulers could be weaned away from the slave trade, if only they would put their slaves to work at agricultural production for export. With the publicity of the Buxton campaign, this

37. N. Macdonald, Annual Report for 1850, PP, 1851, xxxiv [C. 1421], p. 192.

38. H. S. Scott, "The Development of the Education of the African in Relation to Western Contact," The Year Book of Education, 1938 (London, 1938), p. 711; N. Macdonald, Annual Report for 1851, PP, 1852, xxxi [C. 1539], p. 183; Grey to Winniett, 6 August 1849, CO 96/9; M. Laird and R. A. K. Oldfield, Narrative of an Expedition into the Interior of Africa by the River Niger in 1832-4, 2 vols. (London, 1837), II, 394-95; Aborigines Protection Society, Second Annual Report (London, 1839), pp. 22-24; T. B. Freeman to S. J. Hill, Cape Coast, 23 February 1852, PP, 1852, xxxi [C. 1539], p. 189.

39. See, for example: C. Johnston, "The Friends of the African," Simmonds's Colonial Magazine, XIII, 292-96, 435-39 (March–April, 1848), p. 295.

rather narrower usage came into prominence, often replacing the earlier meanings.

This ambiguity merged in turn with a change in the importance attached to "legitimate trade" as a factor promoting African civilization. As we have seen, legitimate trade had appeared in the eighteenth century as a champion capable of defeating the slave trade; but in the first decades of the nineteenth it appeared as a weaker tool, effective only if the slave trade were first destroyed. During the 1830's, and with the new connotations given by MacQueen, its reputation again rose—and especially among those interested in African commerce. Men like Macgregor Laird and Robert Jamieson began to claim that legitimate trade could defeat the slave trade after all.[40]

The new opponents of the anti-slavery squadron carried the argument a step further in the 1840's and 1850's. If, as some claimed, "legitimate trade" could do its work without assistance, the squadron was a useless expense.[41] A still more extreme position could be taken —that any commerce, including the slave trade, helped to spread civilization. From this point of view, the squadron was a positive evil, since, as one spokesman put it, "every obstacle to commerce in slaves even becomes a drawback, in my opinion, to the civilization of the African people."[42]

Humanitarians, on the other hand, began to doubt the civilizing virtues of commerce, whether "legitimate" or not. Missionaries still pictured the "degraded" coastal peoples, even after the slave trade had ceased to operate. Commissioner Madden suspected the influence of European traders, whose personal character was "not calculated to leave many germs of civilization in any barbarous soil."[43] The supposedly "higher" culture of the interior also suggested that "legitimate trade" could not be the only cause of cultural progress. (The

40. Laird and Oldfield, Narrative of an Expedition, I, 3; Jamieson's strongest argument is in R. Jamieson, Commerce with Africa: The Inefficacy of Treaties, 2nd ed. (London, 1859), but the idea occurs here and there in his earlier works. Laird later changed his mind. See [M. Laird], "Remedies for the Slave Trade," Westminster Review, XXXIV, 147 (June, 1840).

41. W. B. Baikie, Narrative of an Exploring Voyage up the Rivers Kwora and Binue (Commonly Known as the Niger and Tsadda) in 1854 (London, 1856), pp. 388–89; F. E. Forbes, Six Months' Service in the African Blockade (London, 1849), p. viii.

42. J. King, Evidence before the Hutt Committee, 9 May 1848, PP, 1847–1848, xxii (366), p. 34, q. 4061.

43. R. R. Madden, Commissioner's Report, 31 July 1841, PP, 1842, xii (551), p. 34.

trans-Sahara trade, being largely in slaves, was not "legitimate" in European eyes.)

Various explanations began to appear, trying to account for the failure of "legitimate trade." A writer in *Blackwood's* explained that commerce brings civilization only at the higher stages of society: savages desire commerce only for the sake of trade gin and guns. The step from savagery to barbarism must come first—then commerce, and progress toward still higher stages.[44] The Wesleyan missionary, T. B. Freeman, suggested another explanation. Aside from the evil of rum as a commercial article, there was also an "unhealthy excitement of petty trading," and commerce developed a "spirit of chicanery." More important still, he held that Africans were spoiled by growing rich and independent too fast, and with only a smattering of education.[45]

For those who began to fear the dangers of commercial intercourse, there were two major alternatives. One was to call for more active government intervention. Commissioner Madden, for example, wanted government regulation to reform the abusive practices, as he saw them, of the British merchants on the Coast. Others called for still more education, more missionaries. As a last resource, there remained the possibility of even more direct intervention. Macgregor Laird came to this in 1842, saying: "The Gambia is in our possession; we put down the slave trade at the Gambia not by commerce, because commerce created the slave trade; we put it down by the moral force of our fort establishment. . . . Moral power on the coast of Africa means a 24-pounder, with British seamen behind it."[46]

The second alternative was to fall back from "legitimate" commerce to agriculture. This was, indeed, the essence of MacQueen's plan: "Commerce must follow agriculture in every country. It is by her agriculture alone, the cultivation of her soil, that Africa can be regenerated. . . ."[47] Buxton's acceptance of this view helped to convince the humanitarians,[48] and it revived many of the older arguments about the superiority of agricultural to commercial development. Even

44. "Africa," *Blackwood's Magazine*, XLIX, 109–13 (January, 1841). See also Huntley, *Seven Years' Service*, I, 400; Ajayi, "Christian Missions," pp. 202–3.
45. T. B. Freeman, 23 February 1852, PP, 1852, xxxi [C. 1539], p. 191.
46. Macgregor Laird, Evidence before West Africa Committee, 15 June 1842, PP, 1842, xi (551), p. 348.
47. J. MacQueen, *A Geographical Survey of Africa* (London, 1840), p. xlvii.
48. See T. Fowell Buxton, *The African Slave Trade*, 2nd ed. (London, 1839), pp. 55–56.

officials, like Governor MacDonnell of the Gambia, began to point out the positive values of agricultural life. He found the roving habits of the ivory hunters and palm-oil gatherers harmful: these occupations required neither foresight nor steady labor, and they were fostered by commerce. Farmers who produced peanuts, on the other hand, had to supply "steady labour and deliberate purpose," thus producing a taste for peaceful pursuits, for European goods, and hence for civilization.[49]

The common ground of all these theories of acculturation was the belief that culture change and economic development went hand in hand. The rival claims of agriculture and commerce as agents of civilization merged with a broader problem of promoting economic development, not only for Africa, but for the whole tropical world, and for Britain herself.

49. Macdonnell to Pakington, 12 July 1852, PP, 1852, xxi [C. 1539], p. 197.

18

WEST AFRICA

IN

THE SOUTH ATLANTIC ECONOMY

British statesmen and publicists at
most times thought of West Africa as a special region with its own
individual problems. When they considered British economic interests
and intentions, however, they thought in broader terms. The tropical
Atlantic was still conceived as an inter-related economic entity, and
with some justice. The flourishing South Atlantic System of the eighteenth century was no longer fully operating, but it was not yet completely dismantled either. Between the 1780's and the 1830's, each
of the national sectors had undergone its own kind of evolution without destroying the essence of the system—the combination of forced
African labor producing tropical staples in America for consumption
in Europe. British legislation had cut off the labor supply to the British sector in 1807, emancipated the slaves as of 1838, and tried to impede the flow of labor to the other national sectors through the anti-
slavery blockade. Nevertheless, the greater part of the tropical staples
entering world trade was still produced in tropical America, still produced with the labor of slaves, still maintained and expanded by the
slave trade from Africa.

There had, of course, been important changes. The supply of slave labor to the southern United States no longer came from the slave trade, but from the normal population growth of the slave caste. With Saint Domingue out of the system—now the Republic of Haiti and relatively unproductive for world markets—the French sector was very much reduced in size. Whether because of abolition and emancipation, or for other reasons, economic growth in the British sector lagged behind the pace set in Cuba and Brazil.

Britain was not, by this token, any the less involved. Two vital changes, which affected her relations to the international system as a whole, had taken place since the 1780's. First, even before the real beginning of the free-trade era, trade barriers between the national sectors of the South Atlantic System had broken down. Each European power tried to protect its national economic interests, but none of them made a serious attempt after 1815 to recreate a complete and self-sufficient empire of trade and plantations. As a result, trade and investment flowed in broader channels. North American and British capitalists invested in Cuba and Brazil. Only a fraction of Cuban and Brazilian agricultural production was sold in the Iberian peninsula. The very illegality of the slave trade opened it to international participation. Typically, a Baltimore-built ship, manned by a polyglot crew, might carry British-made textiles and iron ware to the coast of Africa in return for slaves destined for Havana.

In addition, Great Britain was by far the world leader in economic growth during this half century. It produced the cheapest manufactured goods, consumed an increasing share of the raw materials entering trade, and served as the world's principal money market. Wherever political control might rest, the economic metropolis was London. This was especially true for the fastest growing portion of the whole system—the cotton kingdom of the American South. The southern United States had been peripheral to the eighteenth-century South Atlantic System with its emphasis on sugar, but the southern states were central to the modified and industrialized version of the early nineteenth century. Still, there remained genuine and important British interests south of the Straits of Florida. The British West Indies supplied most of the British demand for sugar and coffee until the 1850's, and British exports went everywhere in the South Atlantic. During the six years, 1847-52, when West Africa took .89 per cent of British exports and the British West Indies took 3.14 per cent, Brazil took 4.16 per cent—more than both the others combined. In addition, Cuba and the other foreign West Indies took 2.18 per cent.[1] In short, the truly tropical sections of the old South Atlantic System still took about 10 per cent of all British exports.

The British had been forced since the 1780's to reconsider the South Atlantic System and their relations to it, with a peculiarly important line of decisions from the Emancipation Act of 1833 to the 1850 decision to keep the blockade on the African coast.

West Africa was implicated both directly and indirectly. The dream of an African eldorado was still alive. For some at least, West Africa was still a place where, "nature seems everywhere bountiful and prolific, and the animal and vegetable worlds develop a countless variety of forms; and even the processes of their decay and reproduction go on more rapidly than in almost any other country. The soil is so fertile that grain is sowed and reaped in the space of three months . . . ."[2]

The economic faith underlying Buxton's plan was the same dream of plenty which had tempted the projectors of the 1780's. Only the promised commodities changed in pace with changing British needs. The tropical woods, nuts, gums, coffee, and sugar of the earlier aspiration were now joined by gold, iron ore, and cotton—especially cotton.[3] British manufacturers were more and more concerned about their dependence on the United States for this key raw material. Though Africa was not alone among possible alternate sources of supply, the promise of cotton gave West Africa another claim to attention—something beyond its claims on British charity or its pitifully small share of British trade—and enthusiasts for African empire were eager to exploit the opening. In 1849, James MacQueen told the Lords' Committee on the slave trade: "there is no country in the world which can produce such an immense quantity of cotton of a quality so fine; it is finer cotton than any description of cotton we know in the world: common cotton in Africa I have seen and had in

    1. J. R. McCulloch, *A Descriptive and Statistical Account of the British Empire,* 4th ed., 2 vols. (London, 1854), II, 20.
    2. J. Howison, *European Colonies in Various Parts of the World, Viewed in their Social, Moral and Physical Condition,* 2 vols. (London, 1834), I, 34.
    3. T. Fowell Buxton, *The African Slave Trade,* 2nd ed. (London, 1839), pp. 200–220; *The Remedy: Being a Sequel to the African Slave Trade* (London, 1840), pp. 19–61.

my possession which was equal to the finest quality of American cotton."[4]

Still another West African possibility was perennially attractive. The enforced labor-mobility of the slave trade appeared to be uneconomic. If, as the enthusiasts claimed, African soils were unused and as rich as those of tropical America, tropical crops could be grown more cheaply in Africa itself. This economic concept underlay a whole succession of projects for African development, from the seventeenth century down to the period of MacQueen and the Buxton plan. Earlier opposition to these projects had justified the slave trade as a nursery for seamen, and mercantilist doctrine had favored production within the existing British colonies. In the light of free-trade economics, both arguments fell to the ground. If the lowest costs of production for tropical raw materials were to be found in Africa, then African production should be encouraged. There was still no empirical evidence that African products *were* cheaper, but the economic reasoning was persuasive. In theory, at least, the old South Atlantic System was inefficient.

Great Britain had, indeed, been trying since 1807 to stop the trans-Atlantic slave trade (though not entirely for economic reasons). The economic results by the 1830's, were not very promising. To the extent that the anti-slave-trade policy was successful—and it was successfully enforced only in the British sector of the System—it seemed merely to impede the economic growth of the British West Indies. African development was still retarded by the continued illegal slave trade. Brazil and Cuba received the slaves and expanded their production of sugar and coffee at the expense of the British colonies. It appeared by 1840 that the foreign slave trade was not only morally wrong but economically disastrous to British interests. Furthermore the slave trade was economically viable in at least one sense. Cuban and Brazilian planters could afford to pay the high cost of smuggled labor and

4. PP, 1849 (Lords), xxviii (32), p. 341. For the special promise of cotton see also MacQueen, Memorandum of 12 January 1839, CO 2/22; C. Johnston, "The Friends of the African," *Simmonds's Colonial Magazine*, XIII, 292–96, 435–39 (March–April, 1848), p. 293; Macdonald to Grey, 18 August 1851, PP, 1851, xxxiv [C. 1421], p. 173; Sir George Stephen, *The Niger Trade Considered in Connexion with the African Blockade* (London, 1849), p. 66; W. B. Baikie, *Narrative of an Exploring Voyage up the Rivers Kwora and Binue (Commonly Known as the Niger and Tsadda) in 1854* (London, 1856), pp. 385–86.

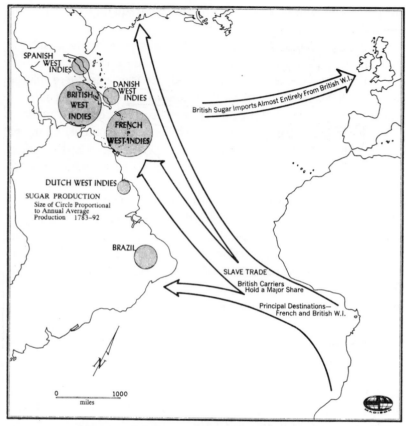

Map 20. Britain in the South Atlantic, 1780's

still compete in world markets. Clearly, then, there was a marked difference between what ought to have happened and what had happened.

Those who thought of the slave trade in economic terms saw it as
a matter of supply and demand. As long ago as 1792, Edmund Burke
had warned that demand for slaves was a natural economic demand,
which would be filled (whether legally or illegally) as long as it continued.[5] After three decades of trying to impede the slave trade by
force and diplomatic pressure, Burke's warning seemed all the more
valid: it went on because it was profitable.

Buxton's adaptation of MacQueen's economic reasoning was designed to render it unprofitable. Britain had failed to stop the eco-

5. E. Burke, "Letter to the Right Honourable Henry Dundas . . ." in *Works,* 16
vols. (London, 1803–1827), IX, 278–79.

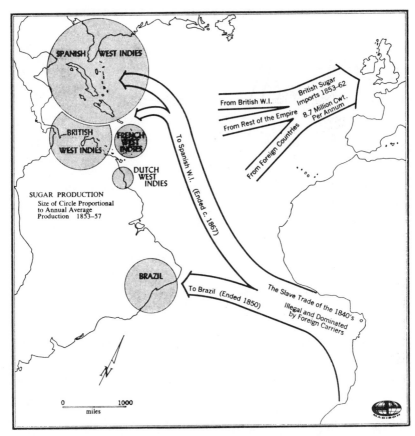

Map 21. Britain in the South Atlantic, 1850's

nomic demand for slaves, but it might be possible to change the cost conditions on the supply side, in Africa itself. Buxton showed that a slave sold in Brazil was worth £100, while the same slave in the interior of Africa brought only £3. The spread between these two prices was the economic force that drove the slave trade. It existed because there was no effective demand for labor in Africa itself. It could be cured when the African authorities had learned "the superior value of man as a labourer on the soil, to man as an object of merchandise."[6] Economic development in Africa would raise the price of slaves, make it unprofitable for the Brazilians to buy them, and thus bring the slave trade to an end. The blockade would still be necessary as an interim

6. Buxton, *The African Slave Trade,* p. 195.

measure, but the permanent end of the slave trade would have to be found in economic change.[7]

This line of reasoning could attract a broad following. Humanitarians would support it because of the ultimate goal of slave-trade abolition. Enthusiasts for African development would support it for its own sake. Some British economic nationalists would support it, because it promised a greater sphere of British interests and the ruin of the American slave-holders—a popular prospect, as much because they were American as because they were slave-holders.

The position of the West India interest was a mixed one. The British planters had been forced to accept legal emancipation in 1834 and the end of a transitional "apprenticeship system" in 1838. The change to a system of wage labor had been peaceful but unhappy. Neither the planters nor the ex-slaves were accustomed to wage payments. The problem was further complicated by the fact that West Indian planters were under-capitalized and saddled with an outmoded scale of production. Their costs of production were high in comparison with those elsewhere, and the British West Indian sugar and coffee industries kept going as well as they did only because they sold their products in the protected British market. On the one hand, they feared the potential competition of the more modern, slave-run plantations of Cuba and Puerto Rico. They, therefore, opposed the slave trade. But they also feared new production from Africa and opposed the Buxton plan as well.

The favorite solution of the West India interest was to lower British West Indian costs. The planters were naturally conscious of the regular payroll as a new item in their accounts. Their own assessment of their plight therefore stressed a wage bill that was "too high." Many British analysts agreed. The money wages commonly paid in the West Indies after 1838 were higher than those paid to English agricultural laborers, but this evidence was misleading. Price levels were also normally much higher in the West Indies than in England so that comparisons of money wages had no meaning in real terms.[8] British economic thought nevertheless followed West Indian,

---

7. Buxton, *The Remedy*, esp. pp. 155–56.

8. The error of comparing money wages was occasionally pointed out at the time. See, for example, *African Colonizer*, 6 March 1841, p. 158. Wages also differed very markedly from one West Indian colony to another. See P. D. Curtin, "The British Sugar Duties and West Indian Prosperity," *Journal of Economic History*, XIV, 157–64 (Spring, 1954), p. 163.

and concentrated on the problem of lowering the cost of West Indian labor.

Regarding labor costs, the most common affirmation of the classical economists had been that free labor would be cheaper than slave—at equilibrium. The equilibrium wage rate would, indeed, be the bare cost of subsistence. Any lower rate would bring about a decline of population, thus a shortage of labor and a return to equilibrium. Any higher rate would bring about population growth and new hands to compete on the labor market.

The known demographic trends in the West Indies seemed to confirm the belief in a labor shortage. When the immigration of slaves was cut off in 1808, the population of many islands declined slightly before it began to rise again in about the 1830's. Even then, the rate of increase was low at first.[9] The apparent scarcity of labor was also influenced by the fact that many colonies—almost all except Barbados—contained tracts of land unused by the plantation economy but perfectly suitable for cultivation. On emancipation, many of the ex-slaves preferred to farm on their own rather than accept wage labor on the plantations. The existence of this alternative to plantation labor made it difficult to depress wages by tacit agreement among the planters. As long as the planters were forced to accept a free market for labor, and as long as they believed the wages they had to pay were far above the equilibrium rate, the logical alternative was to encourage immigration in order to force the wage rate back to its "natural" level.[10]

The idea of induced immigration was especially attractive in the two West Indian colonies acquired during the Napoleonic Wars—Trinidad and British Guiana. Neither had been intensively developed in the heyday of the South Atlantic System. Both had large areas of new land where modern sugar plantations could be laid out. Their superior prospects for development were reflected in the value of their slaves at the time of emancipation. Field slaves were worth £170 each in Guiana, £110 in Trinidad, but only £75 in Barbados and £67 in Jamaica.[11] In effect, both British Guinana and Trinidad con-

9. G. W. Roberts, *The Population of Jamaica* (Cambridge, 1957), pp. 40–45.

10. See H. Merivale, *Lectures on Colonisation and Colonies,* 2nd ed. (London, 1861), pp. 300–332, for an authoritative summary of these views. See P. D. Curtin, *Two Jamaicas* (Cambridge, Mass., 1955), pp. 133–41 for the local application of these ideas in Jamaica.

11. Merivale, *Colonisation and Colonies,* p. 333.

tained a potential planters' frontier at the time of emancipation, but it could only move forward with a large supply of imported labor.

The economic fortunes of the West Indies and West Africa were thus related, and in three different ways. West Africa was the ancient source of labor supply, and might some day again furnish immigrants to fill up the land and make development possible. Meanwhile, it provided the labor on which the prosperity of Cuba and Brazil was based. In the more distant future, West Africa itself might be an economic competitor with its own plantations.

For a British theorist wishing to maximize the value of the South Atlantic economy for the Empire as a whole, Buxton's scheme had certain disadvantages. Even if it worked, it would have beggared the British West Indies along with the rest of tropical America. Other schemes had therefore already made their appearance, beginning shortly after the emancipation of the slaves. Macgregor Laird thought he had discovered a way to ruin the slave trade and the competitive position of Latin American producers, and yet preserve the prosperity of both the West Indies and West Africa. His project was first sketched in 1837 and then developed more fully in 1840. He took the economic viability of the slave trade as his point of departure. If the slave trade were profitable, aiding labor mobility across the South Atlantic could be considered a natural and proper economic activity, though not in its current form. For Laird, the way to ruin the slave trade was to introduce even greater mobility for free labor. His plan called for a government-operated shipping service, offering free passage for contract laborers from West Africa to the British West Indies and subsidized by the West Indian colonies. He tried to forestall humanitarian opposition by insisting on careful controls over contracts, limited in any case to one year and further guarded by the provision that each group of migrants must contain both men and women in equal numbers. After a year, they would have a right to free return passage to Africa.[12]

Where the MacQueen-Buxton plan sought to raise costs on the supply side of the slave trade, Laird's scheme sought to alter the demand side by subsidizing British, wage-labor migration at the expense of Latin, slave-labor migration. In the longer run the Brazilian and Cuban demand for slaves would dry up at the source through failure

---

12. M. Laird and R. A. K. Oldfield, *Narrative of an Expedition into the Interior of Africa by the River Niger in 1832–4,* 2 vols. (London, 1837), II, 357–76; [M. Laird], "Remedies for the Slave Trade," *Westminster Review,* XXXIV, 155–59 (June, 1840).

of their slave plantations to compete successfully with British, wage-labor sugar and coffee. The two plans also differed in another important respect. Laird would have abandoned the expensive naval blockade. The Spanish and Brazilians would be left free to carry on the slave trade, though forbidden to buy slaves within defined spheres of British interest. In these spheres, a scheme of economic development similar to the Buxton plan would be undertaken. Laird looked to the Niger Delta-Cameroons region, supported from a base on Fernando Po. His plan included an agricultural school to provide instruction and a series of treaties with the riverine states of the Niger and Benue to secure British interests in the hinterland. This sphere was expected to grow, partly through the influence of returned laborers from America and partly through a series of small expeditions to explore the further interior.[13]

Laird's plan had an obvious appeal for all those who opposed the Buxton plan—either because of its threat to West Indian prosperity, its threat to established African trade, or its Evangelical base. W. R. Greg brought out a pamphlet presenting Laird's arguments in terms of classical economics and Benthamite legal theory.[14] The Government itself tacitly accepted many of Laird's ideas along with Buxton's, and the full West African project of 1840 was a modified combination of the two. The blockade was to be strengthened, the Niger Expedition itself was to commence African economic development, and the preliminary investigation for a labor-migration scheme was assigned to Dr. Madden.[15] In this way the Niger effort was coupled with a broader intent to reform the whole South Atlantic economy.

In the initial stages of 1840 and 1841, the emphasis lay with African development. After the Niger failure, however, the Parliamentary Committee of 1842 altered the balance in favor of the West Indies. Government assistance for inter-continental migration might appear to be contrary to the ideals of laissez faire economics, but a decade of agitation by the Colonial Reformers had already had its effect. The Australian colonies had begun to subsidize emigration out of money received for the sale of land. The idea of "systematic colonization" was given metropolitan approval in 1840 with the creation of a Board of Colonial Land and Emigration Commissioners,

13. Laird, "Remedies for the Slave Trade," pp. 139–162.
14. W. R. Greg, *Past and Present Efforts for the Extinction of the African Slave Trade* (London, 1840).
15. Lord John Russell to R. R. Madden, 26 November 1840, CO 267/170.

empowered to supervise assisted emigration from Britain to Australia. It was an easy transfer to shift the basic scheme from temperate to tropical colonies. Sir John Jeremie wanted to remake the Buxton plan into a close copy of Wakefield's schemes for the settlement of Australia, but substituting colored West Indians for European immigrants.[16] Where Jeremie wanted an eastward migration, the *Colonial Gazette*, principal organ of the Colonial Reformers, described the more common project for a westward migration as "systematic African colonization," thus emphasizing its similarity to the accepted scheme for colonizing Australia.[17]

Some problems remained, including Dr. Madden's objection that genuinely free emigration from Africa to America was not possible, but the Parliamentary Committee listened more sympathetically to Macgregor Laird. He now appeared before them with quantitative estimates: two steamers could transport 12,000 Africans a year in either direction at a one-way cost of £6 each. The Committee's report followed Laird's recommendations and called for African labor to redress the competitive balance in tropical America.[18]

The scheme was launched in 1843 with ships in charge of government officials and the cost of migration borne by the West Indian colonies. Three ships were initially placed in this service, mainly to carry recaptives who would otherwise have been settled at Sierra Leone. The migrants signed a five-year contract with a promise of free repatriation at the end of the term.[19] In all, some 14,000 free emigrants were taken to the West Indies under this and successive schemes during the 1840's, but the plan was not a success. The free emigrants of a whole decade were only a fraction of the number making a similar trip each year as slaves. They were not enough either to outdo the Cubans in economic growth, or to depress the wage levels of the British islands.

By the mid-1840's, the promise of Laird's first plan, which might have attracted broad support for the joint development of both sides of the South Atlantic, had come to nothing. The West India interest were dissatisfied with the government controls on immigration, which

16. Sir John Jeremie, *A Letter to T. F. Buxton on Negro Emancipation and African Civilization* (London, 1840), pp. 20–23.
17. *Colonial Gazette*, 2 February 1822, p. 65.
18. R. R. Madden, Commissioner's Report, PP, 1842, xii (551), pp. 255–57 and 265–67; M. Laird, Evidence before West Africa Committee, 11 July 1842, PP, 1842, xi (551), p. 572; Report of the West Africa Committee, PP, 1842, xi (551), p. x.
19. Stanley to Macdonald, 6 February 1843, PP, 1843, xxxiv [C. 438], pp. 3–5; PP, 1841, xxxiv [C. 1421], p. 189.

they regarded as onerous restrictions on their labor supply. Humanitarians tended to oppose emigration from Africa, even with controls, since it could easily turn into a disguised slave trade. They objected to the methods of recruitment in Sierra Leone, and the missionaries in particular resented the removal of liberated Africans from their own chosen training ground for the civilization of Africa through "native agency." British opinion gradually hardened into two camps —a humanitarian, pro-African group and an anti-humanitarian, West Indian group.[20] Meanwhile, the hope for tropical development under British aegis on either side of the Atlantic was unfulfilled.

A third possibility appeared during the 1840's, with the rise of the economic doctrine of free trade. Instead of promoting economic growth in either the British-West Indies or a British sphere in Africa, the free-traders urged Britain to buy in the cheapest market. For sugar, the cheapest market was the slave economy of Latin America. Both the humanitarians and the West India interest were unhappy at the prospect. Both argued that moral considerations made it necessary to protect the British sugar colonies with their new systems of wage labor. They were answered by the cry for cheap sugar and claims for the ultimate morality of the "unseen hand" of economic law.[21] As for the West Indian plantations, it was argued that free trade might be painful in the short run, but open competition would be to their long-run advantage.

When the Corn Laws fell in 1846, the sugar duties followed, being scaled down gradually to reach equality for all imported sugar in 1854. The price of sugar in London dropped by 44 per cent, and the British consumption per capita doubled between 1845 and 1854. Part of the new demand was met by the planters of the British West Indies, but much more of it came from foreign colonies or other parts of the British Empire.[22]

Free trade in sugar radically altered the British view of West Africa in the South Atlantic economy. It was especially important in changing the British attitude toward the anti-slavery blockade. Objections to the blockade had been heard from the time of the Buxton

20. For representative opinions on either side of this controversy see: W. R. Greg, "The Slave Trade and the Sugar Duties," *Westminster Review*, XLI, 243–58 (June, 1844) and Dandeson Coates to Lord Stanley, 26 November 1844, PP, 1845, xxxi (158), pp. 3–8. See also the House of Commons debates of 25 February 1845, 3 H 77, cc. 1173–1203.

21. For a summary of the argument see H. Merivale, *Lectures on Colonisation and Colonies*, 2 vols. (London, 1841–1842), I, 201–2.

22. Curtin, "The British Sugar Duties," p. 160.

plan, and Laird's first scheme would have abolished it. After 1846 the older arguments that it was expensive, useless, and inhumane were joined by new considerations. The general philosophy of the free trade movement was unfriendly to government expenditure, to the use of force, and to "artificial" adjustments of the society or the economy. Its rising popularity eroded away some support for anti-slavery patrols. More directly, the end of the sugar duties ended the attempt of British tariff policy to favor the British West Indies over Latin America. It was generally conceded that non-discriminatory sugar duties would lead to an increase of Cuban and Brazilian sugar production. Higher production would necessarily call for still more slaves. To impede the slave trade with the squadron, while favoring it in tariff policy, seemed a contradiction, and one that sacrificed a profitable form of control while keeping an expensive form. Not only the free-traders took this line. Many protectionists used the same argument, with a slightly different conclusion. If the public had to pay in some form or other for the anti-slavery cause, let them buy the expensive, free-labor sugars from the British West Indies. In return, let them give up the expensive anti-slavery blockade. Finally, merchants in the Latin American trade argued that Britain's best interest lay in the growth of the Latin American market, which would develop more rapidly and humanely with a properly organized and regulated slave trade.[23]

All these tendencies of thought merged with the decline of humanitarian fervor, the rise of a tougher minded kind of racist sentiment, and the continued fact that the anti-slavery blockade did not prevent the slave trade. In 1845, William Hutt launched the Parliamentary campaign to abolish the blockade, beginning the six-year effort that was only barely defeated in 1850. The campaign has often been written off as a manifestation of economy-minded isolationist sentiment. It did, indeed, appeal to those who wanted lower taxes, but the ultimate intention was more complex. Hutt himself was no isolationist. He had served on the West Africa Committee of 1842, and he was both a free trader and a Colonial Reformer. This combination of interests made him especially conscious of labor immobility, and his attack on the blockade was part of a broad program—often in-

---

23. These trends of thought and sentiment are found widely scattered through the indexed debates of Parliament on the subject of the blockade and the sugar duties between 1845 and 1851 and in the hearings of the two Parliamentary Committees on the Blockade, 1848–1850. The subject was also widely discussed in the press, especially in *The Times*.

tentionally imprecise in detail—covering the whole of Britain's South Atlantic policy. Its initial objective was the removal of the squadron, for the usual variety of reasons. More positively, Hutt proposed a broad encouragement of African trade (but not agriculture) through the establishment of a series of small posts all along both coasts of Africa. This much was in line with the proposals of the 1842 Committee. Even more important, he wanted to allow the British West Indian governments to import "free" workers without interference from the imperial government, and in greater numbers than the rival slave trade.[24]

Hutt and his followers were rarely specific, but it was already clearly understood that really large numbers of Africans could be recruited only by purchase through the usual channels of the slave trade. The workers' freedom would therefore have been somewhat illusory, though they would have received wages from the time of arrival in America; and sooner or later they would have been allowed some freedom of choice in renewing their contracts.

Other plans, however, took a different line. Some were more genuinely liberal. Macgregor Laird, for example, modified his earlier scheme. In 1848, he came up with a project for absolute trans-Atlantic mobility of African labor. In place of contracts or repatriation guarantees, he wanted a system of free transportation. The British government would establish a steamship service between West Africa and the West Indies. Any individual of African descent could then obtain passage without cost in either direction at any time, and the whole operation would simply be written off as a British subsidy to tropical development.[25]

At the other extreme, some of the plans presented at the time of the Hutt Committee were openly designed to revive the British slave trade. William Allen, one-time commander of the Niger Expedition, was among the more forthright. He believed that the blockade could never stop the slave trade in tropical Africa, and that tropical exuberance would prevent a successful system of pure wage labor in tropical America. In his opinion, Britain should give up opposition to the slave trade and create an international, regulated slave trade under her own control. According to this scheme, Britain would supply

24. W. Hutt, Commons, 24 June 1845, 3 H 81, cc. 1156–1172.
25. M. Laird, Evidence before the Hutt Committee, 11 April 1848, PP, 1847–1848, xxii (272), pp. 203–4.

slaves to the remaining slave-holding territories in America, but with a limitation on the length of service. Each slave would be tattooed with his date of arrival in America. After a period of slavery in Brazil or Cuba he would be transferred to one of the wage-labor territories, such as the British West Indies, there to serve another period as an "apprentice." After this double servitude in tropical America, he would be returned to the African coast.[26]

A similar scheme was outlined to the Hutt Committee by Jose E. Cliffe, a North American turned Brazilian citizen, and a former slave trader. Cliffe explained to the Committee that Africans were natural slaves, created as such by God, who had placed them in the one region where white men could not live. It seemed part of the divine plan that they should serve as a reservoir of tropical labor. The British effort to stop the slave trade was, therefore, contrary to God's will, and the British had already been punished by the ruin of their West Indian colonies. According to Cliffe, the remedy was a system of "free immigration"—that is, the purchase of slaves in Africa for service in America. Like Allen, Cliffe would have tattooed the date of purchase on each slave, granting emancipation in America at the end of eight to ten years of slavery.[27]

Whether the justification came from a theory of tropical exuberance or teleological racism, the result would have been much the same; and both proposals had another weakness. Neither system would have given British planters an advantage over their Latin American competitors. Other suggestions, however, took this problem into account. J. L. Hook, formerly of the Sierra Leone emigration office, thought that "free" emigration could be monopolized. According to his scheme, the government should enter into contracts with African chiefs, providing an annual subsidy equal to their former profits from the slave trade, in return for the exclusive right to purchase slaves as "free immigrants."[28] Another variant suggestion was to withhold "free immigrants" from Brazil and Cuba unless they emancipated their slaves and thus put themselves on the same footing

26. William Allen, *A Plan for the Immediate Extinction of the Slave Trade, for the Relief of the West India Colonies, and for the Diffusion of Civilization and Christianity in Africa, by the co-operation of Mammon and Philanthropy* (London, 1849).

27. Jose E. Cliffe, Evidence before the Hutt Committee, 16 May 1848, PP, 1847–1848, xxii (366), pp. 72–74.

28. J. L. Hook, Evidence before the Hutt Committee, 9 May 1848, PP, 1847–1848, xxii (366), p. 27.

as the British West Indies.[29]

The strongest opposition to any of these proposals for a disguised slave trade came from predictable sources. The humanitarians; some naval officers, who took the attack on the blockade to be an attack on their profession; Lord Palmerston, who was committed to a diplomatic solution—all these united to stop the Hutt group in Parliament. There was, however, another current of opposition from a less expected source. The West Indian planters were angered by the repeal of the sugar duties, and their initial reaction was to seek a new supply of cheap African labor. But then there were second thoughts. Barbardos already had plenty of labor, and some highly placed Barbadians were even thinking of settling part of their redundant population in Africa. Jamaica had little unused land that was really suitable for sugar. The older West Indian sugar colonies as a group soon recognized that they could be ruined just as effectively by the competition of Trinidad and British Guiana as by that of Cuba and Brazil. In the summer of 1849, an organized campaign in favor of the blockade swept Jamaica. It was partly an effort to help the humanitarians on the blockade issue in return for humanitarian help with the sugar duties, but the fact remained that West Indian sugar producers would not stand together and demand large-scale immigration from Africa.[30]

The school of Africa developers were still more adamant. For them, it was clear that more intensive slave raiding in Africa would ruin any hope of realizing their dream of African agricultural bounty. They opposed the Hutt plan for a disguised slave trade as they had opposed the foreign and undisguised slave trade. If forced to choose, many would have favored the British West Indies over other parts of tropical or sub-tropical America. To this end, they occasionally suggested leaving sugar to the West Indies, while West Africa concentrated on cotton.[31] It was a useful tactic to soften West Indian opposition. It was also a claim to British support for their plans, if African development could promise to ruin the Latin American sugar planters and the North American cotton planters at one blow,

29. J. King, Evidence before the Hutt Committee, 9 May 1848, PP, 1847–1848, xxii (366), pp. 30 ff.

30. [D. Turnbull] (Ed.), The Jamaica Movement for Promoting the Enforcement of the Slave-Trade Treaties and for the Suppression of the Slave Trade. (London, 1850); PP, 1849, xix (308), pp. 152–55; James MacQueen, Evidence before Lords' Slave Trade Committee, 5 July 1849, PP, 1849 (Lords), xxviii (32), p. 347.

31. Edward Nicholls, Memorandum of 20 July 1842, enclosed in Nicholls to Canning, 28 July 1845, FO 84/616.

and yet preserve the West Indies' prosperity. MacQueen told the Lords' Committee on the slave trade that the slave plantations of America would be finished the minute West Africa exported a half million bales of cotton and two or three thousand tons of sugar.[32]

From the point of view of the African school, the final outcome was a stalemate. The Niger Expedition failed. The repeal of the sugar duties was allowed to stand. The projects for African labor emigration failed, and the Hutt proposals were defeated by Parliament.

But, on the whole, the decade of the 1840's ended more hopefully than it began, and the decade was marked by a whole series of new projects or alternatives to the Niger Expedition. In all these plans, the Niger project was the point of departure, drawing in, as it did, many threads of past suggestion. The Niger project had, indeed, been something of a catch-all. It included a primary emphasis on trade, but it also had a European-managed plantation in the form of the "model-farm." The model farm itself might have been a form of technical assistance—a genuine model for African entrepreneurs to copy —or it might have been the model for future European-run plantations. The only missing element was the suggestion that Africans might develop economically by producing and trading more efficiently among themselves.

When the projectors of the 1840's began to re-write the Niger plan, they could emphasize any aspect they chose. In so doing, they raised anew all the problems of economic development—trade vs. agriculture, open trade vs. monopolized trade, peasant proprietorship vs. European-managed plantations.

The most popular kind of project was to emphasize trade and let African production rise to meet the effective demand. Most projectors also preferred an open trade to monopoly. Buxton himself had a certain bias toward free trade. (He had hoped to make Fernando Po a free port, on the model of Singapore, without duties or discrimination of any kind.)[33] The more extreme supporters of laissez faire, however, disapproved of all government assistance, even that given to the Niger Expedition. The most consistent pamphleteer in this cause was Robert Jamieson, who was willing to compete with the slave traders but not with government expeditions. His economic case against the Niger Expedition was based on the superiority of free

32. J. MacQueen, Evidence before Lords' Slave Trade Committee, PP, 1849 (Lords), xxviii (32), p. 342.

33. Buxton, The Remedy, pp. 161–62.

enterprise. With government aid, his argument ran, Europeans would engage in agriculture. Once engaged in agriculture, they would want a chartered company. If they formed a chartered company, they would want monopoly powers. If they were given a monopoly, they would drive down the prices offered to the African producers. If the Africans were not paid fair prices, they would return to subsistence farming. When that happened, all development would end.[34]

Non-commercial observers were also concerned about the level of prices offered the Africans. Henry Venn took up the kind of watchdog activity the Quaker, William Allen, had once sponsored in Sierra Leone, keeping a check on the prices paid in Africa in relation to prices on the London market. From time to time he laid out a little of his own capital in arrowroot or ginger as a way of keeping the African prices as high as possible.[35]

Most projectors thought economic development would require some government assistance. MacQueen had always wanted a chartered company with a legal monopoly, on the order of the later Royal Niger Company. Dr. Thomas Kehoe, who had served with the army on Fernando Po, would have settled for something like the Niger Expedition restricted to its commercial aspects. That is, government subsidy to steamers on the Niger and a government entrepôt at the confluence of the Niger and Benue, but no missionaries, no model farm, and no agriculture managed by Europeans.[36]

By contrast, Sir George Stephen, brother of the Permanent Under-Secretary, wanted government commercial enterprise on a much more elaborate scale. Stephen believed in free trade for developed countries, but he held that "Whatever is done for Africa, must for many years to come, be done upon the responsibility of Government; we dare not entrust the responsibility elsewhere."[37] If trade were to appear where none had flowed in the past, the producer had to be assured a firm price, a fair price, and a regular market. This automatically called for monopoly, since a free market was a fluctuating market. It also called

34. R. Jamieson, *An Appeal to the Government and People of Great Britain against the Proposed Niger Expedition* (London, 1840); *A Further Appeal against the Proposed Niger Expedition* (London, 1841); and especially *Sequel to Appeals made to the Government and People of Great Britain, against the Niger Expedition before its Departure from England* (London, 1843), pp. 10–12.

35. Henry Venn, Jr., "Notice on African Commerce," in William Knight, *The Missionary Secretariat of Henry Venn, B.D.* (London, 1880), pp. 540–41.

36. T. Kehoe, *Some Considerations in Favour of Forming a Settlement at the Confluence of the Niger and Tchadda* (Waterford, 1847).

37. Stephen, *The Niger Trade*, p. 57.

for government monopoly, since only the government could guarantee regularity of demand at a firm and fair price, willingly sustaining losses if necessary. On the basis of these considerations, Stephen arrived at a plan nearly foreshadowing the Marketing Boards of the twentieth century. The government would monopolize the Niger trade, offering a steady demand to the African producer. The goods purchased would be stored in government warehouses on Fernando Po and Annobon, where private merchants would always be sure to find a cargo.[38]

This was all very well, but the Colonial Office (and even more, the Treasury) took a narrower view. When Earl Grey was Secretary of State from 1846 to 1852, however, the Colonial Office offered at least a form of technical assistance. Grey tried to abolish shifting cultivation in Sierra Leone, and he favored peasants over plantations for the development of Gold Coast cotton. He thought that African peasants might well respond to economic demand. They were more likely to produce for export (alongside subsistence farming) than to give up subsistence agriculture and transform themselves into wage workers. Grey therefore encouraged European capitalists to set up cotton gins and buy uncleaned cotton at a firm price, rather than grow it themselves.[39]

Other projectors combined technical assistance with ideas for government investment. Governor MacDonnell of the Gambia wanted to attract migratory peanut farmers from neighboring territories by preparing plots in advance and letting them in return for a quitrent.[40] This idea of settling peasants in planned villages was persistent, and it recalled some of the early experiments at Sierra Leone. Edward Nicholls wanted to lay out villages on Fernando Po and elsewhere, letting the land on perpetual lease for 6 per cent of the gross production.[41]

Far more grandiose projects for government investment also turned up from time to time. The same Edward Phillips who thought African barbarism was caused by the alternation of wet and dry seasons sought a remedy and an impetus to economic growth in the provision

38. Stephen, *The Niger Trade, passim.*
39. Grey to Officer Administering Sierra Leone, 24 January 1849, CO 268/43; Winniett to Grey, 22 May 1850 (minuted by Grey), CO 96/18; Grey to Winniett, 14 August 1840, CO 402/2.
40. Macdonnell to Pakington, 12 July 1852, PP, 1852, xxxi [C. 1539], pp. 193–208.
41. Nicholls, Memorandum of 20 July 1842, enclosed with Nicholls to Canning, 28 June 1845, FO 84/616.

of irrigation works. In spite of his general ignorance of African conditions, he chose the interior delta of the Niger as the most promising site—exactly where the dams and cotton scheme of the *Office du Niger* were to rise a century later.[42]

Other projects emphasized technical assistance to African states beyond the range of British control. Brodie Cruickshank advanced a plan for persuading Dahomey to give up the slave trade: Britain should open a consulate in Ouidah, staffed by a diplomatic representative and a professional planter. The planter's salary would come from the British treasury as a subsidy to Dahomean economic development.[43] The King of Dahomey would provide land and labor for an experimental plantation, and retain title to the crop. In time, he would recognize his true advantage and transform himself from a slave merchant into a princely planter.

Most projects conceived in terms of large plantations, however, assumed that Europeans would be managers and owners, not mere technical advisors. But European ownership and management was difficult without European political sovereignty, and the government was set against territorial expansion. Occasional projects were nevertheless brought forward. The most elaborate was promoted in 1842 by R. Dillon Tennent, who issued a prospectus calling for a capital of £40,000 to develop part of Fernando Po and the nearby Amboizes Islands. Some of the land was to be in large plantations, "as if they were West India Estates." The rest could be let out to African, rent-paying peasants. Tennent planned, in addition, to have his own shipping line to Europe.

The project of the Barbados African Colonization Society of 1848 was similar, if more vague. They hoped to found a settlement on the coast of Africa, where members of the Barbadian planting class could take up estates. The nucleus of a labor force would be imported from Barbados and settled as peasants on labor tenures—that is, owing three days of free labor each week in return for the use of their plots. In time, it was thought that local Africans might also be brought into the colony.[44]

Plantation projects raised a further problem of the greatest importance in any plans for the development of tropical agriculture.

42. *Simmonds's Colonial Magazine*, X, 4–8 (January, 1847).
43. B. Cruickshank, Report of 9 November 1848, PP, 1849 (Lords), xxviii (32), p. 189.
44. African Agricultural Association, *Prospectus* (London, 1842); PP, 1849, xix (308), pp. 152–55.

African societies were almost all slave-holding societies, in the sense
that some individuals were in a special status of personal subordination to others. African slavery was never the same as the chattel
slavery of the Americas, and the better informed Europeans recognized this fact; but they also saw the lack of a regular system of
wage labor as a bar to economic development following Western
capitalist norms. The Europeans themselves had not used capitalism
exclusively in their earlier ventures in tropical agriculture. From the
sixteenth century through to the early nineteenth, they had depended
on some form of forced deliveries, forced labor, or slavery. In theory,
they justified the practice as an accommodation to the social forms
of non-Western society, or as the only possible way of making people
work under conditions of tropical exuberance.

From the 1830's onward, however, wage labor was the official
policy for the British colonies. Slavery was still tolerated in India
and a few other places, but the dominant ideology of those who
wished to civilize the world called for the export of British norms—
including the British labor system. Yet the transition from slavery
to wage labor had raised many problems in the West Indies and
South Africa. European managers in the tropics remained convinced
that some kind of forced labor was still a necessity. They might not
want an outright return to slavery, but they were as inclined as ever
to think in terms of tropical labor systems involving something more
than the mere payment of wages.

James MacQueen, and virtually all the others who hoped for agricultural development beyond the area of direct British control, assumed that African authorities would simply put their slaves to work,
rather than selling them. The result would have been slave production in Africa, but an end of the inter-continental slave trade.

The question of slavery in Africa was deftly handled in the pre-
liminaries to the Niger Expedition. Buxton himself was intentionally
imprecise. While it is clear that he accepted MacQueen's view—that
African chiefs would use slave labor—he neither drew attention to
this aspect of the plan, nor defended its morality. He insisted, indeed, that slavery should be forbidden in any territory Britain might
acquire in Africa, but British territory, even in the original project,
would merely have been a series of enclaves. Shortly before the expedition sailed, Buxton asked the Government to create one enclave
of about one hundred square miles in which wage labor might be

used as a demonstration. Otherwise, he was willing to accept slavery in Africa as a better alternative to a continued slave trade. In the end, the Niger Commissioners were only ordered to investigate the possibility of a British sovereign enclave. The Niger Expedition therefore sailed with the expectation that African economic development would rest on slavery.[45]

Protests from anti-slavery circles were surprisingly few, and most humanitarians seem to have accepted Buxton's compromise. The *Eclectic Review,* however, took the line of high principle: "In taking away from the marauder the musket with which he has been making slaves of other tribes, this scheme will put into his hands the lash by which he will aggravate the slavery of his own. He will be transformed from the slave-hunter to the slave-driver."[46]

Buxton was not alone in his compromise with forced labor in Africa. Other men who were normally humanitarian and liberal accepted its alleged necessity. George Maclean, Brodie Cruickshank, William Allen of the Niger Expedition, and Sir George Stephen all did so explicitly.[47] By the later 1840's, disappointment with the economic success of West Indian emancipation (and disappointment with the speed of African acculturation) made the compromise easier. By 1850, the *Westminster Review* felt free to justify slavery as a proper transitional measure—a "stepping stone from barbarism to civilization."[48]

At this juncture, James MacQueen, radical as ever, stepped into the position deserted by the humanitarians. He reversed himself and told the Lords' Committee on the blockade that any form of slavery in Africa would be disastrous for economic development. Slave hunting for the internal slave trade would increase in order to supply labor for the regions of greatest economic growth.[49]

Even within the British colonies and posts, officials often saw the labor problem as one requiring coercion, though outright slavery was

45. Buxton, *The Remedy,* p. 165; Lord John Russell to Treasury, 26 December 1839; Buxton and Lushington to Russell, 7 August 1840; Russell to Niger Commissioners, 30 January 1841; PP, 1842, xlviii [C. 472], pp. 1–2, 15–18.

46. "The Niger Expedition," *The Eclectic Review,* VIII (n.s.), 467–68 (1840).

47. R. R. Madden, Commissioner's Report, PP, 1842, xii (551), pp. 81–87; W. Allen and T. R. H. Thomson, *A Narrative of the Expedition to the River Niger in 1841,* 2 vols. (London, 1848), II, 432; Stephen, *Niger Trade,* p. 68.

48. "African Coast Blockade," *Westminster Review,* LII, 258 (January, 1850).

49. James MacQueen, Evidence before Lords' Slave Trade Committee, 5 July 1849, PP, 1849 (Lords), xxviii (32), pp. 351–52.

illegal. In Sierra Leone, recurrent suggestions called for forced labor from the liberated Africans.[50] An alternative was government plantations worked by African "soldiers" under military discipline.[51] Governor Winniett of the Gold Coast was anxious to introduce cotton cultivation, but he believed continuous and voluntary labor for wages would not be offered: "the Gold Coast Native desires no greater happiness than to eat the bread of idleness, which the extreme fertility of the soil enables him to do in rich abundance, without sacrificing more of his ease than is necessary for healthy recreation."[52]

Governor Winniett seems to state the usual opinion of the time— that the supply curve would quickly become non-linear, since tropical men would prefer leisure to wages once they had achieved the minimum of subsistence. But he made another point as well. He believed the free African might well offer his labor at a "rate of wages that would permanently ameliorate his condition," but not for "such fair and equitable wages, as business with moderate profits would allow."

In order to pay wages at a rate that might be effective in that labor market, in short, the employers would have needed a higher world price. Since the world price could not be altered, the alternatives remained: either no cotton for export, or cotton produced by some kind of forced labor.

Winniett decided in favor of forced labor and thought it might be obtained by using the coercive power of the chiefs within the British quasi-protectorate. If the chiefs would agree to a Labor Act, he considered that it might provide for three different kinds of forced labor. First, chiefs should hire out their slaves to British capitalists, to the advantage of both, since the slaves were only "idle profligates" in any case. Second, planters should "redeem" pawns, a plan analogous to the "redemption" of slaves, after which the ex-slaves repaid the purchase price by a period of forced labor. Finally, Winniett thought that African merchants who cheat Europeans might well be set to work at forced labor in place of a jail sentence.[53]

Earl Grey at the Colonial Office was suspicious of this scheme, fearing that it would merely make the local slave-holders rich. But he was not opposed in principle to forced labor. He believed that some special "command of labour" was necessary to permit "the

50. T. Whitfield, Evidence before West Africa Committee, 18 July 1842, PP, 1842, xi (551), pp. 629–30.
51. J. Duncan, *Travels in Western Africa*, 2 vols. (London, 1847), I, 40.
52. Winniett to Grey, 22 May 1850, CO 96/18.
53. Winniett to Grey, 22 May 1850, CO 96/18.

systematic cultivation of Cotton and other articles of Tropical produce on a large scale." As an alternative to Winniett's project, he
suggested that British capitalists might be allowed to hire slaves from
their masters under government supervision, giving half the wages
to the master and half to the slave.[54]

The plan was never tried, and Earl Grey had long since developed
an indirect form of coercion, which he thought would be preferable.
At the time of the Emancipation Act, Grey, then Lord Howick, had
been Parliamentary Under-Secretary at the Colonial Office. He had
then unsuccessfully advocated a system of stiff direct taxation to force
disciplined labor from the ex-slaves.[55] When he returned as Secretary
of State in 1846, he revived his old idea and made it into a comprehensive system of tropical development. Its theoretical principles
were given in his famous dispatch to Lord Torrington in Ceylon. It
began with the familiar belief that people in temperate regions had
made progress because of the challenge of a difficult climate. There,
necessity was the mother of invention, while in tropical countries
man's physical wants were abundantly supplied by nature. Progress
in the tropics, however, might be encouraged by providing an artificial challenge, and Grey found that challenge in direct taxation. In
fact, opposite fiscal policies were appropriate to the two climatic
zones. In temperate climates, taxation should bear on the poor as
little as possible:

> But the case is very different in tropical climates, where the population is
> very scanty in proportion to the extent of territory; where the soil, as I have
> already observed, readily yields a subsistence in return for very little labour;
> and where clothing, fuel, and lodging, such as are required, are obtained very
> easily. In such circumstances there can be but little motive to exertion, to men
> satisfied with an abundant supply of their mere physical wants; and accord-
> ingly experience proves that it is the disposition of the races of men by which
> these countries are generally inhabited, to sink into an easy and listless mode
> of life, quite incompatible with the attainment of any high degree of civiliza-
> tion.[56]

Taxation in tropical countries should, therefore, bear on the poor,
forcing them to work for wages in order to meet the tax bill. The
revenue would incidentally provide for education, roads, health services, and other essential aids to development.

54. Grey to Winniett, 14 August 1850, CO 402/2.
55. Henry George, third Earl Grey, *The Colonial Policy of Lord John Russell's Administration*, 2 vols. (London, 1853), II, 284.
56. Grey to Torrington, 24 October 1848, printed in George, Earl Grey, *Colonial
Policy*, I, 81–82.

This policy, based on West Indian experience and first suggested for Ceylon, was applied with local variations in Natal, Sierra Leone, and the Gold Coast. For the Gold Coast, Grey suggested a moderate house tax, the proceeds to be used for the support of a local military force, for roads, and for schools of the industrial as well as the intellectual variety. Since the Gold Coast was still only an informal British sphere of influence, any taxation required the consent of the chiefs. A general meeting was held in 1852. The chiefs agreed, and collection actually began late that year; but the plan failed. The tax was an annual poll tax of only one shilling—hardly enough to force anyone to work for wages—and the tax collections immediately began to decline. Nothing at all was received after 1862, and the attempt was abandoned.[57]

For Sierra Leone, Grey proposed a tax on both houses and land, and it was approved with official alacrity. Even before Grey's proposal, some officials had hoped to use direct taxation to encourage the recruitment of labor emigrants to America. Governor Benjamin Pine also shared Earl Grey's belief that shifting cultivation was an evil system, and the tax on both land and houses would force peasants to improve a "limited and fixed spot of ground."[58] Here too there were unforeseen problems. A suitable ordinance was not passed until 1852, and the tax proved so difficult to collect that it was abandoned in 1872.[59]

In either case, Earl Grey was gone from the Colonial Office before the failures were apparent. Regressive taxation nevertheless remained one of the favored devices of British policy in Africa, and the object was that of Earl Grey's proposals—the coercion of labor under conditions where the workers would not respond voluntarily to the wages offered. In West Africa, however, the failure of these first attempts was political rather than economic, and it was so interpreted. The lesson, especially on the Gold Coast, was that Britain could act efficiently only where it was sovereign. It thus led back to the troubled problem of exerting British influence without sovereign control.

57. Grey to Winniett, 20 January 1849, CO 402/2; Grey to Winniett, 18 December 1850, CO 96/19; D. Kimble, *A Political History of Ghana* (London, 1963), pp. 168–79.

58. Grey to Officer Administering Sierra Leone, 24 January 1849, CO 267/43; Benjamin Pine, Annual Report for 1848, 2 November 1849, PP, 1849, xxxvi [C. 1126], p. 298.

59. N. A. Cox-George, *Finance and Development in West Africa. The Sierra Leone Experience* (London, 1961), pp. 65–67.

19

THE THEORY AND PRACTICE

OF

INFORMAL EMPIRE

Political objectives were conspic-
uously missing from the British discussion of African affairs. Not
only was government policy firmly opposed to annexation; few of
the publicists for African activity even stressed the desirability of
empire for the sake of empire. Few suggested that the power to
command was worth having as a primary value, or that British
dominion over Africa might be sought as a sign of British national
glory and greatness. The desired ends of British policy were either
wealth or the civilizing mission, or a combination of both. Only the
means were political.

Yet it was clear that British power had to be exerted, as it was
certainly exerted against the foreign slave-traders at sea and occasionally against recalcitrant African rulers on shore. But the British
rarely discussed their relations with West Africa as relations based
on physical force. At bottom, they most often assumed that African
interests and British interests were congruent. The key to a successful
policy was persuasion, though behind persuasion there always lay the
"moral power," as Macgregor Laird so aptly put it, of the "24-

pounder with British seamen behind it." Potentially, this moral force might have to become physical force, but Laird's statement reflected the genuine sentiment of his generation. Military power was thought to be moral in both senses—it was effective by its presence rather than by its use, and it enforced morality as understood in Britain.

Britain's moral right to intervene in Africa was never doubted, and it was justified in stronger language than ever before. It might be set in the time-honored terms of mutual material advantage—"to benefit Africa and the world," in MacQueen's phrase.[1] It might be set in terms of a right, or even a duty, to develop a "vast, neglected estate."[2] Alternatively, the duty might be that of carrying civilization to the uncivilized, and the material rewards could be seen as the due recompense of those who did their duty.[3] In the view of the Parliamentary Committee on Aborigines in 1837, however, England's material greatness came first, the God-given means for carrying out the work of civilization:

The British Empire has been signally blessed by Providence, and her eminence, her strength, her wealth, her prosperity, her intellectual, her moral and her religious advantages, are so many reasons for peculiar obedience to the laws of Him who guides the destiny of nations. These were given for some higher purpose than commercial prosperity and military renown. . . . 'Can we suppose otherwise than that it is our office to carry civilization and humanity, peace and good government, and, above all the knowledge of the true God, to the uttermost ends of the earth.'[4]

But the call to intervene was limited, especially in the eyes of those who saw Britain's power linked to a moral duty. That duty could also demand a respect for the rights of others. Standish Motte took these rights of non-Western peoples to include:

1. Their rights as an independent nation. That no country or people has a right by force or fraud to assume the sovereignty over any other nation.

2. That such sovereignty can only be justly obtained by fair treaty, and with their consent.

3. That every individual of a nation whether independent or owing

1. J. MacQueen, Memorandum of 12 January 1839, CO 2/22.
2. "Expedition to the Niger," *Edinburgh Review,* LXXII, 457 (January 1841).
3. Report of the Committee on Aborigines, PP, 1837, vii (425), p. 5; J. Harris, *The Great Commission* (London, 1842), p. 238; W. Howitt, *Colonization and Christianity* (London, 1838), pp. 504–5; R. M. Martin, *History of the British Possessions in the Indian and Atlantic Oceans* (London, 1837), p. 338.
4. Report of the Committee on Aborigines, PP, 1837, vii (425) p. 76. See also H. Merivale, *Lectures on Colonisation and Colonies,* 2 vols. (London, 1841–1842), II, 212–13.

allegiance to any other power has a right to personal liberty, and protection of property and life.[5]

Motte's list was more extensive than most commentators would have allowed. The majority recognized rights, but tempered in varying degrees by the "facts" of barbarism or racial inferiority.

A second kind of limitation, and one of greater practical importance, was the fact that Britain simply lacked the means for unlimited intervention simultaneously in all parts of the world. In spite of his humanitarianism, James Stephen opposed the Niger Expedition, as he opposed any extension of Britain's sphere of activity in West Africa. The core of the argument was presented in a famous sentence, addressed to Lord Stanley in 1842 after Stanley had decided to do otherwise.

But to what end to trouble you with a discussion to prove that the value of these African Settlements to our Commerce, or that their utility as preventives of the Slave Trade is enormously exaggerated—that in fact they are nothing else than Factories kept up at the expense of the Nation at large for the profit of half a Dozen inconsiderable Merchants who avail themselves of our national sensibility on every subject in which the Commercial wealth or National importance of Great Britain is concerned—that the Trade of all of them put together is of less value to us, present or perspective, than the Trade with the Isle of Skye—that we are recklessly increasing and dispersing our Colonial Empire in all directions and creating a demand for Naval and Military force which there are no means of meeting, except by weakening the Force where its presence is most needed—that in short neither the Gambia nor the Gold Coast are worth retaining—or that if retained they should be placed exclusively in the hands of Mulattoes or Negroes from the West Indies, and left to maintain themselves like the American Settlement of Liberia?[6]

Stephen's fears were shared by others,[7] but it was still possible to steer a course between the moral demand for intervention and the moral and physical limitations on that demand. That course has been called "informal empire," located in theory somewhere in the twilight zone between influence and sovereignty. To achieve it in practice raised a further series of strategic, legal, and administrative problems.

West Africa enjoyed a very narrow place indeed in the world picture of British strategic interests. Whatever effort the government

5. S. Motte, *Outline of a System of Legislation for Securing the Protection of the Aboriginal Inhabitants of all Countries Colonized by Great Britain* (London, 1840), p. 14.
   6. James Stephen, Memorandum of 26 December 1842, CO 96/2.
   7. Lord Ingestre, Commons, 16 February 1841, 3 H 55, cc. 693–95; Richard Cobden, Commons, 19 July 1850, 3 H 113, c. 42.

made in Africa would have to be limited in economic cost, and hence in geographical focus. The earlier concern about the strategy of entry into the Western Sudan, therefore, continued long after the routes were known and the interior partially explored. Strategic discussion after 1830, however, was different from that of the earlier century. The Niger entry was the undoubted favorite, and the importance of the palm-oil trade of the delta kept a British concentration on the Bights, even when Niger exploration itself was inactive.

Each apparent failure on the Niger, however, opened up at least a tentative suggestion of alternatives. Perhaps the most common re-action was simply to get out and leave West Africa alone with its deadly "climate." Better conditions in South Africa opened dreams of civilization advancing northwards. The highlands of Ethiopia were also more attractive from the point of view of safety, and even Lower Guinea between Mount Cameroons and the Congo had its appeal.[8] But the presumed riches of Africa were still located in the savanna belt of West Africa, and there too was the region of "highest civilization" and greatest potential for further development.

Of the three alternative routes of entry from British-held points on the Guinea coast, Sierra Leone and its neighborhood dropped from sight after 1830. The rivers were only navigable a short distance, and the overland routes were often closed to trade. The Gold Coast possibility was obscured from British view during the merchant's government of the 1830's; though it recovered some of its promise in the mid-1840's, when the Madden scandals died down and more was known of Maclean's judicial protectorate.[9] Meanwhile, the Gambia rose somewhat from its customary neglect. Like the Niger, it was navigable for some distance inland, and its far hinterland was relatively "civilized." Buxton's original plan called for steamships on the Gambia as well as the Niger, and for the establishment of the seat of government at MacCarthy's Island well upstream. The Gambia effort was one of the aspects cut from Buxton's plan by the Government, but Lord Glenelg had intended to follow up the Niger Expedition with one to the Gambia. That particular project died when he left the Colonial Office, but the Parliamentary Committee of 1842

8. *Quarterly Review*, LXXXVIII, 40 (December, 1850); "Ethiopia," *Blackwood's Magazine*, LV, 269–91 (1844); Commander H. J. Matson to Aberdeen, 28 March 1844, PP, 1847–1848, xxii (272), pp. 90–91.

9. T. F. Buxton, *The Remedy: Being a Sequel to the African Slave Trade* (London, 1840), pp. 80–98 and 108; Grey to Winniett, 20 January 1849, CO 402/2.

still thought the Gambia settlements were the most valuable of all British possessions on the Coast.[10]

The Niger nevertheless retained its pre-eminence, and new knowledge about conditions along the river opened new stratgic questions on the Niger itself. One of these was the problem of commercial strategy. There were three possibilities in the Niger trade, to some extent competitive, though not mutually exclusive. The first of these was to maintain and increase the existing flow of trade through the city-states of the Niger Delta, where merchants from towns like Brass and Bonny picked up European goods and went inland to the principal markets in the palm-oil belt, delivering the oil to European merchants at the coastal entrepôts. At any time after 1830, this trade was an established interest, which the African merchants and their British associates were anxious to defend. The Africans might try to defend it by force in the creeks of the delta, and Matthew Forster, M.P., of the firm of Forster and Smith, defended it consistently in the halls of Parliament.

The other two possibilities depended on breaking through the delta monopoly and entering the Niger by steamer. One was to enter into more direct contact with the palm-producing country, which began where the mangroves of the delta left off and extended inland for about a hundred miles. It might be possible to redirect the trade so that palm products flowed to European entrepôts on either side of the Niger, rather than southward through the maze of creeks to the coast. Macgregor Laird recognized this possibility in 1832, and he remained its principal advocate until his death in 1861. The economic advantage in this case was not the technological superiority of the river steamers, but the breach of the African monopoly.

Upstream from the modern city of Onitsha, however, palm production dropped off gradually on account of increasing seasonal aridity. From there to the confluence with the Benue, and beyond, the trade of immediate importance was in ivory, but the ultimate hope was cotton growing for export. To develop this trade would not be merely to shift the profits of existing trade from African to European hands; it would be a genuine economic innovation. It was this third

10. Buxton, *The Remedy*, p. 99; Glenelg, Memorandum of 18 February 1839, CO 2/22; Report of the West Africa Committee, PP, 1842, xi (551), p. vii. See also Captain Belcher, R. N., "Extracts from Observations on Various Points of the West Coast of Africa, Surveyed by His Majesty's Ship Aetna in 1830–32," *Journal of the Royal Geographical Society*, II, 278–304 (1832), p. 296.

possibility that appealed especially to Buxton and served as the basic strategy of the Niger Expedition.[11]

Special problems of political strategy ran parallel to those of commercial planning. The several African economic interests on the Niger were represented in the political goals of African states or groups of states. In the south, the delta states had an obvious interest in preventing steamers on the Niger at any cost, but those further inland might have a different attitude. The key position here was held by Abo, at the apex of the delta. Abo was strategically placed to control the passage of goods up and down the river, and it was also in a position to exert pressure on the non-food-producing delta towns by cutting off their food imports from the north. An alliance with Abo was both natural and essential in any effort to short-circuit the coastal monopoly.

Further north, just below the confluence, Igala was reckoned the most important local power. The Attah of Igala was also in a difficult political position. In addition to internal problems, he was threatened by the power of the Fulani Empire, which reached down through Zaria to the Benue and through Nupe to the Niger. Fulani raiders even appeared from time to time in Igala territory. In this situation, any of the British expeditions stood a good chance of forming an entente with Igala. Friendship with Igala, however, might also alienate the Fulani and cut off the ultimate extension of trade into the wider northern hinterland. If, on the other hand, the British were to advance beyond Igala and establish friendly relations with Nupe, they would leave an unfriendly Igala in their rear to threaten peaceful passage up and down the river, to say nothing of reducing the profits of trade in the Igala markets.[12]

The full complexity of the choice implicit in these facts of political power and interest was not immediately clear, but it emerged during the course of the 1830's and gave rise to an interlocked strategic controversy. An initial choice had to be made between Brass, Bonny, and the other delta states on one hand and the riverine powers between Abo and Igala on the other. This choice was, in fact, made implicitly at the sailing of the Niger Expedition. By the nature of its mission it favored the middle group against the delta traders.

11. This discussion of the Niger strategy is based on K.O. Dike, *Trade and Politics in the Niger Delta, 1830–1885* (London, 1956) and C. C. Ifemesia, "British Enterprise on the Niger, 1830–1869" (Unpublished Ph.D. thesis, London, 1959).

12. Ifemesia, "British Enterprise," esp. pp. 217–68 and 305–41.

Further upstream, however, there remained the choice between Igala and a possible entente with Nupe which would open the whole Fulani Empire to British trade. The earliest strategy for the Niger had been invented before the British even knew about Igala. MacQueen picked the confluence for its physical, not its political position. Buxton, however, was concerned with political goals. On the basis of Clapperton's reports, he chose the two great powers of the interior as the major objectives, hoping to sign treaties with the Fulani Sultan of Sokoto and the Mai of Bornu.[13] But any hope of coming to terms simultaneously with Igala, Bornu, and the Fulani was nearly impossible at the outset.

When the expedition arrived in 1841, they found Ocheji, the Attah of Igala, pleased to offer hospitality to such well armed strangers and perfectly willing to settle them at the confluence—on the marches of his own territory where they were bound to come into conflict with the Fulani. The Commissioners then selected a tract of land on the west bank of the Niger, stretching some sixteen miles downstream and five miles inland from the present town of Lokoja. It is doubtful that the Commissioners realized how thoroughly they were committing themselves to an Igala policy. Even after the treaty with Igala, they hoped to proceed to Nupe and sign another with the Etsu, but the sickness came first and they withdrew from the river.[14] A fully conscious decision to support Igala against the Fulani was therefore postponed; but Commander William Allen emerged with a strong anti-Fulani bias, and his actions suggested a pro-Igala policy.[15]

Meanwhile, the British Fulani policy was discussed in Europe and drew in still broader questions of policy toward Islam in Africa. Gustav d'Eichthal in France gave some detailed advice. Since he believed the Fulani were racially superior, culturally superior, and had in Islam a religion superior to African polytheism, he urged the British to work closely with the Fulani Empire. A show of force might be necessary, in the initial stages, to make the Europeans "feared and respected," but, after that, the British could build their informal empire around the existing power of Sokoto. Such a policy would, of course, force them to abandon Christian proselytization, but, in d'Eichthal's view, Islam was a civilizing religion, and it could be "purified." In

13. Buxton, *The Remedy*, pp. 5–7, 10–15, and 65–67.
14. Ifemesia, "British Enterprise," pp. 317–18.
15. William Allen to Lord Stanley, 9 February 1843, PP, 1843, xlviii [C. 472], p. 136.

any case, accommodation to Islam was preferable to a long religious war. D'Eichthal's general line of argument soon gained a British following.[16] In the early twentieth century, indeed, a variant was put into practice in Northern Nigeria; but there was no immediate possibility, once the Niger Expedition had failed, of moving further in that direction.

The principle of working through an African client state, however, was applicable elsewhere, and it was applied. Maclean's regime on the Gold Coast led to a de facto alliance with the Fante states and other coastal peoples. The missionary concentration on Abeokuta was a less official, religious equivalent, though the government was ultimately involved there as well. In both, the choice of a client state limited other possibilities of action. The Gold Coast "protectorate" made it difficult to remain friendly with Ashanti. British support for Abeokuta cut short the effort to cooperate with Dahomey in schemes for technical assistance. The end result was further commitment—in one case the series of Ashanti wars, and in the other the seizure of Lagos.[17]

The alternative political strategy was to seek a much broader network of alliances, and particularly to seek alliances with the strong states—not merely with those like Abeokuta and the Fante, who were anxious for support. Sir George Stephen advocated a grand design of this kind. He saw the African state system in the hinterland of the Bights as one dominated by six major powers—Abo, Igala, Benin, and the Fulani Empire controlling the Niger basin, while Dahomey and Ashanti dominated the forest zone and southern savanna to the west. If these six would fall into line, the smaller states would automatically come under British influence as well.[18] Diplomatic activity on this scale, however, would have required an over-

16. G. d'Eichthal, "Histoire de origine des Foulahs ou Fellans," *Mémoires de la Société Ethnologique*, I (2), 1–296 (1841), pp. 148–53, 164–65; R. Mouat, "A Narrative of the Niger Expedition," *Simmonds's Colonial Magazine*, II, 138–53, 311–24, 446–65; III, 117–26 (May–October 1844), III, 120; W. B. Baikie, *Narrative of an Exploring Voyage up the Rivers Kwora and Binue (Commonly known as the Niger and Tsadda) in 1854* (London, 1856), p. 393.

17. See J. F. Ade Ajayi, "Christian Missions and the Making of Nigeria, 1841–1891" (Unpublished Ph.D. thesis, London, 1958); S. O. Biobaku, *The Egba and Their Neighbours 1842–1872* (Oxford, 1957); G. E. Metcalfe, *Maclean of the Gold Coast* (London, 1962); C. W. Newbury, *The Western Slave Coast and its Rulers* (Oxford, 1961).

18. Sir George Stephen, *The Niger Trade Considered in Connexion with the African Blockade* (London, 1849), pp. 41–55.

whelming show of British military power. It was inconceivable in the circumstances of the time.

Even the more limited effort to create by treaty an area of British influence raised some serious theoretical and practical problems. Europeans still made international agreements with African states, but the old principle of international equality for all sovereign states, no matter how "barbarous" their culture, began to weaken toward midcentury. British international lawyers kept the principle in the text books until after the 1870's, but British opinion was already beginning to change. The Parliamentary Committee on Aborigines recommend that no treaties should be signed with the aborigines in British colonies, on grounds that genuine agreement was not possible between such unequal parties. The Committee also held that treaties were certain to be misunderstood in societies where formal and written international agreements were not customary.

William Cook, one of the four Commissioners of the Niger Expedition, used a similar argument against the validity of treaties the Commissioners had signed with Abo and Igala. He doubted that the rulers of Abo and Igala had the constitutional right to sign treaties, or the power to enforce them once signed. But Cook and other British officials on the coast recognized that treaties were useful. Even if they had to be enforced by a continuing display of British power, they gave Britain certain rights against other European powers, and they helped to avoid inconvenient legal difficulties in the British courts.[19]

Treaties were, therefore, signed in great numbers, and often in circumstances of doubtful legality. Many of the documents called treaties were really only private contracts. Merchants sometimes signed treaties with African authorities, and these agreements often contained the same provisions found in agreements between sovereign states; but they were neither signed with the Crown's authority nor ratified by the Foreign Office. Oldfield, acting as agent of the African Inland Commercial Company, for example, signed a treaty of commerce and friendship with the Attah of Igala. It may even have contained a clause promising military assistance.[20]

Other treaties lay in a half-light of semi-legality, where they might

19. Report of the Aborigines Committee, PP, 1837, vii (425), p. 80; W. Cook to Lord Stanley, 11 March 1843, PP, 1843, xlviii [C. 472], p. 158; Commander H. J. Matson to Lord Aberdeen, 28 March 1844, PP, 1847–1848, xxii (272), p. 90; MacDonnell to Grey, 16 June 1849, PP, 1849, xxxvi [C. 1126], p. 324.

20. Ifemesia, "British Enterprise," p. 230.

be picked up by the British government for later recognition and enforcement. Each of the three colonial governments at the Gambia, Sierra Leone, and the Gold Coast signed treaties and in effect conducted their own foreign relations. Some of their agreements were reached after consultation with the Foreign Office and were formally ratified. Others were strictly local in character and do not appear on the official lists of British treaties. In the Gambia, for example, the governors of the 1840's maintained regular diplomatic relations with some twenty-five separate African states, and occasional relations with about twenty others. Twenty treaties were considered to be in force in 1849.[21]

A similar web of international relations stretched out from Freetown and Cape Coast—into the hinterland where Britain would one day rule. The principal emphasis at Sierra Leone was the payment of subsidies to African authorities in return for keeping the trade routes open. The agreements on the Gold Coast were more various, ranging from major peace settlements, like the Ashanti Treaty of 1831, to confirmation of small subsidy payments, of which the original purpose had long since been forgotten.[22] The more important development of the judicial protectorate during the 1830's was carried out without benefit of treaties of any kind. It was only in 1844 that the Bonds were signed to confirm in law what existed in fact.

Above and beyond the accretions of local treaties and agreements, anti-slave-trade treaties came into fashion from the time of the Niger Expedition. These were signed on metropolitan initiative, mainly through the diplomatic agency of naval officers from the blockading squadron, and they followed a number of set forms prepared in London.

This system of treaties originated partly from the precedent of ancient custom on the Guinea coast, and partly from Buxton's elaborate plan for a great confederacy of chiefs covering all of West Africa south of the desert. The essence of Buxton's plan, in its political aspect, was, indeed, an especially extensive informal empire. The cement for the whole edifice was to be a series of bilateral treaties between Great Britain and the African rulers. Buxton assumed that treaties could be signed without the use of forceful persuasion—partly in return for a small financial consideration, partly because

21. MacDonnell to Grey, 10 June 1849, PP, xxxvi [C. 1126], p. 324.
22. Minutes of the Gold Coast Council, 10 August 1835, copy in AG, Acc. 68/1954.

the Africans would recognize "their own forlorn and disastrous condition" and wish to improve it, and partly because they would distinguish between the good, anti-slave-trade British and the other Europeans. Only the debased slave-trading chiefs near the coast were expected to be uncooperative. In spite of his confidence that Africans would willingly sign, Buxton had no intention of offering them an agreement between equal partners, with an equivalence of consideration. His treaties were conceived as bonds between superiors and inferiors who recognized themselves as such.[23]

The Niger Expedition sailed with instructions incorporating Buxton's optimism about African subservience, but James MacQueen had already submitted a long memorandum to the Colonial Office, suggesting a more hard-headed appeal to self-interest. His model was the treaty with China which gave Britain special rights in Canton. The African ruler would be asked to abolish the slave trade, to grant British subjects free access to his territory, freedom for economic transactions, the right to purchase land, and a promise of security for their property. The ruler would also have to limit customs duties chargeable on imports from Britain, and British subjects would enjoy extra-territorial jurisdiction under British law. Taken together, these concessions amounted to a real infringement of African sovereignty, and MacQueen was realist enough to understand that they would not be granted merely out of deference to a white skin. He therefore proposed a substantial *quid pro quo*, consisting first of all of a defensive alliance (or even an offensive and defensive alliance). In addition, the Africans would receive most-favored-nation treatment for their exports to Britain and an annual subsidy equivalent to their profits from the slave trade. MacQueen expected this subsidy to run at the handsome figure of about £100,000 a year for West Africa as a whole.[24]

The treaty forms actually sent out with the Niger Expedition contained half of MacQueen's suggestions—the half that granted privileges to Britain—and two additional concessions were demanded. The African signatories were asked to promise toleration for the preaching of Christianity and to allow Britain to place a resident agent in their countries. The financial consideration was reduced from a real subsidy to a gift—the customary small change of African diplomacy,

23. Buxton, *The Remedy*, pp. 5–7, 17.
24. James MacQueen, Memorandum of 12 January 1839, CO 2/22.

worth about £50 for Abo and £100 for Igala. These two states signed, but they signed in the presence of the armed ships, and ceased to honor the treaties as soon as the ships withdrew.[25]

At the withdrawal of 1842, the treaty net of informal empire in the interior was given up, but the treaty policy was continued on the coast. The form of the coastal treaties, however, was much less rigorous than that offered on the Niger. Six were signed in 1841: none of them set a limit on import duties. Only one granted extra-territorial jurisdiction. The coastal treaties of the later 1840's fell into this milder pattern. The crucial clause was the promise to give up the slave trade, usually buttressed with promises to notify the British cruisers on the arrival of a slaver and permission for the British armed forces to land in suppression of the slave trade. Commercial provisions were limited to most-favored-nation treatment for British goods.[26]

Forty-two anti-slave-trade treaties of this kind were in effect by 1850, but their only real consequence was to legalize the actions of the cruisers. None of the major African powers were represented— no Dahomey, no Ashanti, no Benin. The result was thus a far cry from Buxton's dream of informal dominion, but it probably represents approximately the limit of the "moral force" of the squadron. Further concessions required either real subsidies or the application of physical force.

Toward the end of the 1840's, both methods were attempted. Brodie Cruickshank, was sent to Dahomey in 1848 with authorization to offer $2,000 a year in return for an anti-slave-trade treaty. He decided not to press the offer when he found out that the slave-trade revenues of the Dahomean state were in the neighborhood of $300,000 a year.[27] More forceful and less expensive diplomacy was possible nearer to the coast and the naval squadron. After 1849, John Beecroft, as Her Majesty's Consul for the Bights of Benin and Biafra, was able to intervene more extensively in the affairs of the Niger delta city-states.

The naval attack on Lagos in 1851 was followed by a stiffer kind

25. Lord John Russell to Niger Commissioners, 30 January 1841, and H. D. Trotter to G. W. Hope, 1 April 1842, PP, 1843, xlviii [C. 472], pp. 5 ff. and 57–58.

26. Admiralty, "Instructions to Senior Officers of the African Station" (1844), PP, 1844, 1 [C. 577]; PP, 1849, xxviii (32), appendix pp. 43–62; PP, 1852–1853, xxxix (920), p. 214.

27. B. Cruickshank, Report of 9 November 1848, PP, 1849 (Lords), xxviii (32), appendix, pp. 183, 186.

of treaty than that of recent years. The Lagos treaty of 1852 contained the usual articles for the suppression of the slave trade, but it also provided for the abolition of human sacrifice and the protection of both missionaries and Christian converts. A separate commercial engagement limited Lagosian import duties to 2 per cent and export duties to 3 per cent ad valorem, and it established a mixed court of African and European merchants to settle commercial disputes.[28]

Informal control short of genuine territorial empire might be sought in other ways as well. One of the favorite suggestions of past decades had been to extend the existing pattern of trading-post enclaves into the interior. MacQueen, the Buxton plan, and the Niger Expedition all combined trading posts with the treaty policy, but in some projects the trading-post empire stood alone. A Gloucestershire gentleman named Paul Read sent a plan of this kind to the Colonial Office in 1832. He was even less well informed than most of the other projectors and conceived of West Africa as a stateless area, where political institutions could only be created by the establishment of British centers of "steady and permanent power" on islands or on the banks of the Niger and its tributaries. Each post was to have an armed steamer to police the river, a garrison to protect the fort, and a complement of British convicts to grow food for the garrison.[29]

The trading-post enclave also played a role in the later projects of Thomas Kehoe, Macgregor Laird, Sir George Stephen, and Edward Nicholls. These different plans visualized the trading post in varying terms. It might or might not be colonized by British settlers. It might or might not imply the extension of British sovereignty over the surrounding country. In spite of the health problem, the idea of limited settlement was still brought forward. Read would have confined the sacrifice to convicts, but Governor Rendall of the Gambia, F. Harrison Rankin, and Governor Winniett of the Gold Coast all believed that a managerial force of capitalist colonists would be necessary.[30]

28. Treaty of 1 January 1852, engagement of 28 February 1852, PP, 1862, lxi [C. 2982], pp. 1–4. For the change to a policy of intervention see Dike, *Trade and Politics*, pp. 128–52; Newbury, *The Western Slave Coast*, pp. 49–76.

29. Both the original plan of 1832 and a later version of 1840 are found in CO 2/22. The second version was published as P. Read, *Lord John Russell, Sir Thomas Fowell Buxton, and the Niger Expedition* (London, 1840).

30. J. Rendall to Glenelg, 3 January 1839, CO 2/22; F. H. Rankin, *The White Man's Grave: A Visit to Sierra Leone in 1834*, 2 vols. (London, 1836), II, 24–29; Winniet to Grey, 22 May 1850, CO 96/18.

At an early stage in the formation of his project, Sir George Stephen could still picture really large scale white settlement: "If we found settlements in Africa, colonization must follow; wherever the British flag is raised, thousands, and tens of thousands will seek protection under it; it is sheer hypocrisy to pretend that this is not the consequence of our civilization plans, if fairly carried out. . . ."[31]

Nothing of the kind was at all likely; but the speculation remained alive, and Dickens' caricature of the Niger Expedition changed the trading post at the confluence into "Boriaboola-Ga," a colony for white settlers.[32]

By whatever devices informal empire was to be furthered, it posed special problems of administration. A variety of administrative forms had been tried in the past, from the full monopoly for trade and the power to govern, granted to the Royal Africa Company in the seventeenth century, through the device of a regulatory company such as the Company of Merchants Trading to Africa, down to the system of Crown Colony government tried experimentally in Senegambia before 1783, in Sierra Leone after 1808, and in the other posts after 1821. But Crown Colony government was designed to rule sovereign British territory, not to exercise influence beyond it. The Foreign Office was the usual institution for dealing with British interests beyond the sphere of British sovereignty, but it was equipped to negotiate and report, not to exercise continuous informal influence. No existing British institution quite met the need, and it was partly for this reason that British influence on the Coast was exercised through so many channels in the 1830's—the merchants' government on the Gold Coast from 1828 to 1843, royal colonies at Sierra Leone and Gambia, naval officers as de facto diplomats in a variety of different circumstances. The shifts and turns of administrative organization may be explained in large part as an effort to solve the problem of informal empire.

Various publicists pushed for their own favorite forms of government or influence. The merchants of the coastal school would have preferred a broad expansion of merchants' control on the Gold Coast model,[33] but the Gold Coast itself was returned to royal control

---

31. G. Stephen, *Letters to the Right Honourable Lord John Russell, on the Plans of the Society for the Civilization of Africa* (London, 1840), first letter, p. 28.

32. C. Dickens, *Bleak House* (London, 1853), Ch. IV.

33. Martin, *History of British Possessions*, p. 337; Stanley to Hill, 30 December 1844, CO 402/2; Petition of "Native Merchants" of the Gold Coast, 14 August 1850, CO 96/19.

on the grounds that merchants' government was too informal. James MacQueen had begun with the ideal of a single great Chartered Company, and he kept up his pressure for this form even after the Niger Expedition.[34]

Some planners drew up complex administrative projects, designed specifically to meet the problems of informal empire. One such plan was the work of Governor Rendall of the Gambia, who proposed to unify all British government agencies on the African coast under a single command located in the Banana Islands. The supreme government would then have control over four lieutenant-governors in Bathurst, Freetown, Cape Coast, and Fernando Po as well as the naval forces of the anti-slavery blockade.[35]

An even more elaborate plan was submitted to the Parliamentary Committee of 1842 by Edward Nicholls. He proposed that full powers over British African affairs from the Sahara to the Namib Desert should be given to a Governor based on St. Helena. The whole coast could then be divided into five superintendencies, with a sixth on Ascension to administer a normal school and health station. Each superintendent would have authority to acquire sovereignty over any territory or persons that might freely offer themselves. The problem of governing widely separate colonies and spheres of influence would be met by keeping either the Governor or Lieutenant-Governor constantly on the move by steamship. Nicholls estimated that a round trip to all the superintendencies would take about 81 days. The two chief officials could thus make about four circuits each in the course of a year.[36]

The mere fact that Nicholl's own estimates put the cost of his plan at £400,000 a year was enough to keep it from serious consideration. Instead, the government drifted along with the older forms, even though they were not quite appropriate. The three Crown Colonies that emerged as independent entities in 1843 continued as such, and the Foreign Office took over the informal sphere in the Bights with the establishment of the Consulate in 1849.

The internal government of the Crown Colonies posed another kind of political problem, and one with less immediate, but more

34. MacQueen, Memorandum of 12 January 1839, CO 2/22; MacQueen to Aberdeen, 6 September 1844, FO 84/555.

35. J. Rendall to Lord Glenelg, 3 January 1839, CO 2/22.

36. E. Nicholls, Memorandum of 20 July 1842, enclosed in Nicholls to Canning, 28 June 1845, FO 84/616.

long-range importance. As rulers of alien societies, however small, the British believed they had certain obligations. These were not necessarily the political obligations they felt toward the colonies populated by English settlers, who were entitled to English law and to English representative self-government at the local level. In Sierra Leone, the principal obligation was already conceived as a trusteeship over the welfare of the liberated Africans. Elsewhere the obligations were barely defined, but the ultimate question was already present— what political and legal institutions are appropriate to an African society?

Various answers were implied by some of the new ideas about race and culture, trusteeship and conversion, but the dominant position in government circles, however vaguely stated, remained the expectation that somehow and sometime Sierra Leone would become a "free African colony," as Sir George Murray had promised in 1830. The idea that African settlements should move toward independence under British influence came from other directions as well. A British African Colonization Society was formed in 1833 to establish a settlement for colored British subjects, similar to Liberia. It had patronage of the Duke of Sussex and the active support of Thomas Hodgkin, but it failed in its own aims and ultimately merged with its American counterpart.[37]

The idea of exerting British political authority in Africa through the agency of Westernized Africans, however, recurred in many different contexts. It was, indeed, the ultimate political implication of the idea of conversion. As T. Perronet Thompson told the House of Commons in 1850, "for a European nation desiring to exert itself in Africa . . . there is an instrument ready made, God's tropical man." The ultimate goal for Thompson was a multi-racial British Empire, based on the "English principle" of uniting "all races and bloods under the name of Englishmen."[38] More specific projects for an all-black colony followed the failure of the Niger Expedition, and Sir George Stephen's scheme for government-controlled trade assumed that all posts, including the highest, would be filled by Africans.[39]

37. *African Colonizer,* 20 February 1851, p. 151.
38. T. P. Thompson, Commons, 19 July 1850, 3 H 113, c. 53.
39. Allen and Thompson, *Narrative of the Expedition,* II, 435; W. Allen, Evidence before the Hutt Committee, 28 March 1848, PP, 1847–48, xxii (272), pp. 71–73; Stephen, *The Niger Trade,* p. 58.

In spite of the ordinary xenophobic tension on the Coast, the government recognized officially only one kind of racial difference—that of immunity to disease. At the Colonial Office, both James Stephen and Herman Merivale, who succeeded him as Permanent Under-Secretary from 1847 to 1859, held the line against overt racial discrimination.[40] Merivale, indeed, believed in both racial equality and racial mixture: "Diversity of races is an evil only when the law has recognized a difference in privileges; where the white is taught from infancy to regard himself as superior to the negro or the Indian, the Englishman to the Irishman, the British colonists to the Canadian *habitant.* Let all be placed on a footing of equality—let intermixture be encouraged, instead of reprobated—and all prejudice will cease to exist."[41]

The practice of the 1830's and 1840's was generally that of appointing Africans to the government service, with some local variation according to the recent death rate of Europeans and the racial opinions of the governors. Governor Alexander Findlay, for example, kept the settlers out of all important posts in Sierra Leone between 1830 and 1833. Between 1836 and 1839, however, an important group of Afro-West Indians were given key positions when the yellow fever epidemic began to kill even the older European residents.[42]

With the 1850's a shift in attitude took place all along the coast. The declining European mortality brought stiffer competition for the better government posts. Theoretical racism of British origin began to be imported to Africa with a new generation of officials. Resentment against the "educated Africans" increased markedly, and even the normally liberal Herman Merivale was to stigmatize them in a biting minute as "half-caste and half-educated."[43] Merivale's attitude was not so much racial as cultural prejudice, but cultural prejudice alone could raise doubts about the wisdom or possibility of European-style political development for Africa.

These doubts were symptomatic of a shift from ideas of conversion

40. See, for example, J. Stephen, Minute of 27 July 1848 on Doherty to Glenelg, 10 December 1837, CO 267/141. In 1851, Earl Grey stopped Governor Macdonald of Sierra Leone from instituting racial segregation in the colonial hospital. (Grey, Minute on Macdonald to Grey, 10 September 1841; Grey to Macdonald, 20 November 1851, CO 267/22.)

41. Merivale, *Colonisation and Colonies,* II, 315–16.

42. C. Fyfe, *A History of Sierra Leone* (London, 1962), pp. 188–189, 211.

43. H. Merivale, Minute of 29 February 1855, CO 96/31.

to ideas of trusteeship. The change was rarely explicit, but it was clearly present when the British turned their attention to legal and political institutions. British Gambia and Sierra Leone had begun with English law, but without British forms of representative government. By the 1830's, some authorities began to doubt that English law was appropriate in all cases.

One suggestion was to preserve the forms of English law, but to set non-Europeans in a special position under that law. Even in the fully conversionist era, the fate of the aborigines in the settlement colonies suggested that they needed special protection. The status of legal minority seemed appropriate. Herman Merivale thought it should be imposed on the aborigines of Canada and Australia. In place of full freedom of contract, for example, they would receive special protection (and special disabilities) appropriate to their minority.[44]

Merivale's idea thus approached concepts of trusteeship, but with some differences. His long-run intention was to suppress native law by allowing freedom of appeal to English law, and the status of minority was a temporary measure, to be enforced only until such time as the aborigines were fully conversant with English legal norms and able to protect themselves. The full-blown doctrine of trusteeship that was to emerge later in the century laid much less stress on the shift to English norms, and the period of minority was seen to stretch off into the indefinite future.

Another solution to the problem of legal conversion worked somewhat differently. Rather than shifting immediately to English law, the non-Europeans were to be left with their own law; and that law itself was to be changed gradually until it fell into line with Western legal norms. Standish Motte's study of the problem concluded that each different society required its own appropriate legislation, based on its own peculiarities.[45] Commander Allen of the Niger Expedition hoped to begin with African law in any colony he might plant on the Niger, letting legal reforms come through the spread of British influence.[46]

George Maclean had already done something similar on the Gold

44. Merivale, *Colonisation and Colonies*, II, 161–69.
45. Motte, *System of Legislation*, pp. 11–12.
46. W. Allen and T. R. H. Thomson, *A Narrative of the Expedition*, II, 424–25.

Coast. His area of jurisdiction outside the British forts was informal, by the consent of the Africans themselves, and the law he enforced was African law with certain amendments.[47] Maclean produced no theoretical defense of his methods, but Matthew Forster, the Africa merchant and Member of Parliament produced one for him before the Committee of 1842:

> Experience has shown us that political reforms, even in civilized states, should always be based upon their original institutions, and that the new should retain as many features as possible of the old customs and principles. Our own constitution contains abundant evidence of the rudeness of our original institutions in the semi-barbarous forms and maxims it preserves. On the coast of Africa, then, we should bend the state of society we find into better forms, not plant foreign institutions, as unfit to resist the climate as the officers who are to manage them. Let us modify the native customs so as to render the natives themselves not incapable hereafter of administering them in their amended state. The success of our administration on the Gold Coast may fairly be ascribed to this, that the officers in command at the different forts had the wisdom to take the native laws and customs as their rules, extracting from them, and bringing forward, that basis of justice which will always be found in the laws of the most debased tribes, and throwing into the background the cruelties and absurdities which, in a negro, as in an European code of laws, are corruptions only. In such judicious administration and combination of their own, with more enlightened principles, you will have the sympathy and assistance of the natives.[48]

Forster's argument was clearly based on a Burkean conservatism, with the belief that effective conversion must be gradual, but it was still conversionist. Here as with Merivale, however, a further shift to the late-century doctrine of trusteeship was easy. In the hands of racists, the complete transition was not expected to take place: the Africans would continue with a partially Westernized law, appropriate to their partial ability to become "civilized." Or, in still another version, the goal could be changed from Westernization to development under Western trusteeship, but development "along their own lines" and not toward "civilization," as the West understood it.

However the legal transition was to take place, it raised certain practical problems so long as British influence was only informal; and some of these problems could be very disturbing to a trained lawyer

---

47. See Metcalfe, *Maclean,* pp. 145–78.
48. M. Forster, Evidence before the West Africa Committee, 27 July 1842, PP, 1842, xi (551), p. 713.

like James Stephen at the Colonial Office. It was normal for a British official to enforce British law in British territory, and even outside British territory in special cases authorized by the legislature. But for a British official to decide questions according to alien law in alien territory seemed to stretch a point beyond the legitimate authority of the British Crown.[49] The issue was met for Maclean's jurisdiction by removing it altogether from the British sphere. Judicial Assessors after 1844 were Crown officials, but the authority they exercised outside the forts was not derived from the British Crown. It was held to depend solely on the consent of the "Sovereign Power of the state within which it is exercised.[50] Thus, while the goal was still conversion to Western culture, it was to be achieved by changing African culture slowly, under African authority, and not by substituting British authority and British institutions.

Meanwhile, a similar discussion was taking place on the theory and practice of representative government. Perronet Thompson and the *Westminster Review* had already raised the issue for Sierra Leone before 1830, and they kept up the demand, calling for a constitutional transition toward self government.[51] Colonial self government was no longer a contradiction in terms. The Canadians were moving toward an executive responsible to the local legislature for all local affairs. A similar transition might be possible for Sierra Leone, especially if the electoral franchise were limited to Africans of wealth or education. The demand was occasionally made; but the government could always plead the necessity of special controls to guard their special responsibility for the early training of the liberated Africans, and no significant changes were made.

The situation on the Gold Coast was different, but there the problem was to extend British influence into an informal sphere, rather than over sovereign territory. Various possibilities were considered after Earl Grey's accession to the Colonial Office. The Gold Coast was given a Legislative Council in 1850, but it was wholly appointed by the Governor and had jurisdiction only over the forts themselves. Grey was concerned to expand the informal British sphere in order to

49. J. Stephen, Memorandum of 26 December 1842, CO 96/2. See Metcalfe, *Maclean*, pp. 288–93.
50. Stanley to Hill, 22 November 1844, CO 402/2.
51. *Westminster Review*, XVI, 246 (1832). See also G. Stephen, *Letters to Russell*, first letter, pp. 24–28.

establish direct taxation within the judicial protectorate. To collect the tax required the consent, and hence the representation of the chiefs. As with the judicial sphere, there was a choice between British and African political institutions. Grey chose the African, hoping "to preserve whatever is capable of being rendered useful in the existing customs and institutions of the people." He suggested that the chiefs be formed into a Council of Chiefs, initially to authorize the direct tax but in time to meet more frequently and ultimately to become "responsible Public Officers."[52] This was an important departure from the earlier idea of ruling through the chiefs: the chiefs were to be formed into a new political unit, amalgamating the small, pre-existing units.

The idea was taken up on the Gold Coast by Brodie Cruickshank and James Bannerman, an African merchant who was also a government official. Together they drafted a memorandum of their own proposals for a Gold Coast constitution. For the forts themselves, they asked for a representative element in the Legislative Council to express the opinions of the merchant community. As for the protectorate, they wanted the Council of Chiefs made into a regular Assembly of Native Chiefs, empowered to pass laws subject to the confirmation of the Governor. Bannerman and Cruickshank also wanted the chiefs brought into the administration, with regular salary from the government, serving under a code of administrative regulations. Their justification stressed the necessity of communication between the people and the government, so that government could respond to the needs of a changing society.[53]

The Cruickshank-Bannerman proposals were a high-water mark of projected representative institutions. Grey gave only limited approval, and in a way that would have reduced chiefly functions from legislative responsibility to mere administrative work for the Cape Coast government.[54] By 1851, Bannerman and Cruickshank had themselves changed their minds and decided that representation was premature. S. J. Hill, the new Governor, disapproved, and Grey accepted this opinion.[55]

52. Grey to Winniett, 6 August 1849, CO 96/19; Grey to Winniett, 14 August 1850, CO 402/2.

53. B. Cruickshank and J. Bannerman to Winniett, 22 August 1850, CO 96/19.

54. Grey to Winniett, 18 December 1850, CO 96/19.

55. Hill to Grey (Confidential) 27 October 1851, CO 96/23. Minutes of the Gold Coast Legislative Council, 1 April 1851, copy in AG, ADM 14/1.

Incipient efforts to foster political development therefore came to an end. Grey's successors were no longer interested in the kind of informal political extension represented by the Bannerman-Cruickshank proposals. Similar efforts to join African and British political institutions, however, were to emerge during the 1860's and 1870's in both the Egba state of Abeokuta and a revived effort to unite the Fante chiefs. In both cases the initiative came from Westernized Africans rather than the metropolitan, or even the colonial, government. The Gold Coast constitutional discussions of the early 1850's were nevertheless something more than a futile exchange of correspondence. They were an attempt to grapple with the problem of Westernizing or modernizing African polities, so as to help meet the West on something like equal terms. In this sense, they were in line with the era of humanitarianism, with its insistence on cultural conversion and a limitation to informal empire.

These political trends and political suggestions were among the most fragile parts of the early-nineteenth-century image of Africa, since they were to be cut off during the 1880's and 1890's by the formation of territorial empires throughout West Africa. Nevertheless, they did not simply disappear: some aspects were taken up later on in connection with administrative devices like indirect rule. Echoes from still others were to reappear during the 1940's and 1950's, when Britain was again concerned with "political development" in West Africa. Indeed, the British theory of African empire, as it first emerged in the era of humanitarianism, showed a remarkable tenacity in the face of new conditions. As Africa entered the colonial period, the image of Africa was to be modified and developed in many new directions; but it set the base lines and became the point of departure for the British colonial regime.

POSTSCRIPT

Perhaps the most striking aspect of the British image of Africa in the early nineteenth century was its variance from the African reality, as we now understand it. There was also a marked lack of the kind of "progress" one might expect to find in a body of ideas that was constantly enlarged by accretions of new data. This is especially hard to explain, given the fact that nineteenth-century social scientists were trying to be methodical, working to a standard that was conceived as rational investigation.

One source of error has already been suggested: reporters went to Africa knowing the reports of their predecessors and the theoretical conclusions already drawn from them. They were therefore sensitive to data that seemed to confirm their European preconceptions, and they were insensitive to contradictory data. Their reports were thus passed through a double set of positive and negative filters, and filtered once more as they were assimilated in Britain. Data that did not fit the existing image were most often simply ignored. As a result, British thought about Africa responded very weakly to new data of any kind.

It responded much more strongly to changes in British thought. The travellers (and, even more, the analysts at home) took the European *weltanschauung* as their point of departure. They did not ask, "What is Africa like, and what manner of men live there" but, "How does Africa, and how do the Africans, fit into what we already know about the world?" In this sense, the image of Africa was far more European than African.

479

In considering the nature of racial differences, for example, the scientists studied African races in order to answer questions posed for them by the existing state of biological theory and knowledge. Some African data were of immense importance, especially the data about differential mortality between blacks and whites on the African coast, but these data were selected because they seemed to answer problems set in their European context. In much the same way, the interdependence of race and culture was assumed because that assumption helped explain something in which the Europeans were very interested—their own leadership in the world of the nineteenth century. It was not built up by careful examination of data from Africa, or any other part of the world overseas.

At a more personal level, many affirmations about Africa were made for political, religious, or personal reasons. Prichard's belief in monogenesis came, first of all, from his desire to prove that science was congruent with Scripture. Nott and Gliddon's polygenesis came from their desire to prove that Negro slavery was licit. It is hard to avoid the conclusion that some of the wilder ravings of Knox's "transcendental anatomy" came from a blighted career, not merely from the currents of evolutionary thought.

In this way, the British image of Africa was intimately related to other strands of Western thought and life, and all the particular facets of that image were more closely related to one another than can be briefly stated. All these bodies of thought—about medicine, race, history, or political and economic development—were equally integrated with the world of events, both as cause and effect. They helped to form the plans for Sierra Leone or the Niger Expedition. They responded, in turn, to the lessons of experience, though these lessons were filtered in the same manner as other data.

The image of Africa, in short, was largely created in Europe to suit European needs—sometimes material needs, more often intellectual needs. When these needs allowed, it might touch on reality; as it did in the empirical victory of tropical medicine. Otherwise the European *Afrikaanschauung* was part of a European *weltanschauung*, and it was warped as necessary to make it fit into the larger whole. To say this, however, implies neither a moral nor an intellectual judgment of the nineteenth-century Europeans. They sought knowledge for their guidance, and the very magnitude of the effort remains as a kind of monument. Their errors, nevertheless, did as much to mold the course of history as their discoveries.

REFERENCE

MATTER

MORTALITY IN WEST AFRICA

$\mathbf{M}$ortality statistics for West Africa are, at best, approximate. The groups for which they are available were generally speaking too small to have statistical validity. Very few calculations differentiate between the new arrivals and the old residents—an important distinction since old residents would be expected to have acquired a degree of immunity.

The initial attempts at colonization	*Death Rate*
Province of Freedom (within the first year)[1]	
European settlers	46%
Negro settlers	39%
Bulama (April 1792 to April 1793)[2]	
Europeans	61%
Sierra Leone Company (first year, 1792–1793)[3]	
Europeans as a whole	49%

1. Includes mortality on the outward voyage from England. R. R. Kuczynski, *Demographic Survey of the British Colonial Empire, Volume I: West Africa* (London, 1948), 43–45.

2. Philip Beaver, *African Memoranda* (London, 1805), p. 89; A. Johansen, *Description of Bulama Island* (London, 1794), p. 8. Figures include both the outward voyage from England and the homeward voyage of those who left Bulama before the end of the first year.

3. Sierra Leone Company, *Account of the Colony of Sierra Leone From Its First Establishment in* [*sic*] *1793* . . . (London, 1795), pp. 47–49.

Upper servants	17%
Lower servants	49%
European settlers	72%
European soldiers	69%
Nova Scotian Negro settlers at least	17%

Sierra Leone Company (second year 1793–1794)
Remaining Europeans   10%

European personnel on exploring expeditions, 1805–1830[4]

Park's Second Expedition (May–November 1805)
Mortality on overland trip from Gambia to the Niger   87%
Ultimate mortality   100%

Tuckey's Expedition to the Congo   37%

Clapperton—Lander penetration from Badagri to the Niger   83%

Coastal posts in the early nineteenth century

Colonial Office estimate of deaths per year among "the better class of society" (*c.* 1825)[5]
Gold Coast   12.5 %
Sierra Leone   8.3 %

Church Missionary Society, total European personnel (1804–1825)[6]
89 sent out; 54 died   60.5 %

Officials of the Company of Merchants Trading to Africa (1812–1823)[7]
95 officials sent out; 44 died of disease   46.0 %

Gold Coast Government Officials (1822–1825)
111 officials (including military officers) sent out; 55 died of disease   45.0 %

European personnel arriving in Sierra Leone over the five years 1821–1826[8]
Civilians: 44 sent out; 20 died   44.5 %
Military and Civilians together: 1,612 sent out; 926 died   56.5 %

4. See M. Laird to Clarendon, 5 March 1855, printed in S. Crowther, *Journal of an Expedition up the Niger and Tshada in 1854* (London, 1855), pp. viii–x.
5. Unsigned memorandum, 2 July 1825, CO 267/65. These estimates probably reflect the death rate of "acclimatized" Europeans with reasonable accuracy.
6. William Fox, *A Brief History of the Wesleyan Missions on the Western Coast of Africa* (London, 1851), p. 617.
7. Kuczynski, *Demographic Survey*, I, 532.
8. PP, 1826–1827, xv (7), p. 209.

Total European troops sent out to all West Africa (1810–1825)[9]
    5,823 sent out; 1,912 died   33.0 %

African troops stationed in West Africa (total for 1810–1825)[10]
    Of 6,769, 254 died   3.75%

Major Tulloch's Investigation of Military Mortality[11]
    European other ranks, annual average mortality from disease only
        Sierra Leone Command, strength 1,843 men (1819–1836)   48.3 %
        West Indian Command, strength 4,333 men (1817–1836)   7.9 %
        Troops stationed in Britain (1819–1836)   1.5 %
    European officers, annual average mortality from disease only
        Sierra Leone Command (1819–1836)   20.9 %
    African troops, annual average mortality from "fevers" (1819–1836)
        Sierra Leone Command   .24%
        Windward and Leeward Command (West Indies)   .46%
        Jamaica   .82%
        British Honduras   .44%
        Bahamas   .56%

Exploring expeditions and small groups of newcomers, 1830–1850

Laird's Niger Expedition (1832–1833): 49 Europeans, of whom 40 died[12]   83%

Quorra Expedition to the Niger (1835): 6 Europeans; 1 died[13]   16%

---

9. Report of Commissioners Wellington and Rowan, PP, 1826–1827, vii (312), pp. 106–8. As the commissioners themselves noted, these reflect both the mortality of newcomers, which ran at about 50 per cent per annum, and that of older residents, which was much lower.

10. PP, 1826–1827, vii (312), pp. 106–8.

11. PP, 1837–1838, xl (138), pp. 5–7; PP, 1840, xxx [C. 228], pp. 16–17 and 24. Major Tulloch's survey may be considered the most careful and reliable of those conducted during the first half of the nineteenth century.

12. M. Laird and R. A. K. Oldfield, *Narrative of an Expedition into the Interior of Africa by the River Niger in 1832–4,* 2 vols. (London, 1837), II, 410–11.

13. C. C. Ifemesia, "British Enterprise on the Niger, 1830–1869" (Unpublished Ph.D. thesis, London, 1959), p. 165. The Europeans in this case were apparently recruited in Africa and hence "acclimatized."

Government Niger Expedition (1841–1842): 159 Europeans;
55 died[14]   35%

Wesleyan Missionary Society, new European personnel sent
out to Sierra Leone (1838–1850): 21 sent out; 7 died   33%

Wesleyan Missionary Society, new European personnel sent
out to all of West Africa (1838–1850); 67 sent out; 25 died.[15] 37%

Mortality of the anti-slavery blockade

Annual average mortality (1825–1845)[16]

From all causes	6.49%
From disease	5.44%
From "epidemic fevers"	3.00%

Comparative mortality from disease at other naval stations
(1825–1845)[17]

South American Stations	.77%
Mediterranean Station	.93%
Home Station	.98%
East Indian Station	1.51%
West Indian Station	1.81%

Mortality of officers and men of the blockade, percentage of
total mean strength[18]

1840	4.1 %
1841	7.9 %
1842	5.5 %
1843	2.1 %
1844	2.8 %
1845	5.0 %
1846	3.3 %
1847	2.5 %
1848	2.2 %

Annual average, 1840–1842   5.8 %

Annual average, 1846–1848   2.7 %

14. PP, 1843, xxxi (83), p. 1.
15. Fox, *Brief History*, p. 617. These figures for the period of improving mortality make an interesting contrast with the CMS mortality of 1804–1825 (above).
16. A. Bryson, *Report on the Climate and Principal Diseases of the African Station* (London, 1847), pp. 177–78. These figures differ slightly from some other published figures on blockade mortality, since Bryson constructed them from the pay books rather than the medical reports. The category "epidemic fevers" is therefore not a clinical description but a measure of the number of simultaneous deaths on a single ship.
17. Bryson, *Principal Diseases*, pp. 177–78.
18. PP, 1850 (Lords), xxiv (35), appendix, p. 221.

Annual average mortality of the West African squadron,
1858–1867[19]   2.2 %

Mortality of fever victims

Gallinas Raid (1840): 130 men, 7 days up river; 23 fever cases
3 deaths[20]

Niger Expedition (1841): European personnel only[21]
  Albert: 64 days up river, 62 men; 55 fever cases, 23 deaths.
  Wilberforce: 45 days up river, 56 men; 48 fever cases, 7 deaths.
  Soudan: 40 days up river, 27 men; 27 fever cases, 10 deaths.

19. PP, 1867–1868, lxiv (158), p. 7.
20. R. R. Madden, Commissioner's Report, PP, 1842, xii (551), p. 226.
21. J. O. M'William, *Medical History of the Expedition to the Niger During the Years 1841–42* . . . (London, 1843), p. 126.

The sources for a work of this kind have no clear limits. Ideally, it should be based on a careful reading of every work concerned in any way with West Africa, on all the periodical literature, the newspapers—all the archives of the missionary societies, the merchant houses, and the governments. Perfection would demand a similar knowledge of the German, French, and American works on Africa, but the demands of perfection meet practical limitations. I have followed leads into the European and American literature, when works from abroad seemed to have a peculiar importance for the development of British thought. Printed books and articles published in Britain have been covered more thoroughly, and Chapters 1, 8, and 13 are in part bibliographical essays.

Among the non-specialist journals, special attention has been paid to the *Anti-Jacobin Review*, the *Eclectic Review*, the *Westminster Review*, the *Quarterly Review*, the *New Monthly Magazine*, and *Blackwood's Magazine* as broadly representative of the kind of journal the educated middle class without a special interest in Africa might have read. More specialized journals are discussed in the bibliographical chapters.

Archival sources and the personal papers of key authorities are also too extensive to be used exhaustively. They have been consulted with special reference to key periods of changing policy. At these times the official correspondence often went beyond problems of day to day administration, into those of theory and planning. Among the more important manuscript sources have been those of the Public Record Office, London, the National Archives of Sierra Leone, the National Archives of Ghana, the Nigerian National Archives, the Clarkson papers in the British Museum, the archives of the Church Missionary Society, the Archives of the Methodist Missionary Society, the papers of the Anti-Slavery Society and the Aborigines Protection Society.

Special attention has been paid to the government correspondence which was printed for Parliament, partly because it was available to the public and partly because it included the important suggestions and statements of policy. Where possible, citations have indicated the more readily available Parliamentary Papers, even when a document may have been consulted in the archives.

INDEX

Abd Shabeeny, El Hage, 200–201
Abeokuta: growth of, 156, 313; foreign relations, 314–15, 464; mentioned, 478
Aberdeen, Earl of: reference, 362
Abo, 462, 464, 465, 468
Abomey, 31, 155
Aborigines: theories about extinction of, 372–75, 376, 381, 420; legal status of, 474–75
Aborigines Committee. *See* Commons, House of
The Aborigines Friend, 339
Aborigines protection movement, 299, 375
Aborigines Protection Society: foundation of, 329–30; legal studies of, 417–18; archives of, 489; mentioned, 266, 339, 374; reference, 330, 428
Acclimatization: recognition of, 82–83; artificial acquisition of, 83, 191–92; promoters' reaction to, 178
Accra, 9, 169, 307, 312
Acculturation. *See* Culture change
Acherknecht, E. H.: reference, 81, 182, 195
Adam and Eve: racial nature of, 40
Adamawa, 201, 311
Adams, C. D.: reference, 12
Adams, H. G.: reference, 386

Adams, Capt. John: strategic views, 163; commercial guide, 200; on slave trade, 255, 271; reference, 12, 163, 200, 211, 254, 255, 271
Adams, Rev. John, 24
Adams, Robert: pretended trip to Timbuctu, 164; reference, 165
Adangme: ethnographic report on, 329
Adanson, Michel: in history of botany, 12n; investigations in Senegal, 15–16, 220; mentioned, 23, 59; reference, 12
Adelung, J. C.: linguistic studies of, 222
Administration, colonial: discussions of 1808–1821, 159–64; discussions of 1800–1830, 277–79; problems of, in informal empire, 470–71
Admiralty: sponsors exploration, 151, 172, 200, 311–12; scientific investigations of, 334; mentioned, 162; reference, 468. *See also* Navy
Africa: relation to West Africa, 292–93; British trade with (1829–1852), 294
African Agricultural Association: reference, 451
African Association: foundation of, 17; expeditions of, 17–18, 144–46, 151; and geographical scholarship, 22, 199; and belief in healthy interior, 86–87; 87n;

315–16, 429, 441, 444–47; pamphlet publications about, 341; influence of free trade on, 443–44; mortality rates of crews in, 486–87; mentioned, vii, 271
Blumenbach, J. F.: race classification of, 38, 230–31; on racial ranking, 39; on origin of race, 41; anti-racist writings of, 47, 240–41; influence of, 47–48; mentioned, 230, 386; reference, 38, 39, 41, 47, 230, 241
Blyden, Edward W.: defense of Africans by, 386; reference, 386
Boahen, A. A.: reference, 12, 144, 150, 151, 166, 167, 172, 174, 195, 311
Board of Colonial Land and Emigration Commissioners, 441
Bocage, J. D. Barbié de: reference, 22
Boers: spread into the interior by, 292
Boilat, P. D.: reference, 412
Bolama Island. See Bulama Island
Bold, Edward: pilot guide by, 200
Bonds: Gold Coast, 307, 466
Bondu: relations with Europeans, 310
Bonny: in Niger commercial strategy, 461; mentioned, 14, 202, 410
Bontius: and beginnings of tropical medicine, 71
Bopp, Franz, 397
Boriaboola-Ga, 470
Bornu: European reports about, 20, 205, 208; in "Popicola's" project, 164; relations with Tripoli, 166–67; Clapperton-Denham-Oudney expedition to, 172; description of, in juvenile literature, 216; mentioned, 146, 201, 408, 411, 463
Bory de Saint-Vincent, J. B. G.: support for polygenesis from, 230
Botany: investigations in Africa, 15–16
Botany Bay: convict settlement at, 95
Boteler, T.: reference, 200
Bourguignon d' Anville, J. B. See D'Anville, J. B. Bourguignon
Bovill, E. W.: reference, 10
Bowdich, Thomas Edward: expedition to Ashanti, 167–69; as translator of French works, 170, 201; reporting by, 201, 211; as enlightened traveller, 209; press reactions to work of, 213; linguistic studies by, 221; opinion about African cultures, 226; historical theory of, 257; on creation of client-states, 282–83; on importance of firearms, 283; mentioned, 170, 213, 319, 328; reference, 169, 202, 211, 221, 257, 270, 283
Bower, Archibald: reference, 12

Boyd, M. F.: reference, 73, 81
Boyle, James: on classification of fevers, 347–48; on prevention of fevers, 351; on bleeding of fever victims, 357; mentioned, 344, 358; reference, 344, 348, 351, 352, 353, 359, 360
Brachycephalic: origin of category of, 366
Brandenberg: participation in South Atlantic System by, 5
Brass: in Niger commercial strategy, 461
Brazil: trade of, 8, 157, 294–95, 433–34; British relations with, 141, 158–59; slave trade of, 157–58, 436–37, 446, as source of geographical data about Africa, 202; anti-slave-trade legislation of, 300, 316–17; influence of British free trade on, 443–44; mentioned, 334, 440, 447
Bridge, Horatio: reference, 322
British African Colonization Society, 472
British and Foreign Anti-Slavery Society, 316, 339
British and Foreign Bible Society, 142
British Association for the Advancement of Science: and ethnography, 329, 331–33; mentioned, 364, 368; reference, 329, 332
British Guiana. See Guiana, British
British India Association, 340
British Medical Council: reclassification of "sun stroke," 195
British Museum, 489
British North America, 292. See also Canada
"British system," educational practices of, 264
British West Indies. See West Indian colonies
Britons: as relatives of the Fulbe, 411
Broca, Paul: and revival of polygenesis, 369
Brookings, R.: reference, 393
Broussais: on causes of fevers, 347
Browne, P. A.: reference, 370
Bruce, James: writing about Ethiopia, 25
Brunonian school, 193
Bruns, P. J.: reference, 199
Brunton, Henry: linguistic studies of, 220, 266
Bryant, Jacob: on nature of the Africans, 53
Bryson, Alexander: study of naval medicine, 334, 345; and yellow fever terminology, 346–47; reform of naval medicine, 349; empirical discoveries of,

Index

Index

Index 507

Index

Index

Index